HO$TILE
MONEY

HO$TILE MONEY

CURRENCIES IN CONFLICT

PAUL WILSON

The
History
Press

The author wishes to thank Professor Paola Subacchi (now of Queen Mary's University, London) and John Plender for their encouragement. Special thanks also to Forrest Capie, Professor Emeritus of Economic History, Cass Business School, City University for his constant support and advice.

First published 2019

The History Press
The Mill, Brimscombe Port
Stroud, Gloucestershire, GL5 2QG
www.thehistorypress.co.uk

British Library Cataloguing in Publication Data.
A catalogue record for this book is available from the British Library.

ISBN 978 0 7509 9079 0

Typesetting and origination by The History Press
Printed and bound in Great Britain by TJ International Ltd

CONTENTS

INTRODUCTION

Money or currency – for the purposes of this book the two terms will be interchangeable – is generally accepted as having three functions: it is a store of value, a medium of exchange and an accounting unit. It is a medium of exchange designed to make transactions easier than they were in the simplest societies where only barter functioned (although at times of direst necessity, people in the most sophisticated societies will revert to barter when monetary systems break down through war or economic mismanagement). As a store of value, money is a relatively reliable means of preserving our wealth beyond the short term. Not as good perhaps as land, but certainly better than foodstuffs, which are a necessity but which lose their value fairly rapidly as they degenerate. As well as these two very material attributes, money also performs a rather more abstract function as an accounting unit, a standardised way of measuring the value of our transactions or stores of value. This aspect of the nature of money is preserved in certain cases by the name of the currency we use. The pound sterling derives its name from the pound of silver used in the minting of a very fixed number of silver pennies. And the lira, the former – and perhaps future – currency of Italy, comes from the Roman term for a pound of pure silver. Similarly, the livre – a pound weight in French, and therefore originally a measure of weight – was used to determine how many coins could be produced from a pound of silver. The dirham of Middle Eastern currency systems and the Greek drachma from which dirham originated were likewise units of weight.

In the beginning, however, long before even the simplest form of currency emerged, transactions between people were carried out by means of barter: the direct exchange of one or more goods or services in return for other goods or services.

But the particular ingenuity of some ancient societies gave rise to new means of recording transactions and these new methods performed some of the functions of money – particularly those of the unit of exchange. In this way, clay tablets from Mesopotamia dating back to the period of 1600 BC act as promissory notes, setting out exactly what goods may be claimed in return for the tablet. These tablets assign no abstract, monetary value to the transaction but occupy the midpoint between simple barter and money.[1]

In China, a form of currency in the shape of spades and knife blades began to appear as early as about 1000 BC, followed by the introduction of coinage in about 229 BC, attributed to the first Chinese Emperor Qin Shi Huang.[2]

From an early point, the imperial authorities in China were at pains to ensure that the public should accept the 'nominal' value of coins, rather than weigh the coins as a means of valuing them on the basis of their metal content.[3] They promoted the so-called cartalist view – the view that the value of money is determined by government – as an expression of imperial power, but also because it offered the opportunity to manipulate the value of those coins. Attempts by the government to increase the nominal value of coinage over and above its intrinsic metal value prompted counterfeiting, inflation and currency collapse.

The valuable commodities that were eventually to become money – gold in ingot form, for example, in Egypt and Mesopotamia – may have started out as stores of value rather than media of exchange and, submitted as tribute to the rulers of those lands, remained locked away in treasuries rather than permitted to circulate.[4] At some point someone in authority decided that the precious metals silver and gold might perform a useful function in mediating between the participants in barter transactions, setting an objective measure of value acceptable to both parties. It is generally believed that Lydia in western Asia, a region possessed of quantities of easily mined gold ore usually found in the natural alloy with silver called electrum, was the first to introduce gold coinage as a unit of exchange and as a store of value at some point around 700 BC. Local rulers adopted the measure of stamping the coins as a way of reassuring the populace that the quality of the precious metals used was of a reliable standard of fineness. The impress of the ruler's symbols was therefore a guarantee of value offered by the central authority in the land.

If the silver content of coins was reduced, but the 'nominal' value remained the same, the coin would be said to be debased and its value consequently depreciated by the population. When the precious metal content of the currency in circulation was known to be debased, traders might start to demand more coins for their products and services than they had previously demanded when the currency was known to be of a better quality. Prices expressed in the unit of exchange, therefore, went up. The ruler's guarantee as expressed by the face value was not worth what it once was. The market preferred to apply the 'metallist' view of currency.

However, some alternatives to coins and banknotes persisted in certain societies, long after those societies had had the opportunity to monetise transactions. Ingots and bars of gold and silver might be used for high-value international settlements or for preserving large amounts as a store of value. In an interesting but unsurprising parallel with the social behaviours and monetary policies of the late Roman Empire, gold was held in Han China (206 BC–AD 220) in ingot form and tended to be mostly in the possession of the wealthier aristocratic classes. A thousand years later, during the Sung dynasty (AD 960–1279), silver ingots were still used as stores of value and held in treasuries as tax receipts; when bronze coinage was in short supply, they also counted as the 'backing' for paper currency in circulation.[5]

A complete breakdown in the national monetary system of a country might lead the population to adopt the currencies of another country, or resort to barter, or counterfeit the currency that until recently had been circulating efficiently in that country. By 1294 – the final year of the reign of Kublai Khan – the paper notes issued by his government in Yuan dynasty China had so depreciated that the population not only reverted to barter, but also resorted to trade tokens such as 'tea tick-ets' and 'flour tickets' and 'bamboo and wine tokens', facilitating trade in certain commodities.[6] The authorities perceived these initiatives as a threat to the official currency and attempts were made to ban them.

Production of small denomination coins in Britain had waned in the late eighteenth century when the Royal Mint's production was focused very much on gold coins. The situation was aggravated by decree of George III in 1775, who commanded that the Mint should cease production of copper coins. Those copper (and silver) coins that were circulating were being melted down and the metal recycled as lighter counterfeits. Large numbers of agricultural labourers had moved to towns to find work in the factories created during the Industrial Revolution. Unfortunately, factory owners were unable to secure access to sufficient volumes of smaller denominations and resorted once again to privately produced copper tokens. As the British government had neglected the demand for smaller denominations, the private sector was forced to meet the challenge. As an exigency of war, officially produced copper coins were sanctioned by a proclamation of George III in 1797. In 1816, the government at last took on responsibility for production of smaller denominations in copper and private coinage was rendered illegal by the 1817 Act of Suppression.[7]

Thus, the story of token production in Britain in the second half of the eighteenth century represents a case study in the competition between government and market in the supply of money and the effect of major social movements of monetary systems. But it also demonstrates the impact of war on established monetary systems. Economic and social conditions drove up a demand for money that the government not only ignored, but wilfully resisted. Private enterprise filled the gap with an unofficial money in the form of tokens whose production was facilitated by the combination of an easy supply of raw materials and the arrival of ground-breaking technology in the form of steam presses. This failure to provide sufficient currency for the purposes of trade also became a problem for Britain's fledgling colonies.

Together with debasement and failures in the usual sources of supply, other threats to monetary systems emerged: counterfeiting, coin smuggling, and competitive attempts by neighbouring states to draw large volumes of precious metals in the form of coins to their own mints away from those of the country of origin. Every so often in these circumstances, monetary systems based on commodities such as gold and silver would fall into such disrepair that a major operation to renovate the system would become necessary.

The next stage in the development of money after the replacement of ingots by coins was the introduction of paper money, which had long circulated in China and in Iran before its accidental emergence in Western Europe in the seventeenth century. It began as a certificate of deposit for copper coins in China in the ninth century and in Sweden eight centuries later, by coincidence, the prototype banknote was nothing more than a certificate of deposit for copper coins – of a sort. But, in the case of Sung China when the government over-issued paper currency, it resulted in depreciation and inflation to the point where that currency became worthless. Instead, unminted silver and silk were adopted as substitutes by the population.[8]

The money that we now handle every day in our minor transactions takes the form of banknotes and coinage (as well as the now rare cheque); but in our age, banknotes and coins make up only a very small part of the overall 'money' circulating within and between countries. And, increasingly in our times, more transactions – even minor ones – are carried out electronically, using a smart card or a mobile telephone. The quantitative easing that in recent years has often been described in journalistic shorthand as 'money printing' involves electronic transfers rather than paper and ink. From a pound weight of silver to a string of digits, money evolves, while its three purposes remain constant.

Increases or decreases in population, agricultural and industrial activity and innovation in new forms of money would all have a major effect on a country's monetary supply. And then there were other factors that could have a dramatic effect on a nation's currency system. Among these are wars, revolutions, diplomatic alliances and the secession or independence of one state from another. There is also the effect that the policies of one country can have on the monetary system of another country through political counterfeiting, sanctions and monetary operations short of outright hostility.

Wise monetary policies are vital to the economic well-being of any country. But the application of wise policies presupposes not only the technical capacity to apply them, but also the power to govern the system. When power is seized or empires extended over some otherwise independent country, the ascendant power usually take control of the issue of money as a matter of some priority. Whoever controls the supply of money commands the army, the civil service and other public services. The stability of the money system and of prices in the market place reflects not only good economic and monetary policy, but also confidence in the political stability of the regime.

Threats to monetary systems can also be internal in origin. When Germany was beset by civil disorder in the aftermath of the First World War, strikes developed into armed revolt involving the Communist Party of Germany and the radical revolutionary Spartacist League. When these armed insurrectionists seized the means of banknote production in 1919, the leaders of the western Allies, Presidents Wilson and Clemenceau for the US and France, and Prime Ministers Lloyd George and Orlando for Britain and Italy, secretly debated how best to restore control of banknote production to the legitimate authorities. As the four powers planned the settlement of Europe and the dissolution of empires in the aftermath of that war, security of the means of production of Germany's money was a factor in their calculations.

To maintain control over the monetary system as well as over the other instruments of public policy, autocrats had to maintain the loyalty of their armies. And in order to maintain that loyalty the pay that troops received had to be 'good' money, that is, not debased. Armies can march without pay for some time, but there is a limit and even if troops are content in some exceptional cases to perform their duties without payment so long as they are fed and clothed, the supplies themselves must be financed. History records instances of armies rebelling or simply melting away when their pay was cut or debased or ceased altogether.

The very basis of a monetary system may turn out to be its weakness, exploitable by hostile forces. When coins of precious metal are replaced by paper notes of little or no intrinsic value, a monetary system based on cheap tokens presents a vulnerability to be exploited by hostile powers. Paper money, unbacked by gold and issued by American and French revolutionary authorities in the late eighteenth century, was easily and cheaply counterfeited by Britain in an attempt to undermine her opponents' finances. 'The surest way to destroy the capitalist system is to debauch its currency', a maxim that J.M. Keynes attributed to Lenin in the early twentieth century,[9] had in practical terms been tested more than a hundred years earlier, although the observable results do not necessarily prove the maxim to be true. Even without such deliberate acts of hostile attack directed towards a foe's monetary system, national currency systems are weakened, undermined, overturned or totally destroyed as a result of war or civil war; an incidental consequence of the turmoil, uncertainty and breakdown in confidence of the markets and of the civil population in their own money.

Money gets swept up in the storms of history and either floats or founders. Carthage's currency went the same way as that state: ultimately overcome by Rome, the majority of Carthage's coins were melted down for use in the victor's own currency. Carthage's currency was deleted. Britain's wars against France in the late seventeenth and early eighteenth century marked the first steps of sterling's emergence as the leading international currency, a position it was to hold unrivalled from the end of the Napoleonic wars to the First World War. Sterling's reputation was the monetary endorsement of Britain's power in the same way that the international credibility of the US dollar is as much based on Washington's military and diplomatic power as it is on the real productivity of the American economy. Empires of currency rise and fall.

While the purposes of money may be constant and its forms evolving, conflict, diplomacy and politics apply a seemingly infinite variety of factors to the way in which it operates. Attempts to overthrow a regime or undermine another country in war or peace have often consciously involved a policy of attacking its currency or replacing the existing, authorised currency with an alternative, or indeed resulted in the collapse of the currency as a by-product of war or revolution. This is true whether the currency concerned is based on metal, paper or digital systems.

And in the era of the internet, when it is easier than ever to make transactions across borders, the vulnerability of national monetary systems to hostile attack, now by hackers, especially of the state-sponsored type, is greater than ever.

1

REBELLION, RIOT AND MILITARY COUPS

'A disordered Currency is one of the greatest political evils.'
Daniel Webster, Secretary of State of the United States

When civil war broke out among rival emperors of Rome in AD 192, the winner, Septimius Severus, granted the troops a pay increase and paid for it by increasing the number of silver denarii in circulation. This increase in money supply could only be achieved by means of a debasement of the silver content to 48 per cent. An old denarius thus had only the same nominal value as Septimius Severus' new denarius but had a much better silver bullion content. Inevitably, the older, finer coins began to disappear – to be melted down for their higher bullion value. So, a vicious circle would have been created: the emperor minted more coins to pay the army; in order to do so, he debased the silver content of the coin; that in turn caused the older, finer coins to disappear out of circulation, being melted down for their finer silver content. This in turn created a demand for more money – of poorer quality – to be minted and issued to replace those that had disappeared from circulation. Unless the state was able to access entirely new stocks of silver – usually by conquest – the only way to issue new coins was by taking in older ones with good silver content, melting those down for their silver bullion and reducing the amount of silver added to the newest issue of coins. The effect may have been a net transfer of wealth from some sections of society to the army and perhaps an increase in the speed with which money changed hands. The discovery of new mines and their exploitation in conquered countries might to a certain extent hold off debasement. But, if the economy were to expand too quickly and army pay increased too dramatically – and if supplies of new bullion could not keep pace – there were limited means of coping with the problem: debase the coinage, replace some payments with goods in kind or replace the lowest denominations with base metal.

The demand for an increased money supply to pay armies is clearly understood by figures for the average annual pay of a Roman soldier:

Reign	Average annual pay in denarii
Julius Caesar (46 BC)	225
Domitian (AD 81–96)	300
Septimius Severus (AD 193–211)	600
Caracalla (AD 211–217)	900
Maximinus (AD 235–238)	1,800

Source: Williams, Jonathan (ed.), *Money: A History* (British Museum Press, 1996).

The same source also reports one estimate that during the middle of the second century, 75 per cent of the Imperial budget of 225 million denarii was spent on paying the army of 400,000 troops. The cost of paying a single legion, according to one source,[1] amounted to around 1,500,000 denarii a year. Tacitus relates the case brought against Publius Vitellius in AD 32, during the reign of Tiberius, who was charged with 'offering the keys of the Treasury and the Military Treasury for seditious purposes'.[2] Clearly, with such a large proportion of the budget allocated to the army, control of the Military Treasury would make the difference between a successful and an unsuccessful conspiracy or coup.

The demand for increased money supply to pay the army in turn required a substantial increase in coin production capacity. New mints had been established in Gaul, Britannia and elsewhere by rival emperors who had broken away from Rome's central authority during the third century. The situation in the third century had been aggravated by the fact that army and civil servant salaries had not kept pace with inflation, forcing the authorities to make up the shortfall with supplies in kind.

Coin production capacity increased but raw materials were not forthcoming in sufficiently large volumes to keep pace with the enhanced production capacity; the silver content of the denarius was consequently debased to eke out the available silver stocks.

The observation of Milton Friedman that periods of war increase the demand for money[3] finds clear support in the record of inflating salaries for Rome's troops; but it could equally be said that the demand for an ever-increasing issue of money to pay the armies continued during peacetime to guarantee their loyalty in societies where armed forces do not feel themselves to be subordinate to the civil government.

China

In the China of the early Sung dynasty, the army grew in size from 378,000 in AD 975 to 912,000 in AD 1017 and 1,259,000 in AD 1045 and, as it grew, so too did the troops' demand for additional allowances and perks. The government had no choice but to increase the issue of money on a major scale to cope with these demands. Improved methods of producing silver and copper, increases in the availability of raw materials and in spending on defence led to a massive surge in money supply, the state budget expanding from 22,200,000 'strings' of cash (a cash being a bronze coin and a string consisting of 1,000 coins) in AD 1000 to 150,800,000 in AD 1021. Inflation was the inevitable result.[4]

Primitive efforts to dupe the military with debased coinage rarely survived exposure and the hostility of the intended victims. Late in the sixteenth century, the authorities in the province of Zhejiang in Ming-era China attempted to force the circulation of state issue coinage by paying one-third of military salaries of the Hangzhou garrison in coin at the official rate of 1,000 bronze coins to a tael of silver, a tael weighing anywhere between 34g and 40g according to the region of China in which it was used. However, it soon became apparent that the market rate was 2,000 coins to a tael of silver, reducing the promised 30 per cent of salary in coin to 15 per cent in real terms, and depriving the troops of the remaining 15 per cent. The predictable result: the garrison mutinied and, without a force to impose law, the city was left in a state of disorder and exposed to rioting mobs protesting against unrelated, but punitive taxation.[5]

The Power of the Military in the Ottoman Empire

Authorities ignored at their peril the willingness of a military caste to revolt when its demands for payment in sound money went unfulfilled. Until the early nineteenth century, the Janissary corps of the Ottoman Empire was one of the most powerful elements in that empire. Only the elite Janissaries were up to the task of meeting the best European troops head to head and the decision to increase threefold that part of the army demanded a corresponding increase in expenditure.[6] However, not only did the Empire have to increase the level of its military expenditure for an expanded Janissary corps, it also had to ensure that the quality of the money was acceptable to this powerful sector of society.

During the reign of the Ottoman Sultan, Mehmed II (1451–81), the Janissary corps revolted in response to regular debasements.[7] The sultan had two periods of rule, the first standing in for his father in 1444 when Mehmed II was only 12 years old. That year the Janissaries were paid in newly issued silver akçe, which had been debased by 11 per cent in silver content and weight. Alert to a reduction in the external exchange rate against the Venetian ducat, which was the international standard of monetary reliability, and wise to the likelihood of an increase in prices, the troops gathered around a hill outside the capital city of Edirne and demanded a return to the old standards of silver content and weight or an increase in their salaries. The government buckled and increased the troops' pay by about 16 per cent. Although this event, known as the Buçuktepe incident after the name of the hill, is viewed as only partly down to the government's imprudent action in debasing the currency, it and other rebellions in Ottoman Turkey that involved the issue of the quality of money demonstrate the importance in certain militarised societies of maintaining military salaries at an appropriate level to offset the effects of debasement and inflation.

The pattern repeated itself in the late sixteenth century. The army had expanded as a result of lengthy wars with Persia and Austria and, to cope with vastly increased national expenditure, the sultan's government debased the silver coinage, leading to a drop of 230 per cent in the external exchange rate. The fixed rate of pay of the Janissary corps was insufficient to cope with the inflation in prices and the problem came to a head when, in 1589, the government chose to pay them in debased coin rather than in the older, higher quality coin. Almost inevitably, the Janissaries revolted, demanding the execution of the high official deemed responsible for the debasement, a demand to which the sultan acceded. The episode became known as the Beylerbeyi incident after the unfortunate scapegoat.[8] Prior to this event, the demands of the military caste for 'sound money' had had a curiously stabilising effect on the Akçe over a period of about a hundred years from 1481 onwards, with one single exception of debasement in 1566.

By the end of the sixteenth century, the Ottoman administration appeared to have learned the lessons of these mutinies. A very high proportion of payments from the Ottoman Treasury went towards the payment of troops. To get a measure of the importance of securing the army's loyalty: documentary evidence of Treasury payments over two sample periods, the first over a period of nearly a year from July 1599 and a second period of two years beginning in 1602, indicate that 70 per cent of all disbursements went to the army. It is difficult to ignore the similarity with the estimation that 75 per cent of payments from Rome's Treasury were allocated to the army. Moreover, the fact that 67 per cent of payments made to the Ottoman army were in gold, the best store of value, seems to be further evidence that the state had begun to take the army seriously.[9] Even when the state resorted to military payments in the higher quality silver coin known as the *shahi* during wars with the Iranian Empire in the second half of the sixteenth century, it was evident that production of those coins noticeably increased at the mints in the eastern part of the Ottoman empire, the region where there were large concentrations of troops. Conversely, high-volume production slowed down and mints were closed at the end of the war and troops were dispersed.[10]

The power of the military in Ottoman Turkey was undisputed. When Sultan Mehmed IV was deposed in 1687 and replaced by Suleiman II, the new sultan had to pay the obligatory 'accession gift' to the army.

Attempts to raise enough money through new taxes on the population of Istanbul backfired when the people revolted. The administration addressed the challenge by minting copper coins with an enhanced face value of one akçe (previously a denomination reserved for silver coins), using new presses that had been installed the previous year and making use of various sources of copper for the raw material. Additional rooms were added to the Istanbul mint, expanding the minting capacity simply to satisfy the military demand for a gratuity on the accession of a new sultan.[11]

Only the suppression of the Janissary order in 1826 by the reforming Ottoman Sultan Mahmud II, who ruled from 1808–39, removed this powerful obstacle to repeated debasements, the first serious one being implemented during the period 1828–31. The seigniorage yield (the profits a government or central bank can make from the issue of money) as a result amounted to half a year's total revenues.[12]

	Weight of kuruş (g)	Silver content (g)	Exchange rate to pound sterling
1808	12.8	5.9	19
1818	9.6	4.42	29
1828	3.2	1.47	59
1839	2.13	0.94	104

Source: Pamuk, Şevket, *A Monetary History of the Ottoman Empire* (Cambridge University Press, 2000), p. 191.

The power of the military in monetary matters in certain societies could still be seen in the twentieth century.

Chile

The First World War had changed definitively the relative economic strengths of Britain and the United States. The strength of the City of London as a centre for the financing of international business and Britain's position as the world's leading gold standard country prior to the war had given the country a pre-eminent position in world trade. Prior to the war,

America had been heavily in debt to the banks of Britain and France, among others. During the war, however, America's economic position was transformed from that of net debtor to net creditor. Much British gold had been shipped via Canada to America to pay for materiel and food-stuffs. As the war progressed, Britain was forced to take significant loans from America, some of which were passed on to Britain's allies, France and Italy. Emerging from the war years as indisputably the world's leading economy, the US expanded its commercial interests in Latin America and, as the possessor of the world's largest gold reserves and naturally, therefore, a committed adherent of the gold standard, it wanted its trade partners in Latin America to operate on the same system. Contracts denominated in gold-backed convertible currencies where debts could be settled and prof-its repatriated in gold were reassuring. However, the issue of notes detached from a gold standard in Chile in the immediate post-war period, adding to the depreciation of currency that was a feature of South American econo-mies, was not attractive to American government and business.[13]

On the demand side of this relationship, Latin American states were ready to believe that there were benefits to be had from their mem-bership of the gold standard and adoption of other US requirements such as protection for foreign property. American advisers, pre-eminent among them Princeton University Professor Edwin Kemmerer, known as 'the Money Doctor', undertook technical missions at the invitation of various governments in South America. Kemmerer's missions made recommendations on the reformation of local economies and monetary policies, and on fiscal and banking systems.

Different states saw the benefits in different ways, but often the fun-damental attraction was that membership of the gold standard would make it easier for them to borrow on the international markets. For Colombia, adherence to the gold standard enabled the country to borrow on foreign markets to the extent that its public debt increased ten-fold between 1923 and 1930. The military junta running Ecuador in the 1920s believed that accession to the gold standard would bring with it official US recognition of their military regime and that recognition, in turn, would facilitate borrowing on international markets. Following American advice on monetary reform in 1925, Chile's public borrowing increased three-fold.[14]

From the middle of the nineteenth century when Chile's Ministry of Finance was reorganised by a French adviser, currency issue had been based on free banking (the issue of banknotes by commercial banknotes free of central bank or government control), leaving the way open to excessive note issue by private banks apart from a short, deflationary, trial of the gold standard in 1895–98. By the end of the nineteenth century the government had taken over issue of notes, but as the country was now off the gold standard, a renewed period of excessive note issue followed. Between 1900 and 1920, currency in circulation increased six-fold and the peso lost more than 30 per cent of its value on the London exchange.[15]

Government expenditures increased by 90 per cent in the period 1913–27 and public sector salaries over the same period rose 132 per cent. When in 1925 the government of the day hiked government spending by increasing the size of the military and the civil service and by increasing their salaries, it was reflected in the total value of notes in circulation, which increased by 30 per cent between 1924 and 1926. But although the intention had been to secure the goodwill of the military and the public sector, the ensuing inflation simply eroded the value of their increased salaries. The rapidly rising cost of living threatened social disorder. Stabilisation of an inflating currency through adoption of the gold standard became a priority for a cross-section of society: merchants and industrialists found their interests aligned with those of middle-class and working-class workforces. The failure of the reformist government of President Alessandri to stabilise the currency and a deadlock in legislation that occurred when the congress blocked his various bills led to a military coup in 1924.[16]

For the military, the principal reason for action was one of self-interest. Of course, having secured salary increases, both the officer classes and the other ranks needed stable prices; instead, the benefits they had gained were being quickly eroded by inflation. On a professional level, a depreciated local currency also made procurement of foreign armaments much more expensive. But, contrary to the stereotypical portrayal of Latin American military coups as designed to repress the working classes, the coup of 1924 and a counter-coup of 1925 led by a more energetically reformist element in the army sought to defuse the prospect of civil disorder by reform of the currency and by welfare programmes. Thus, when Kemmerer the Money Doctor arrived in Chile in July 1925 to provide advice on reform of the currency, fiscal and banking systems, local political conditions were more than receptive to his proposals. Both the middle and working classes were desperate for reform and the military, which was able to force reforms through by means of its control of the machinery of state, was ready to support his programme. More widely, there was a view that Kemmerer's programme could effectively be kick-started by the military junta, but that it was proper that it be brought to a final successful conclusion by an elected government. Ironically, it was conservative elements in society that were the leading proponents of elected government, fearing that the junta would pursue a programme of social welfare financed by higher taxes. In 1925 Kemmerer's recommendations were passed into law, establishing a central bank and placing the country on the gold standard.[17]

Following the coups of 1924 and 1925 and presidential elections later in 1925 and 1927, one of the 1925 coup plotters, Colonel Ibañez del Campo, emerged as the president with powers vastly increased at the expense of the legislature. For the first two years of his tenure, Chile's economy thrived on the back of US banking loans extended enthusiastically thanks to the country's adherence to the gold standard, with many of the funds provided being invested in infrastructural projects. Within two years, however, the Wall Street crash caused the loans to dry up. As the Depression progressed, Chile's economy suffered terribly. Demand for Chile's exports faltered and then plunged. More than 50 per cent of the central bank's gold reserves left the country in settlement of debts. Exchange controls were introduced to stem the tide, but at last, in April 1932, the gold standard was jettisoned – well after Britain had dropped it and at much greater cost.[18] The gold standard policy of the military junta worked only as long as conditions in international markets facilitated Chile's borrowing.

Ecuador's Military Junta and the end of free banking

As Chile was abandoning its first, short-lived experiment with the gold standard in 1898, Ecuador was going in the opposite direction. In 1897, a conservative government was overthrown by Eloy Alfaro, a military man of liberal persuasion.

Alfaro's primary economic interest was in the development of Ecuador's national infrastructure, with special attention to the building of the trans-Andean railway. This project had for some time been seen as essential to the challenge of linking Ecuador's interior to the coast but had always been deferred on the grounds of cost. Alfaro's determination to drive through this and other projects once he had seized power led him to agree quickly to proposals from New York finance houses prepared to provide the necessary loans against a thirty-three-year mortgage on the country's customs revenues. Although Alfaro's government agreed that the repayments were to be denominated in the local currency, the sucre, the transfers were to be made in gold. Unfortunately, Ecuador was not on the gold standard in 1897 and the prospect of a depreciating sucre with correspondingly smaller payments in gold being made was of concern to the financiers in New York. Almost certainly in response to their concerns, Alfaro took Ecuador on to the gold standard in 1898. But, along with most other countries, it suspended convertibility of paper money to gold in 1914, leaving the way open for excessive note issue.

After Alfaro's monetary discipline, the country's money supply, now off the gold standard, was compromised by the free issue of notes permitted to commercial banks. Based in the port of Guayaquil, Alfaro's home town and the centre of liberal business activity, the bankers and other commercial operators usually found themselves in opposition to the conservatives of the capital Quito, dominated by the Church, the military and central government. By the 1920s, long after Alfaro's death, six commercial banks were competing to issue ever larger volumes of banknotes. The largest among these six, the Banco Comercial y Agricola, set the pace for note issue: of all notes circulating in 1925, this one bank accounted for 50 per cent of the total, in value exceeding the legal limit geared to its gold reserve. [19] There was widespread support for drastic reform of the broken monetary system.

In 1925 a military coup seized power in Ecuador as another had done in Chile in the same year. Also echoing the situation in Chile, this coup was welcomed by both working and middle classes, the latter seeing it as a means to defusing social tensions. In the following year, the junta invited the 'money doctor', Edwin Kemmerer, to visit Quito on a technical mission. Engaging with the Kemmerer mission and accepting its recommendations held certain attractions for various sectors of Ecuadorian society that welcomed the military coup as a route to rapid reform of the economy and its expanded monetary supply. Supporters of the junta in particular hoped that adherence to Kemmerer's proposals would gain US and international recognition for the military government, facilitating borrowing on the international markets. Members of the junta were also hopeful that Kemmerer would be able to find an accommodation between the commercial communities of the coast and the military and conservative interests of the interior.[20]

Kemmerer's proposals for the creation of a central bank as the single note-issuing authority were warmly welcomed by the junta, the leading military members of which were, in contrast to Alfaro, not well disposed to the liberal business community centred in Guayaquil. In addition to the junta's ardent support for Kemmerer, he was welcomed by a wide section of society, which was convinced that his reform programme would be effective in turning around the ailing economy and would consequently raise the country's credibility in the foreign capital markets. Some of the shine was, however, to be taken off Kemmerer's credibility to some extent when it emerged that he was in favour of the junta remaining in place to implement his reforms.

Nevertheless, when the junta handed power back to civilians in April 1926, it was to a government led by the arch-conservative Isidro Ayora, who shared their antipathy towards the banking community supporting his liberal opponents. Ayora was therefore also in favour of Kemmerer's central bank proposals, which would at a stroke dismantle the free-banking bloc. In August of the following year the central bank began operations and Ayora took Ecuador on to the gold standard. Although the junta had by this time turned over power to the civilians, the military in Guayaquil and Quito made it quite clear that they were not prepared to brook any opposition to Kemmerer's plans.[21]

While Chile had at least enjoyed a couple of years of successful exports from 1927 to 1929, Ecuador was less fortunate. The country was exporting a reasonably diversified selection of raw materials, but remained dependent on cacao as its primary export, a luxury for which the demand was already stagnating. As the Depression bit from 1929, matters got worse. Although the market for cacao was clearly in free-fall, Ayora's government refused to accept the inevitable, clinging slavishly to Kemmerer's gold standard prescription. Instead of reducing the proportion of reserves held against currency on issue, thereby permitting more currency to enter circulation, Ayora's government maintained reserves (in gold convertible currencies) in excess of 70 per cent of the value of currency in circulation. Ecuador's economic situation was so parlous that in 1930, it attracted absolutely zero direct investment from the United States, which, despite the Wall Street crash and the ensuing Depression, was still investing in other Latin American countries, albeit at a much-reduced level. The situation was untenable and in 1931 Ayora resigned and Ecuador exited the gold exchange standard. The imposition of the gold standard by military juntas in Chile and Ecuador consistent with the prevailing orthodoxy was proven by market forces to be ill-timed.[22]

Portugal's Banknote Crisis of 1925 and Military Coup

As events in Chile in 1924 moved the country towards military intervention and before Ecuador experienced its own coup in the following year, a major counterfeit banknote conspiracy was being devised that would help to push Portugal towards its own military coup.

In 1924, a convicted Portuguese fraudster, Artur Alves Reis, conceived a plan to persuade the British banknote printing firm of Waterlow and Sons that he was authorised to place an order for notes of various denominations on behalf of the Bank of Portugal, to be used for the financing of projects in Portugal's colony, Angola. Waterlow and Sons were already appointed suppliers of those notes and so held the appropriate printing plates for production of the notes. Reis' plan rested on information made public by Francisco Leal, a former Prime Minister of Portugal, that the constraints on notes issued by the Bank of Portugal were lax and that the bank was able to issue notes neither recording the volumes concerned nor informing the government of the numbers. Having studied the operational weaknesses of the Bank of Portugal, Reis concluded that an order from Waterlow and Sons for banknotes with a face value of 300 million escudos, worth more than £3 million sterling at the exchange rates of the time, would not attract attention. He made contact with the company and presented his credentials as an authorised signatory to banknote contracts.

Rather naively failing to apply stringent checks on Reis and his spurious claims, the company accepted the order and set about producing notes of the 500 escudo denomination. In one sense, this was less of a case of counterfeiting and more a case of an unauthorised production run by the otherwise contracted printer.[23]

Of the banknotes ordered by Reis, notes with a value of 200 million escudos were obtained and laundered by him over the period February–December 1925 in a three-step process and the proceeds then used partly to settle old debts, but also to set up the Bank of Angola and Metropole in mid-1925. Audaciously, Reis went on to use these funds to buy shares in the Bank of Portugal, at that time a private institution. Between June and November 1925, Reis acquired 10,000 shares out of a total target of 45,000 shares, which would have given him a controlling stake in Portugal's national bank. But the establishment of the Bank of Angola and Metropole, the mystery of the origin of Reis' funds and his growing shareholding position at the Bank of Portugal attracted press speculation. The press coverage prompted a counterfeiting expert to carry out an analysis of some of the 500-escudo notes, proving that many of the serial numbers were duplicates.

Reis had covertly increased the money supply by nearly 6 per cent, or 0.8 per cent of GDP. One analysis concludes the inflation in prices would have been directly proportionate to the increase in money supply, although based on other cases it is difficult to infer such a directly proportionate increase in prices. Other calculations suggest to the contrary that prices in 1924–26 were falling and indeed, although the escudo: sterling exchange rate had collapsed from 18:1 to 133:1 over the period 1920–24, it had improved from 133:1 to 94:1 over the period 1924–26. The budget deficit had also improved considerably in the same period.

Thus, despite the increase in currency in circulation caused by Reis' criminal activity, there was no evidence of that reflected in further price increases or a further weakening of the escudo that threatened social stability as it had done in some Latin American countries. Nevertheless, it was one of the pretexts cited in favour of action outside the usual democratic processes.[24]

Reis' plot was exposed in the press in December 1925. To some powerful interests, its revelation was one more indication among others that the republican government of President Bernardino Machado was not in control of the levers of power, even if in the past two years there had been evidence of a fall in prices. Portugal's military taken as a whole might not have had grounds for complaint on the basis of the erosion of purchasing power of all their salaries on average across the ranks, as did Chile's military. However, there had been a deliberate policy on the part of the republican party of awarding proportionately better pay increases to lower ranks in the military and to junior civil servants than to the generals, whose relative wealth had slipped because of the longer-term drop in the value of the escudo since 1920. It is not, then, surprising that it was the senior ranks of the military that took action. Two attempted military coups had gone awry in 1925 but in January 1926 senior army officers again began plotting to overthrow the government, and in May Machado was forced to resign by the military.[25]

Given that the general economic conditions had improved significantly in terms of pricing levels, exchange rates and budget deficit over the previous two years, the generals' economic grounds for a coup would seem to have been subsiding. Did they fear that they had missed an opportunity prior to 1924 when all the macroeconomic indicators were looking irredeemably bad, and did the Reis scandal offer a welcome pretext for action, the straw that broke the back of the republican government's reputation?

In the febrile atmosphere of the 1920s, after a decade of revolutions in Turkey, Mexico and Russia, of the overthrow of imperial dynasties and economic instability released by the collapse of the gold standard and unfamiliar levels of hyperinflation, the coup had become a common enough means of securing the transfer of power. Since 1920, coups had taken place in Iran, Greece, Italy, Spain, Bulgaria, Chile and Poland before Portugal's own 1926 coup. Perhaps if the generals in Portugal had not found a pretext in the banknote crisis for their own coup, they would have found another, equally slender pretext. Even if the banknote crisis did not represent the single most important factor in the decision to mount the military coup, monetary problems in the form of very high inflation and salaries for senior generals were clearly important elements in the mix. Machado's policy of awarding relatively decent pay increases to the junior members of the armed forces would seem to have avoided rebellion on the part of the rank and file that had so plagued other regimes in other eras. However, he had not covered all the bases and in ignoring the position of the generals, had simply shifted the focus of resentment to a different level of the military hierarchy.

The Invergordon Mutiny and the End of Britain's Gold Standard

Military intervention of one sort or another might have dramatic effects on a currency system and sometimes in unforeseeable ways, even in countries that might have otherwise seemed to be paragons of monetary virtue.

Depression conditions in Britain in the late 1920s and early '30s drove a range of cuts in public spending, including a reduction of up to 25 per cent in the pay of naval ratings, who consequently mutinied. For Britain, a country whose security for 100 years had been founded on the strength and reliability of the Royal Navy, a mutiny in the fleet at Invergordon seemed to rock the country's very foundations at a time of severe economic difficulty. The mutiny on 16 September 1931 sparked a run on the pound. British reserves of gold and foreign exchange had declined by £200 million and, taking all government and Bank of England commitments into consideration, would have left Britain with only £5 million in reserves. The severity of the situation was clear enough. Only two days later, the Bank of England reported to the government that it was no longer able to support convertibility in the face of the run. On 21 September, the Labour government took sterling off the gold exchange rate.[26]

That the gold standard was the wrong basis for Britain's monetary regime during the Depression era has long been accepted – at least at the rate of exchange to the dollar at which it was pegged. If the Invergordon event had not acted as the catalyst for a withdrawal from the gold standard, some other destabilising event no doubt would have had the same effect. What Invergordon demonstrated, however, was that mutiny by military (or in this case, naval) forces could still have a dramatic effect on a country's monetary system even in the most developed of economies, especially if that economy was already in a fragile way.

Zimbabwe

The importance of a stable currency in securing the loyalty of the armed forces remains as true in the twenty-first century as it was in previous centuries. The second worst recorded inflation level of the past 100 years is attributed to the Zimbabwean dollar during the period 2007–08. As the Zimbabwean dollar collapsed, shops and other private sector enterprises stopped accepting the local currency and insisted on payment in the US dollar or South African rand. At the peak of the currency crisis soldiers were unable to withdraw money from their bank accounts and rioted in Harare. To contain any prospect of a full-blown mutiny within military establishments, cash was supplied from banks directly to the barracks.

Morgan Tsvangirai, the new Prime Minister in a coalition government, recognised the danger and took to paying the army with US dollars in February 2009. Although senior military officers were opposed to Tsvangirai's inclusion in the coalition government, the payment of all ranks in US dollars had done something to secure rank and file support, making it more difficult for senior ranks to act against him.[27]

Payment of salaries in dollars was subsequently extended to other public sectors and, the private sector having effectively already led the way, Zimbabwe's economy was to all intents and purposes dollarised by 2010. But, having converted to a US dollar economy, Zimbabwe now had to come to terms with a number of problems. The country was unable to grow enough food for its own needs and therefore needed to import proportionately more. In May 2016, the UN's World Food Programme reported that Zimbabwe needed to import 1.3 million tonnes of maize out of its national demand of 1.8 million tonnes – more than two-thirds of the total requirement. This, of course, meant paying in dollars, which consequently left the country. Moreover, the access to dollars declined as the country's GDP had declined since 2012; in one calculation the country's economy halved between 2000 and 2016. Furthermore, as a dollar economy, Zimbabwe was always going to attract many more imports than it could export. Traders in the region wanted to sell things into Zimbabwe in return for dollar payments going in the opposite direction. World Bank figures published in 2017 covering all exports and imports indeed indicated that imports amounted to twice as much in value as exports. This trend would, of course, deplete the country's dollar earnings.[28]

By the middle of 2016, the seriousness of the situation had become apparent. There were simply not enough dollars coming in and too many going out. Troops were subject to limits on the amount of cash they could withdraw from banks and paydays were deferred. Senior officers became sufficiently concerned to request banks supply cash to barracks directly to guarantee payment as they had done in 2008–09. The government was careful to ensure that troops and other security services were the first to be paid among other public sector staff. The government had no alternative but to announce the decision to issue a new form of currency, the bond note, which would, according to the plan, be exchangeable 1:1 with the US dollar. As with all such planned rescue currencies, the issuing authority promised to restrict the numbers of notes to be issued and explained that the issue would be backed by a $200 million loan facility from the Afreximbank, which is owned by the African Development Bank.

The population's experience in 2008 of terminal inflation – inflation at such rates that the currency system is unsustainable – was so shocking and so recent that public confidence in the new bond notes started from a low point. Money changers quickly opted not to accept bond notes at the official 1:1 exchange rate with the US dollar. Digital cash payments

– an alternative to physical cash – were also rejected in favour of US dollars. US $100 bills issued in 2009 and in good condition appreciated to be valued at $115. Leaked reports from the Central Intelligence Organisation warned the government that the army was as unhappy with the new currency plan as the wider population.[29]

It is as true in the twenty-first century as it was 2,000 years ago that governments vulnerable to direct pressure from their own armed forces will have to ensure that the money supplied to those troops is not only adequate in quantity, but also holds its value.

2

REVOLUTION

'The surest way to destroy the capitalist system is to debauch its currency.'
Lenin (attributed to him by J.M. Keynes)

Control of the money supply in political terms was often, but not always, a part of the process of exerting authority over a state and its population. Notable exceptions include the Ottoman administration, which, over lengthy periods, permitted a very open market for foreign currency, allowing the coinage of foreign states, both good and bad in quality, to circulate in Ottoman lands. Similarly free circulation of foreign coinage could be seen in countries where the internal stability and authority of the state was under extreme duress, France during the Hundred Years War being a clear example.

Challenges to the monarch's prerogative over the issue of money had already emerged in some northern European states during the seventeenth century. In England, the king's authority over the national currency had been challenged since the reign of Charles I (1625–49). In the commonwealth of Poland, where a constitutional monarchy with strict checks on the power of an elected king operated, authority over currency passed during the reign of King Ladislaus IV Vasa (1632–48) to the government of the commonwealth dominated by the nobility. In Sweden, the creation of the world's first central bank in 1668 followed the collapse of Stockholms Banco, a private bank that had performed de facto the role of national banknote issuer. The oversight of the new central bank was transferred to the Swedish parliament and away from the king, Charles XI, who was seen to have been too closely involved with the failed Stockholms Banco. Thus, in significant parts of northern Europe, royal authority over the issue of money had been challenged or curtailed in the seventeenth century. In France, royal authority over currency remained unchallenged for a further century or more until the very institution of monarchy itself was overthrown.[1]

And in the process of an entire system of government being over-thrown and replaced by a new social order, there can be dramatic consequences for monetary stability, although, in the case of relatively peaceful, rapidly executed revolution, the damage can be contained: a good example being England's Glorious Revolution of 1688.

The Continentals – A Revolutionary Currency

Money supply in the American colonies became one of a number of issues that drove the colonists to their ultimately successful confronta-tion with the British government. In the early years of their existence, the colonies had got by with a range of commodities, foreign coins and paper substitutes to supply the demand for money. At one end of the scale, commodities such as tobacco and maize were used as media of exchange – only half a step away from barter. Credit notes for tobacco stored in warehouses were adopted as legal tender by the authorities in Virginia. Coinage from the mother country, but also from Spain and Portugal and their South American colonies, and sometimes locally produced paper money, were all acceptable in one colony or another, although as media of exchange, their value would ultimately be con-verted into pounds, shillings and pence as units of account. No fewer than seventeen different forms of money were pronounced legal tender in the colony of North Carolina in 1715.[2]

Much of the coinage circulating in the English colonies originated in Mexico and South America, with which the colonies had a trade surplus. However, regulations imposed on the colonies by the mother country, England, restricted the trade with the Spanish colonies, closing off one of the few means of earning specie. Other means of improv-ing the money supply were sought. Various states of north America had tried to produce their own currency in the early years; as early as 1650, Massachusetts had produced the pine tree shilling to supply the shortage of currency from England, even though minting in the colonies was forbidden at the time. Paper bills of credit were produced, again in Massachusetts, as early as 1690 to make up for the shortfall of coinage during preparations for a military campaign in Canada.[3] Massachusetts' repeated use of bills of credit – which the House of Assembly decreed would be legal tender – provoked the home government in England to introduce new regulations in 1727, requiring the governors of the colonies to reduce dramatically the amount of paper money in circulation.

This was of direct interest to no less a figure than Benjamin Franklin, the elder statesman among the founding fathers and a printer by training, who had been a key figure in the production of paper currency for the state of Pennsylvania. In his paper 'A Modest Enquiry into the Nature and necessity of a paper currency' of 1729,[4] Franklin contended that while an excess of money would be of 'no advantage to trade' (to understate the dangers of inflation), an insufficiency of money would be 'exceedingly detrimental to it'. Franklin specifically attributed the scarcity of currency in Pennsylvania to the activities of English merchants who, in exporting to America, were drawing stocks of gold and silver out of the colonies; he went on to argue that the local production of paper money would be of benefit to English merchants keen to continue exporting to Pennsylvania and other American states at a time when there was no silver or gold coinage to be had. Plainly, Franklin's campaign for more printed money in Pennsylvania – which owed not a little to self-interest – worked: when Alexander Hamilton, first Secretary of the Treasury of the newborn United States of America, issued his report to the House of Representatives on the creation of a national bank in 1790, he singled out Pennsylvania for special and critical attention as it had nearly $1,500,000 of paper money in circulation. To put this money supply for one state alone into perspective, Hamilton's proposal set out a maximum capital stock of no more than $10,000,000 for a federal central bank serving all the colonies.[5]

As Franklin had noted in 1729, what gold and silver there was tended to be drawn out of the colonies in return for imports from Britain under a closed imperial trading system. Individual colonies such as

Massachusetts and Franklin's Pennsylvania produced their own paper currency to make up the shortfall, a natural market reaction to a shortfall in supply that had been the resort of remote colonies ill-supplied by the mother country with currency as far back as the Roman Empire in the late third century. Excessive note issue had, of course, led to inflation, which held its own attractions for small tenant farmers who would find it so much easier to pay off fixed debts to their creditors. But the benefits of paper issue in, for instance, Rhode Island, would even be upheld by establishment figures such as the governor of that colony in 1740 as the reason why it flourished commercially in comparison with other colonies.[6] Ranged against paper were those communities such as merchants and wholesalers who needed adequate access to sterling to trade with England and for whom paper was not advantageous. The Governor of Massachusetts ranged alongside this latter group and against paper, the success of which he attributed to an excess of democracy, observing that 'the ignorant majority ... always sought to tamper with sound money'.

However, the settlement of transactions in paper money rather than specie was, despite Franklin's arguments, unattractive to those British merchants whom he identified as part of the problem. As a result of their lobbying, legislation was passed in London in the form of the Currency Act of 1764, forbidding the production of paper currency in the colonies and setting out a programme for the retirement of the existing paper currency. Demands for the payment of taxes to England in sterling, restrictive trade regulations and an atrophied money supply were together the major factors destabilising the relationship between England and its colonies in North America.[7]

Some thirty-six years after his 'Modest Enquiry' and a year after the introduction of the Currency Act, Franklin found himself in London, a representative of the disgruntled colonies for negotiations with the British government. There Franklin proposed an intriguing scheme as an alternative to the government's heavy-handed schemes of taxation. Bills of credit, printed in the colonies, would be issued to borrowers prepared to pay the colonial treasuries 6 per cent interest. The bills would act as 'running cash': that is, to all intents and purposes banknotes. While the 6 per cent interest would be remitted to the British government in lieu of tax revenues, the colonies would benefit by the substitution of these bills of credit for absent gold and silver coinage.[8] The British government was having none of it, though, preferring to stick to taxation in preference to what was, in effect, usury as a means of raising revenue. The scheme, in any case, did not find favour with the propertied class of Pennsylvania.

With the outbreak of war, the revolutionary forces led by Washington required some recognisable medium of exchange to keep the army in the field. Benjamin Franklin's familiarity with the technical requirements of banknote production made him the obvious choice in 1776 as the man to lead the revolutionary authorities' plans for a series of banknotes – to be known as 'continental dollars'.[9] Although Franklin was charged with developing adequate security features for the new currency, they were ineffective and British counterfeiting of the continentals ran riot, contributing to the collapse of confidence in the revolutionary currency. Depreciation during the course of the revolutionary war was dramatic: wholesale prices in Philadelphia doubled in each year in 1776, 1777 and 1778 and across the two years 1779 and 1780 prices rose by more than 1,000 per cent.[10]

The threat of a complete collapse of public confidence in the dollar was serious enough to threaten also the success of the revolution. John Adams, successively vice president during George Washington's second term of office and then Washington's successor as president, commented in 1776: 'If that [the continental currency] suffers in its credit, the Cause must suffer. If that fails, the Cause must fail.'[11] In the event he was wrong. But the statement casts light on the importance of a stable currency for the revolutionary leadership.

In the period 1775–80, Congress issued $241 million's worth of 'continentals', while individual states issued their own paper money to a total value of $210 million.[12] Paper money produced in New Jersey and Pennsylvania and coins from a variety of European states continued to circulate, for instance, in New York and, although Congress installed the dollar as the standard unit of currency, people continued to trade in pounds, shillings and pence. While the continental dollar remained acceptable in payment of government bills, its rate of depreciation amounted to more than 85 per cent over a period of a little over twelve months.

	Exchange rate to the Spanish gold dollar
October 1779	40
End 1780	75

An interim currency reform involved a cessation of issue by the federal government and an agreement by the individual states to accept continentals in payment of taxes.[13] By 1781 the currency had completely lost its value, although some continental dollars were eventually exchanged for US Treasury bonds at 1 per cent of the dollar's face value.[14]

One wonders exactly how many people thought this transaction worth the effort. In 1783, Congress stopped issuing continentals, and in the following year Alexander Hamilton formed the Bank of New York with the purpose of issuing notes and providing information on exchange rates for the multiplicity of currencies available. However, contrary to the concerns of John Adams, the collapse of the continental dollar did not lead to the collapse of the revolutionary cause. This is a fundamental truth of money: that even where its value collapses altogether, its failure does not necessarily lead to a failure of a regime or a movement.

France

For much of the eighteenth century, during an era when banknotes were well established as a means of exchange in Sweden, England, the Netherlands and elsewhere, specie remained the preferred store of value and medium of exchange in France.

It was the experience of the collapse of John Law's system in 1720 that had inclined the country against banknotes issued by a public bank. Law was a brilliant Scottish adventurer whose persuasive style and mathematical and financial skills had convinced the Regent of France, the Duc d'Orleans, to support various plans including the creation of the Mississippi company, a massive get-rich-quick scheme of investment in France's embryonic American colonies. Tied to this commercial bubble was the idea that shares in the Mississippi company could be converted into notes issued by Law's bank, which in turn would be convertible to gold. The eventual collapse of public belief in Law's extraordinary Ponzi scheme and the inability of its duped investors to convert on demand their shares into notes and then into gold had destroyed confidence in banknotes and in banks in France.[15]

Although in 1776 a Swiss banker founded the Caisse d'Escompte, a bank that again issued banknotes convertible into specie, the idea of banknotes as acceptable money was still tenuous in French minds and this was reinforced by the fate of this bank. Following a compulsory reorganisation and loan of 100 million livres to the king's government, public confidence in the Caisse d'Escompte waned and the convertibility of its notes to gold was suspended in 1788. A year later, the outbreak of the revolution led to the bank's liquidation.[16]

By rejecting banknotes and limiting its ability to create a broader supply of money in this way, France may have created an exceptional constraint on the development of its domestic industries that put it at a disadvantage with England, but this is only one element of the aggregate of problems that led to the revolution. Bad harvests in 1788 left no option but to buy foreign grain, thereby exporting France's gold and silver. An attempt in 1788 by the king's administration to issue interest-bearing paper to act as money came up against widespread disapproval, including from leading politicians such as the one-time bishop and leading diplomatic and political figure Talleyrand, as well as radicals such as Mirabeau, one of the leaders of the social change about to break over the country.

In January 1789, the Estates General (the National Assembly) formally expressed strong opposition to the introduction of paper money and a national bank. The belief in gold and silver as the only credible form of money had deep roots and carried the convictions of even the more forward-looking members of society. Social and economic issues, war with reactionary European states and a flight of capital drove up the national debt to a point where the new revolutionary administration, which had overthrown the Bourbons, desperately searched for a means of paying it down. As late as December 1789, there were opinion-formers in Paris who recognised that money was in short supply but did not see paper money as the solution.[17]

Much of the capital that left the country in the form of gold and silver was in the hands of the nobility and clergy, the estates most threatened by the social instability, who gathered in exile in Turin and Koblenz to establish centres of resistance to the revolution. It was at this point that the bishop, politician and diplomat Maurice Charles de Talleyrand – subsequently to become foreign minister to Napoleon – proposed confiscation of Church lands, an idea that attracted immediate attention, even though it was clear that the produce of the land itself would not be sufficient to cover the immediate problem of the national debt. Only sale of the confiscated land itself would deliver the kind of rapid return that would help to solve the problem.

Consequently, a decree of the National Constituent Assembly (which in June 1789 had succeeded the Estates General) of 2 December 1789 commanded the expropriation and sale of Church land with a total value estimated then at 3.5 billion livres tournois, although the initial offering of Church lands for sale was valued at 400 million livres. The revenue of the sale of these lands would have been slow in coming and so the administration came up with a method of getting the money in sooner. An 'Extraordinary Treasury' (Caisse de l'Extraordinaire) was established in 1789, tasked with the sale of notes called assignats, effectively a certificate of indebtedness or bond bearing 5 per cent interest, notionally giving the bearer a claim on a portion of the Church lands available to the value of the bond at the point when it was due to be redeemed. In fact, assignats would be redeemed not with parcels of land, but by cash obtained from the sale of Church lands within five years.[18]

This initial issue was largely reserved for financiers and contractors to whom the state was already indebted. As wealthier members of society, they had the money to buy the bonds and, by means of their purchases, would be contributing to the paying down of the national debt that, ironically, they had helped to create. In the short to medium term, the assignats could be used by the government's creditors to pay their own creditors, and so on. Assignats would, moreover, unlock the silver and gold that was being hoarded, revitalising the money supply. The link to the lands of the Church and aristocracy seemed to provide the substance that backed the assignats and gave it a credibility that, ultimately, Law's banknotes lacked.[19]

So long as the clergy still held and administered their own lands, however, the legal practicalities were unclear and the assignats were an uncertain proposition to potential purchasers. As a first step in resolving this difficulty, the National Constituent Assembly abolished in 1790 most of the clerical orders, swept away those orders' rights to hold land, and prepared terms and conditions for the sale of the expropriated Church lands.[20]

The total value of this first offering of assignats and the reluctance of moneyed individuals to buy into the scheme led to a rethink. After an interim issue of assignats at a reduced 3 per cent interest in April 1790,[21] the government changed tack. In September 1790 the assignat was designated a banknote with no interest payable. Moreover, purchase of assignats was made available to the general public and not just the small class of financiers, contractors and public employees to whom the state was in debt.[22] Measures were also taken to limit the value of assignats on issue to 1.2 billion francs; assignats paid to the government either for redemption in expropriated land or in payment of other dues were to be destroyed. Even those who had originally opposed the assignat, such as Mirabeau, came to feel that by this time it had become a necessity.[23]

It was not long before the government dropped the pretence of the convertibility of the assignats into land, so that the assignats became an early example of a fiduciary note, relying solely on the confidence of the public in the government's ability to make them work as a means of exchange. It did not work well. As public confidence in them was tested, prices of goods paid in assignats were raised above that of prices for the same goods denominated in gold and silver coin. The high denominational value of assignats contributed to the inflation in goods, which in turn drove a depreciation of the notes.

And, as the assignats had been issued originally in high denominations, the absence of smaller denominations in either paper or coin created inconvenience for the public. Low denomination notes were issued to facilitate the purchase of small items. The assignats, which were only printed with a face value of 1,000 livres in 1789, were, a year later, to be found with a face value, in some cases, as low as 5 livres, but not before private companies and local authorities had taken to producing small denomination notes – *billets de confiance* – to supply a requirement that the national government had ignored. Following the failure of a major private issuer of the billets, the National Assembly moved to ban the private production of such notes in November 1792.[24] Private sector initiative in supplying a gap left by unimaginative or ineffective management of the money supply, followed by government efforts to exercise control of the private sector innovation, is a theme that recurs in monetary history and can be seen in our own times in the emergence of so-called crypto-currencies and the interest in public sector institutions in adopting the block chain technology associated with them.

The external exchange rate of the assignat on the markets in London started to fall as early as 1790–91. In France itself, the assignat depreciated against silver by 18 per cent by November 1791 and by 43 per cent by August 1792. The decline was temporarily reversed by public sentiment following internal political events and the success of the revolutionary army at the Battle of Valmy, driving the assignat back up to 72 per cent of its silver equivalent, but by December 1793 it had fallen again, being traded at 24 per cent of its face value.[25] The discounted value against its original face value continued to fluctuate: up in reaction to successful military operations against reactionary European states, down when another seismic shift took place in the domestic turmoil of revolutionary France – for instance, the toppling from power of the revolutionary leader Robespierre and his execution.

After a brief positive interlude, the assignat assumed the character of 'bad money', driving out of circulation the good money of gold and silver, which came to be hoarded or exported. It was still possible to trade silver and gold until April 1793, but from that point on the revolutionary government took steps to achieve 'forced circulation': assignats could not be traded at a discount to their face value – breach of which law was punishable by death. From a point where the assignat was an interest-bearing bond, limited to purchase by only a limited section of society and backed by land, it had transformed into a fiduciary currency, not bearing interest, not convertible, used by the entire population as a banknote. As ever larger numbers of assignats were held by all sectors of society, their depreciation drove up prices of food. As prices rose and as the assignat became the primary means of exchange, specie having become scarce through hoarding, more and more notes were issued, initially to supply the deficiencies in money supply and then simply to keep up with prices. In this way fiat paper note production echoed the debasement of coinage of earlier times and the consequent inflation. In an attempt to hold back the rampant inflation, the authorities introduced in 1793 the Maximum, an arrangement that set the maximum price that could be charged for certain products. But, by December 1794, the government reversed this decision and the Maximum was abolished, releasing once again the temporary brake on price inflation.

The dizzying rate of issue and the recourse to the printing press, initially as a reaction to inflating prices and rising government debt, can be seen from the following figures:

Issue	Value in livres
December 1790	800 million
December 1794	8 billion
October 1795	20 billion
December 1796	40 billion

Source: Davies, Glyn, *History of Money* (University of Wales Press, 2002), p.558; Vilar, Pierre, *A History of Gold and Money* (Verso, 1984), p.305; Capie, Forrest, 'Conditions in which very rapid inflation has appeared', Carnegie–Rochester Series on Public Policy (1986).

By way of contrast, only 32 million livres of silver were minted over the period 1792–97, a consequence of the shortage of bullion and specie, which had been driven underground.[26]

Public confidence in the assignat was further undermined by announcements by leading members of the old, aristocratic regime that they would not honour revolutionary currency when they resumed the reins of power. The Church, for its part, threatened anyone promoting the expropriation of the Church's property with excommunication. Speculators, furthermore, were encouraged to talk down the value of assignats, buying them at a discount and thereby reducing the price of the Church land that the assignats would buy.

Perhaps one of the most significant factors in undermining the assignat was that of counterfeiting. Emigré conspirators took to a programme of counterfeiting of the crudely produced assignat in Belgium and Switzerland as early as October 1792. The main effort, though, of an organised counterfeiting attack on the revolutionary assignat, was to be in England under the patronage of the government of William Pitt (*see* Chapter 6 on political counterfeiting).[27]

The state, no doubt in part to stimulate confidence in these notes, bought them to use as payment for troops. However, as the notes continued their relentless spiral of depreciation downwards, the value of the note came close to the cost of printing it. In the period of worst inflation – 1794–96 – price rises that could be observed from hour to hour made it impossible for administrators to govern. In one departement it was observed that food was available but the rapidly rising prices made it difficult for local authorities to buy enough to provision hospitals.[28] The printers themselves went on strike and the government recognised the notes' worthlessness by breaking and burning the machinery, plates and paper publicly in February 1796. They were succeeded by a new paper currency, the mandat, later that same month, and in July of the same year the government decreed that *assignats and mandats* could be exchanged at the current value, which was about 2 per cent of the original face value.[29] The rate of depreciation of paper currency compared to the gold ecu, a coin worth 24 livres tournois, fluctuated, but the general trend was clear and dramatic:

Date	1 gold ecu buys assignats:
7 June 1796	585
13 June 1796	1,000
16 June 1796	450
26 October 1796	2,000
30 October 1796	3,450
31 October 1796	2,450

Source: Vilar, Pierre, *A History of Gold and Money* (Verso, 1984), p.306.

A new law enacted on 26 July 1796 had permitted the public to set the payment terms for transactions and almost inevitably gold and commodities were immediately favoured, explaining the sharp drop in the value of assignats between June and October 1796.[30]

An important turning point came in February 1797, when *assignats and mandats* ceased to be legal tender and were from that point onwards no longer acceptable in payment of taxes, always an indication that a government has lost confidence in the quality of its own money. The presses were destroyed.[31]

Further emergency measures were taken to stabilise the situation. Two-thirds of national debt were simply cancelled as the government declared a partial bankruptcy and started to mint increasing volumes of silver coins again, exploiting the flow of specie from England to the continent, brought about by the suspension of convertibility of the Bank of England's notes. Other factors played a part in helping to bring the inflation under control, including good harvests that reduced the prices for foodstuffs. After these interim measures, the assignats were finally consigned to history by the introduction of the franc on a precious metal basis in 1803 during the period of the consulate. By this arrangement, the new franc was set at a specific weight and fineness of gold or silver – a so-called bimetallic system.

Many factors contributed to the failure of the assignats: a long-standing distrust in France of paper money; over-issue by the authorities; large-scale counterfeiting by the enemies of the revolution; a refusal by farmers to send their goods to market in return for worthless paper currency; and the public's lack of confidence in the ultimate survival of the revolution, its institution and, naturally, its money, particularly at times of heightened domestic turmoil or military defeat overseas.

But, was the assignats system a complete failure? Initially, probably not, as it bought some time for the revolution to gain momentum. Indeed, the collapse of the assignats did not signal the end of the revolution.

The early experiences of America and France with a fiat money supply unbacked by specie driving high inflation under conditions of political and military turmoil were to be repeated more frequently in the twentieth century.

Mexico

Revolutions in France in the eighteenth century and in China and Russia in the early twentieth century toppled long-established royal and imperial dynasties. In Mexico, the revolution that began in 1910 struck against a corrupt and politically stagnant regime headed by Porfirio Diaz, a general of relatively obscure background and a self-made man. Against this regime and the vested interests of some sectors of society that found protection under Diaz, a range of opponents found common cause: from true revolutionaries demanding a redistribution of the land in favour of those who worked it, to wealthy individuals seeking to loosen Diaz' grip on power.

After successes as a professional army officer in military campaigns in the middle of the nineteenth century and election as a deputy to the National Assembly, Diaz had seized power in 1876 by virtue of an armed rebellion against the government of the day. Diaz' government lasted so long that the term Porfiriato has come to describe a forty-year era of personal government during which Mexico came to be seen as an economic power of some significance. However, it was also a time when the benefits were bestowed on industrialists and foreign investors rather than on the peasant classes and indigenous communities, even though Diaz himself was the product of mixed Spanish immigrant and indigenous blood. Indeed, some indigenous communities suffered particularly badly during the Porfiriato when their landholdings were divided up and sold off. Diaz' control over society and state was achieved by suppression of the media, manipulation of the courts and the appointment of friends and relatives to the legislature. Northern industrialists prospered but felt that they had no political power.

Since Mexico's independence from Spanish control in 1821, the country had passed through half a century of instability, war and territorial loss. In 1823, Guatemala, El Salvador, Honduras and Costa Rica declared independence in their turn from Mexico. Twenty-five years later, much of Mexico's northern territory – modern California, Utah, Texas and parts of other states – was seized by the United States at the end of a war in 1848. Sixteen years later – in 1864 – a member of the Austrian house of Hapsburg, Maximilian I, was imposed on Mexico as emperor by Louis Napoleon, Emperor of France. Within three years, however, Maximilian's government had been overthrown with American encouragement and the hapless Maximilian executed.

Such external assaults on Mexico's sovereignty did not tell the complete story, though. The individual states that formed Mexico competed against each other in commercial matters, imposing duties on any goods that crossed state lines. Parts of some states seceded from their original parent state; one state might annexe parts of another state. Internally fragmenting and threatened externally, notably by the United States, for a period of fifty years post-independence, Mexico did not enjoy the peace necessary to establish a stable polity that in turn would enable the creation of a stable, unified monetary system.[32]

Matters were made more complicated by the absence of a single central bank responsible for currency issue. Instead, a range of banks were permitted to issue notes. Officially on a bimetallic standard, in reality that changed when the international value of gold compared to silver soared in the 1870s. Mexico was then, appropriately enough as a leading producer of silver, actually on a silver standard in which a peso was defined as a coin containing 24g of silver. Banks issuing notes would redeem those notes for silver coins, but only at the original branch where the note was issued. This constraint meant that a banknote circulating far from its original branch of issue would be discounted, a situation less than ideal for the management of a stable and unified currency system.[33]

In 1881, the Banco Nacional Mexicano signed an agreement with the finance ministry by which only the former's banknotes would be recognised by the federal government. Over the following three years, the government turned repeatedly to the Banco for loans and as the bank became progressively wary of these demands, the government responded in 1884 by merging it with another bank to create the Banco Nacional de Mexico (Banamex). Banamex would be responsible for all government financial activities, from the collection of taxes to payments to suppliers, and would have the sole right of banknote issue, bringing to the bank all the seigniorage that would yield.[34] Other existing banks already issued banknotes, but by the new arrangement, they would pay a 5 per cent tax on their banknote issues that would be capped according to specie reserves held by the relevant bank. Banks chartered after the

Banamex agreement would not be permitted to issue notes. But it was not until 1894 that Banamex's notes could be redeemed one for one for silver pesos at any branch throughout the country, making Banamex the first bank in Mexico to issue a currency that was accepted at face value across the nation. In many respects Banamex had become the central bank and was perceived as such on the eve of the revolution in 1910 by external observers. In other respects, however, it fell short of performing a central bank role as there were still other issuing banks whose notes were not being redeemed at face value elsewhere in the country.[35]

This problem would be solved to some extent by the creation of another bank, the Banco Central Mexicano, in 1899 that guaranteed the redemption of other banks' notes at par throughout the country, up to the limit of those banks' deposits at the Banco Central. The Banco could not, though, issue banknotes itself. Thus, for the last quarter of the nineteenth century and the first years of the twentieth, Mexico's note issue was conducted by multiple banks, inadequately regulated and in a poor position to resist the pressures of revolution and civil war.[36]

Problems in respect of coinage added to the difficulties. Mexico had joined the gold standard in 1905 to help facilitate trade with other gold standard countries. The Mexican silver peso, however, enjoyed an international reputation as a trading currency and for that reason the government decided to leave the peso in circulation as a full-bodied coin, its face value equating to the market value of its silver content. But when the world price of silver surged in 1908, silver pesos inevitably left the country for other markets. This external drain was particularly disastrous for the poorer classes, which depended on the lower denomination silver coins rather than the higher value gold peso. It is not unreasonable to agree with some authors that this was a contributory factor in the revolution of 1910, although it is impossible to calculate just how significant a factor it was.[37] By laws of 1897 and 1908, banknote issue was limited to one bank in every state of the country and two banks in Mexico City. By 1910–11, some 116 million pesos of banknotes had been put into circulation by twenty-four different banks.

In 1908, after more than thirty years in power, Diaz himself was having doubts about his ability to carry on: he indicated that he would not stand for re-election, only to quickly reverse his decision. The disappointment triggered action. Francisco Madero, a wealthy individual of the northern coal-mining state of Coahuila, gathered around himself a group of prominent individuals dedicated to blocking Diaz' re-election. Despite this opposition, Diaz proceeded to stand in 1910 and when he was re-elected it was widely felt that the process had been rigged. But Diaz had plainly lost the stomach for a fight and in the following year a transfer of power to Madero was arranged.[38]

Those who thought Diaz' surrender of power to Madero would solve Mexico's political and social problems were wrong. Madero, who came from a very rich family, had no interest in agrarian reform. The transfer of power did no more than loosen the lid on the sense of deprivation and resentment in rural communities. The cost of maintaining military forces drove state administrations into debt and made economic reform unrealistic. A series of regional rebellions occurred in 1911 and 1912, even spreading to Madero's own state of Coahuila. The cost of containing these rebellions ate into Mexico's reserves. Rural resistance to Madero's government found focus in the south of the country in Zapatismo, a drive to redistribute the land to those who worked it, led by Emiliano Zapata, a political activist from a farming family. Madero's government remained under extreme pressure until he was toppled in 1913 and murdered by a coup mounted by Victoriano Huerta, a general who had enjoyed career promotion under both Diaz and Madero.

Huerta's regime was in turn attacked by a northern 'constitutionalist' movement led by the governor of Madero's home state Coahuila, the self-proclaimed 'First Chief' of the revolution, Venustiano Carranza and its army, led by, among others, the ex-bandit turned northern revolutionary, General Pancho Villa. To finance the fight against the constitutionalists, Huerta's government borrowed excessively, often placing the banks under duress to lend and in at least one case having to use the majority of a loan to pay off the borrowings of the previous Madero government. Even Huerta's extensive borrowing was insufficient, however, and the specie reserves of the Banco de Morelos, in the southern state of Morelos – which was the centre of Zapata's power – were seized to cover costs. In such circumstances, it is hardly surprising that specie fled the country, with much of the gold going to the United States. The peso lost 16 per cent of its value between May and August of 1913, forcing

Huerta to ban the export of gold. Mexico was off the international gold standard. A run on the banks ensued, with the last two willing to guarantee convertibility of paper forced to disburse silver pesos on demand in November. Moreover, the banknotes of the two issuing banks based in Mexico City were declared legal tender throughout the country, effectively cancelling domestic convertibility of their notes into gold or silver in addition to the suspension of international gold payments. Banknotes of state banks were also declared legal tender but only within their specific state of issue.

With the rigorous constraints of the classic gold standard lifted, Huerta was able to opt for monetary financing of the government's expenditure: Banamex was ordered to issue 16 million Mexican dollars' worth of new notes between November 1913 and January 1914. Other issuing banks were permitted to increase the volume of notes they could issue. Half of all government spending in the first quarter of 1914 was covered by notes issued in this way by the banks. Predictably, the gold value of those notes fell sharply in the first quarter of 1914. At the same time, emergency notes of various types were issued by Huerta's regional commanders, who were cut off from their usual sources of currency, particularly in the north of the country. This dire state of affairs was compounded by a collapsing economy. Revenues plunged and public sector expenditure, particularly on military costs, rose. Mining activities dived: silver production was down by two-thirds, gold by 50 per cent, aggravating the shortage of specie.

The constitutionalists under Carranza, who had quickly seized power in the northern state of Sonora, were themselves not beyond aggressive monetary measures. In April 1913, Carranza announced the first issue of paper money by the constitutionalist forces, with strict penalties for those who refused to accept them. It was forbidden to carry out transactions in IOUs or tokens or other money substitutes, although IOUs issued by the constitutionalist General Obregon were designated legal tender, as were notes issued by General Villa. Specie and banknotes were seized and in October 1913 Banamex banknotes were declared illegal in the territories controlled by the constitutionalists. State of Sonora banknotes were issued but were of poor quality and subject to counterfeiting. These in turn were superseded by constitutionalist government notes, which would be issued in all three of the northern states held by the constitutionalists. The notes were produced by an American company in Washington DC and the attempt to transport them to Sonora was initially blocked by the US authorities, who had been tipped off. The notes were seized as contraband of war at Eagle Pass, Texas, where the United States borders Carranza's home state of Coahuila. US authorities, arguing for the seizure of the notes, cited Carranza's own statements to demonstrate that the notes were to be used in the waging of hostilities against Huerta's regime. On that basis, US prosecutors asserted that Huerta's government would have the right to bring a case in the US courts against the company supplying Carranza. It is interesting that, in support of their position, US prosecutors cited a landmark case heard in the British House of Lords regarding unauthorised notes printed for use by Hungarian revolutionaries (*see* Chapter 9 for the case of the Emperor of Austria versus Kossuth and Day).

Following legal appeal, however, the notes were released to the constitutionalist authorities. To compensate for the hoarding of coins and to provide an easy source of cash, small denomination notes were also printed in the springs of 1913 and 1914, the latter issue of notes called cartones after the fact that they were printed on cardboard. By the middle of 1915, the constitutionalists had issued at least 672 million pesos' worth of banknotes.

The combined effect of banknotes issued by Huerta's administration, the constitutionalists and a variety of other forces, as well as private issues by landholders, mining companies and trading organisations, was to cause depreciation of the currency by 54 per cent from 1913 to 1914. Matters were aggravated by counterfeiting, encouraged by the wide variety of notes now entering circulation such that the public could not be sure what was a genuine note and what was not. The staple diet items of corn and beans, which had already doubled in price, now doubled again in 1914. A wave of strikes broke out among both public and private sector workers in reaction to the collapse of the currency. The constitutionalists tried measures to bolster confidence in their currency: a decree of October 1914 imposed a requirement that 50 per cent of all payments to government – taxes or other payments – would be paid in constitutionalist bills. But by mid 1915 the price of corn and beans had increased by more than 2,000 per cent.[39]

Under relentless military pressure by the northern forces that were driving south towards Mexico City, Huerta threw in the towel and fled to the US. After a brief interregnum, the 'first chief', Carranza, was by the end of 1915 installed as president. In September of that year he had begun a process of rationalising the note-issuing banks by investigating and then closing those that had issued more notes than they were legally entitled to issue, even though they were pressured to do so under Huerta's programme of monetary financing. Eighteen issuing banks were consequently closed down in 1916 and their specie reserves seized where they had not already been shipped out to the US. Agile and pragmatic, Banamex quickly adjusted to the shift in power and made arrangements for major loans to Carranza's constitutionalist government, becoming thereby one of the seven issuing banks to survive Carranza's banknote issuing purge.[40]

Typical of a number of military commanders contributing to the problem, the northern general Pancho Villa issued his own currency. While Villa's military star was on the rise, his currency was popular. Supporters believed in his ultimate success and were confident that his notes would ultimately be redeemed at full value. By the end of 1915, following military defeat inflicted by Carranza's leading general Alvaro Obregon, confidence in the peso issued by Villa evaporated, in only two months dropping from 30 US cents to 1.5 US cents in value. The depreciation was reflected in severe inflation. Even Villa's draconian punishments failed to persuade merchants to hold down prices. Instead, they simply refused to offer goods for sale. Here and elsewhere, the temporary capture of territory by one side only to be followed by retreat and surrender of that territory to the opposition led to extreme monetary instability as the incoming military power cancelled the notes of the expelled forces. In those circumstances no currency could hold its value for any length of time.[41]

Initially, notes issued by private banks commanded somewhat more confidence than those issued by the government and so people held on to the former, preferring to part with the government notes that were seen to be worthless. But, from the middle of 1915 to the middle of 1916, public confidence in paper money collapsed and specie was hoarded. From mid 1915 to mid 1916, the peso's value fell from 9 to 2 US cents. Between 1914 and mid 1916, the peso had depreciated by 154 per cent compared to its 1913 value when the peso was still on the gold standard. An attempt was made in mid 1916 to correct the rampant inflation by withdrawing all circulating notes and replacing them with a new series, the *infalsificables* ('unforgeables') printed in America, at the rate of 10:1. As with other cases of currency replacement mid-war, the effort failed. As the population became aware of the withdrawal of the old constitutionalist notes, the value of the latter fell further and people sought to pass them in transactions as quickly as possible, before their value depreciated further. The government produced far too many notes and simply replaced one set of inflationary ones for another.

Prior to the revolution, the total value of notes and coins in circulation in Mexico was 262 million pesos. A government decree announcing the replacement of 'old' pesos issued and in circulation estimated their total value as 700 million pesos. These should have been replaced by a total of 70 million of the infalsificables at a rate of 10:1. But, by the spring of 1917, 400 million pesos of the infalsificables type were in circulation (with a remaining 140 million of infalsificables and other types still in government storage.)[42] Within a month of their issue (May 1916), the new infalsificables were rapidly losing value, the entirely predictable outcome of an attempt to reform currency in the midst of civil war and revolution. In June 1916, one peso of the new currency was worth 9.7 US cents. By December it was worth less than half a cent. The use of barter increased.[43]

Privately issued notes were valuable only so far as people hoped they might be exchanged for specie at some point in the future. In a world where the convertibility of paper currency to gold was the established norm, what seems to us now as wishful thinking was not unreasonable. Indeed, in September 1916, the government presented all its Banamex notes to that bank and demanded conversion to gold. [44]

Having closed down the majority of note-issuing banks in September 1915, the government tightened the screw again in September 1916, demanding the remaining banks halve their note issue or double their specie reserves. Failure would result in the seizure of those banks' remaining specie reserves. The threat pointed towards the true intentions of the constitutionalist government, which was desperately in need of additional funds to cover the cost of the war. By November, the government itself had lost confidence in its own currency to the extent that duties payable to government were to be settled in gold or in paper notes according to their value in gold, with that exchange rate being set every ten days. [45]

From December 1916, it dropped the pretence and began to seize the specie reserve of state banknote-issuing banks, completing the task by the end of 1917. By then the peso had depreciated 2,009 per cent compared to its official gold standard value. In that same year, Carranza fixed prices in terms of gold and silver, a distant echo of the introduction of the Maximum during the French revolution. Indeed, the infalsificables had so lost their credibility that gold and silver coins that had been hoarded during the course of the revolution started to reappear in circulation. Traders priced their goods either high in paper or relatively modestly in gold specie. Workers began to demand a portion of their salaries in specie. Government gave in to the mounting demand and announced that a portion of the pay of public sector employees would be in gold. While no gold had been coined between 1910 and 1916, in the eighteen months from mid-1916 to the end of 1917, 37 million pesos worth of gold pesos was produced. It was as though Mexico's currency, having passed through the point of depreciation where Gresham's law kicks in and bad money drives out good, had now gone full circle so that the good money was replacing the bad. Paper money had reached the terminal point of depreciation and natural market forces rather than a state-managed currency replacement programme had started the process of correcting the problem. [46]

With so many valueless infalsificables still on issue and representing a liability for the government, a novel solution to the challenge of redemption was created: to each peso payable for import and export duties (and a few other duties) was added a surcharge of one peso infalsificable. As these pesos were surrendered to the customs authorities, they were burnt. [47]

From December 1916, specie, rather than paper money, was the main form of payment in Mexico. US dollars were declared the only paper money with legal tender status. Mexico's constitution of 1917, indeed, stated that: 'Wages must necessarily be paid in legal tender and cannot be paid in goods, coupons, tokens or any other instrument intended to substitute the money.' The fact that this clause appears in article 123 of the constitution is in itself significant, as that article is concerned with workers' rights. The insistence on payment in legal tender was plainly aimed at those industrialists and large landowners paying their employees in scrip that they had issued themselves and which in many instances could only be used in shops owned by the same enterprise or estate.[48]

Although he remained president until his assassination in 1920, Carranza faced continuing armed revolt from Zapata, Villa and other regional leaders. He was eventually deposed by his own general, Alvaro Obregon. Obregon's accession to power marked the end of the war and the ensuing period of peace saw reforms in labour relations, education and land redistribution. The reforms did not, however, extend to the establishment of a single authority for the issue of currency. Reviewing the chaotic banking arrangements and the resultant plethora of notes in circulation, Obregon settled on the creation of a central issuing bank together with six provincial banks with rights of issue, less because this was the optimal arrangement for Mexico's economy, but rather because this would create competitors for his favours. The establishment of the Banco de Mexico, the central bank, had to wait until the end of Obregon's term of office in 1924 and succession by Plutarco Calles. The Banco began operations in 1925 and since then has had sole responsibility for currency issue.[49]

China

China had once led the world in matters relating to currency. It had introduced an early form of paper currency in the form of certificates of deposit in the ninth century at a time when the west had only begun to emerge from the Dark Ages. Printed banknotes began to appear in Sichuan in 1024. From earliest times, bronze had been the preferred metal for China's unique knife-and spade-shaped coinage and other coins were produced in copper. During the fifteenth century silver became increasingly favoured for trading purposes and for the payment of taxes and by the late nineteenth century, when almost all of Europe, America and other countries around the world had moved on to the gold standard, China remained on silver.[50]

Being on silver at the end of the nineteenth century was not an ideal position to be in. Some countries had abandoned silver in the last few decades of the nineteenth century simply because they feared being flooded with silver from those countries abandoning it in favour of gold, bringing about a complete collapse in the value of silver. The standard Chinese unit of value and weight for silver, the liang of 36g, had been worth $1.2 US dollars in 1887, but only 62 cents in 1902.[51]

In addition to the plunging weakness of silver, China's holdings of silver were drained by a series of reparations and indemnities levied on her between 1841 and 1897 by foreign powers worth at least 294 million liang, more than $350 million by 1887 values. This included a massive 200 million liang indemnity to Japan at the end of the war of 1895, equivalent to three times the annual revenues of the Chinese government. A further indemnity of 450 million silver dollars payable to foreign powers involved in suppressing the Boxer rebellion was levied in 1901.[52]

Since 1841, Russia, America, Japan, France, Britain and Germany had all succeeded in wringing territorial and trading concessions out of the weakened Chinese state. The shock of the defeat inflicted by Japan on China in 1895 accelerated demands for reform, just as humiliation at the hands of American gunboat diplomacy had led to constitutional change in Japan a generation earlier and in Russia following defeat at the hands of Japan in 1905. Fossilised regimes confronted by well-organised states with advanced armaments gave way and, in the aftermath, searched for lessons in modernisation. After the suppression of the Boxer rebellion in China in 1900, the demands for change and modernisation in China grew louder. The defeat of Romanov Russia by Japan in 1905 was particularly shocking as the first example of the comprehensive defeat of a European state by an Asian one in modern times.

The first serious top-down attempts at reform that were receiving serious consideration by China's penultimate emperor, Zaitian, were rapidly stifled by conservatives led by the dowager empress Cixi, who for the next ten years succeeded in keeping the lid on reform until her own death in 1908. (The emperor himself was unable to take up the reins of reform once again as the dowager empress had had him murdered the day before her own death.) A regency had been established to govern during the minority of the child Emperor Puyi, who was to be the last emperor of the Qing dynasty, and the regency again attempted to introduce limited reforms. It was at this moment, with a feeble regency in control, foreign powers in command of ports where they enjoyed extraterritorial rights to operate their own legal systems, and a fragile economy drained of so much of its main commodity currency, that revolution broke out, with the first uprisings taking place in the south-eastern province of Hunan in 1910.[53]

Opposition to the ruling Qing dynasty took many forms: intellectuals had been pushing for reform of the state for some years, on occasion resorting to violence, albeit ineffectively; middle-class investors reacted against the regency's plans to nationalise the railways; students, many of whom were from the same families as those merchants who were private shareholders in the railways, rebelled; provincial governors also began to rise up against the essentially foreign Manchu dynasty. Further attempts by the conservatives to secure a constitutional monarchy were unsuccessful and by early 1912 the Qing dynasty had been replaced by a republican government. But this in no way meant that a stable unifying government had succeeded to power.

In fact, from the first successful regional rebellion against the Manchu dynasty in October 1911, there followed a succession of more than twenty provincial rebellions reaching out as far as the most remote outposts of Manchu authority in Mongolia and Tibet. In many of the provinces, governors and governor generals had risen to their positions through a career in the military, so it was hardly surprising that the breakdown in loyalty to the Qing dynasty created a leadership vacuum that was filled by assertive military types. Rebellion in almost all of these provinces resulted in the declaration of provincial military governments, while Mongolia and Tibet went further by reasserting their independence. If matters had rested there, it might have been possible to establish a degree of stability and a modus vivendi between the military leadership of the various provinces. It was not, however, going to be that simple. It has been suggested that between 1911 and 1928, no fewer than 140 conflicts broke out between as many as 1,300 military leaders.[54]

Prior to the outbreak of revolution, the regency government had recognised the need for currency reform among many other aspects of government that needed urgent change. China's currency regime was in a parlous state. Commodity currency took many forms: the sycee, a silver ingot that could take various forms and which was produced by silversmiths rather than by a state mint, silver dollars from Latin America and bronze coinage all circulated. Much of the specie would only trade at its nominal value in the province or city where it was issued and at a discount elsewhere. There was good reason for low public confidence in the circulating coinage. Provincial mints had been set up in the late Qing period using modern equipment purchased from European companies. The governors of these provinces were unable to resist the temptation to use this equipment to churn out large volumes of debased coinage with the aim of maximising seigniorage. The authorities of treaty ports also started to mint silver dollars.[55]

Paper currency similarly was issued by various institutions: government notes as well as money substitutes such as scrip issued by the military or private enterprises. Banknotes were also issued by foreign banks operating in the international settlements, which enjoyed extra-territorial rights, that is, were not subject to control by the Chinese government. It is hardly surprising that these notes circulated at their face value only in the settlement where they were issued, but, as with specie, would trade at a discount in other regions. Foreign banks, displaying what they might have considered only as prudence but others as high-handedness, would accept only Chinese notes issued by the Imperial Bank of China.[56]

Chaotic currency arrangements were far from attractive to foreign trading houses and a major syndicated loan had been agreed for the purpose of currency reform by British, German and American bankers, but was put in doubt by the outbreak of the revolution. New Chinese silver dollars were at last minted by the new republican government in Beijing in 1914 and increasingly replaced foreign silver coins as the predominant form of currency. By this time power in China had translated from that of a monarchy to that of a republic. The dominant figure through this transitional period proved to be Yuan Shikai, a general who had risen through various high-profile positions to become, in November 1911, the last Prime Minister to serve the Qing dynasty. Yuan's ambitions, however, did not stop there and, following a unanimous vote in a stooge 'representative assembly', had himself declared emperor in December 1915. Within the year, however, Yuan's government was struggling to raise the revenues it needed to stabilise the state and the economy. In that year, it resorted increasingly to the printing press and issued instructions to government banks to stop converting notes to silver, measures not dissimilar to the 'forced circulation' of paper money as legal tender under the Mexican dictator Huerta, three years earlier. Widespread disapproval among provincial governors of Yuan's self-promotion to the position of emperor led to rebellion in various provinces and after only eighty-three days as nominal emperor, and before the appropriate ceremonies could formalise his elevation, Yuan abdicated and died two and a half months later. There was, though, an unexpected legacy in that silver coins minted with Yuan's portrait became the preferred high value currency for many years after his death, supplanting silver ingots as the preferred medium of exchange while ingots increasingly took the role of bank reserves.

While bullion and coins in the economy were tending to increase by only about 5 per cent per year, paper notes and deposits were increasing over the same period of 1911–36 at a rate of more than 9.5 per cent. Partly because of the government's recourse to printing currency, but also partly because the Chinese banking system was developing at a healthy pace, coins were becoming less important. As a proportion of the M1 money supply (notes and coins in circulation, together with deposits in banks that are not time-limited and can be withdrawn on demand), notes and deposits grew from 22 per cent in 1910 to 83 per cent in 1936.[57]

Only the relatively stable period of government by the Kuomintang, or Chinese Nationalist Party, located in Nanjing in 1927–37 provided the opportunity to begin rationalising China's extraordinarily fissipa-rous monetary system. A new fiat currency, the fapi, was introduced in 1935, free of the burden of convertibility to silver and the associated problems of a drain of silver abroad prompted by rising silver prices.

The high prices that had led to sales of China's silver abroad had at the same time enabled the national government to build up substantial foreign reserves with which the fapi was backed. Although the new banknotes were issued by three different banks instead of a single public-sector bank, the circulation of foreign notes was from this point onwards forbidden. It was a remarkable improvement on what had gone before.[58]

The collapse of the Qing dynasty in 1911 had not so much brought to an end weak government in China, but rather had ushered in a turbulent period of nearly forty years, comprising a brief attempt at establishing a new imperial power, loss of power by the centre over the provinces during the warlord era, a lengthy and bloody attempt by Japan to extend its sovereignty over all mainland China, and finally a protracted civil war between the Kuomintang and the Chinese Communist Party. It was during this final phase of civil war that the Chinese Communist Party emerged triumphant in 1949, but not before China had again suffered another huge bout of revolutionary inflation, with monthly rates reaching 50 per cent in 1947.[59]

Russia

Three years of war and general military and economic failure created conditions in Russia in 1917 for the overthrow of the Romanov dynasty, which had by then only been living on borrowed time. Earlier military defeat by Japan and widespread social and economic unrest had resulted in a revolution in 1905. But this first attempt to effect lasting political change in the country ran up against the loyalty of the armed forces to the status quo and was defused, at least for a time, by political concessions that created a constitution and a multi-party system, and placed some limits on the Tsar's hitherto unconstrained powers. The effect, however, was merely to buy time. When the deferred cataclysm finally did occur in 1917, the transition from monarchical autocracy, via a short-lived socialist government led by the moderate Alexander Kerensky, civil war and foreign military intervention, eventually saw the Bolshevik Communist Party emerge the winners.

The central bank and its banknote production facility initially held out against the new Soviet authorities, refusing to supply notes to the new government or to open an operational account for it. Apparently, a minimal proportion – 0.1 per cent – of the total monetary issue was eventually released to the Bolsheviks after a delay of five days. In an effort to secure control of the bank and the monetary system, the Soviet authorities sacked the senior staff and seized control of the bank's vaults in November 1917. The gold holdings in both specie and ingot form of private banks were to be transferred to the state gold fund.[60] The latter step, together with the planned nationalisation of private banks, so undermined confidence that six months later, in May 1918, Lenin observed that the middle classes were hoarding currency and that a national currency reform would be required to flush out holdings of cash. Until that time, however, the new government compounded problems by continuing to issue currency notes bearing the old Tsarist designs, Treasury notes as issued by the government of Kerensky, and promissory notes bearing 5 per cent interest with denominations from 1,000 to 1 million rubles. State credit notes were pumped out with denominations ranging from 1 ruble to 10,000 rubles. By 1921, there were no fewer than forty-seven different forms and denominations of paper in circulation. Unconvincing attempts were made to persuade the population that new issues of currency were credible stores of value. Thus, a series issued by the finance ministry in March 1920 with face values between 100 and 10,000 rubles was printed with the legend 'Secured by the entire wealth of the Republic'. However much these claims might try to beguile the public, the ludicrously high face values being issued testified to the depreciation of the ruble and the consequent inflation.[61]

Despite the frenzied issue of various forms of paper money or paper money substitutes in the main cities of the republic under Soviet control, hostilities ranging across such a huge country with a poor transport infrastructure impeded the supply of currency to the provinces. When central government in a sprawling empire fails to supply adequate quantities of currency to the further reaches of its supposed authority, regional governments are forced to make up for the deficiency. Thus, regional currencies were issued in Soviet Central Asia and in the Soviet Socialist

Republics of Armenia, Azerbaijan and Georgia, which were effectively operating their own currency systems from 1920 or 1921 with the blessing of the central Soviet authorities in Moscow.[62]

The Cashless Society in Revolutionary Russia

Against this backdrop of multiple forms of circulating paper notes and autonomous currency issue by the remote republics, the Soviet authorities decided to embark on a bold experiment in monetary policy. As early as 1918, that is some years before the Bolshevik party had fully taken control of Russia, a policy of 'military communism' was promulgated to help consolidate the ideological successes the party had already achieved. All trade in grain was to be conducted under a state monopoly and all industry was to be placed under central government control. Similarly, all farms were brought under centralised control. Going even further, the Third Congress of the Council of People's Commissars passed a resolution calling for the abolition of money. Further measures prepared the ground for the realisation of this daring resolution. Free public canteens were made available in Moscow and St Petersburg (renamed Petrograd) and certain public services including mail, telegraph and telephone services were made available to the public and to institutions free of charge. Significant amounts of food were also distributed free of charge.

The idea gained momentum. In January 1920 the central bank was closed, its responsibilities being absorbed by the ministry of finance. A series of decrees issued later in the same year prohibited cash payments by public institutions and enterprises. Payments for prescription drugs, accommodation and utilities including water, gas and electricity, public transport, printed materials and other goods and services were all abolished in 1921.[63]

However, the dream of a cashless society founded on a central command economy did not survive the realisation that military communism was failing with massively damaging consequences for the population. Taking cashless transactions to a very basic but rigidly regulated level, the government attempted to fix the exchange rate of amounts of basic food products such as grain, to measures of other products and commodities. Thus, a certain weight of wheat equated to a set number of spools of thread, or a fixed volume of kerosene or a defined length of cloth. By this means, Soviet authorities aimed to eliminate the need for money as a regulating measure between products in what would otherwise be a barter process. But the programme foundered on the opposition of agricultural communities unwilling to part with basic foodstuffs on these highly regulated terms. Resentment at the heavy-handed imposition of many of these policies was aggravated by forced seizure of grain to feed Soviet troops. Other factors including variations in agricultural and industrial productivity, poor transport infrastructure and unreliable utilities services also contributed to the decline and failure of the system. The disruption of food supplies to the urban populations prompted a large-scale migration to the countryside. Dozens of revolts broke out in protest at the desperate conditions generated by the military communism programme, the most prominent of which, among sailors of the Soviet Baltic Fleet based at the naval fortress Kronstadt in the Gulf of Finland, was suppressed by a major military operation with much loss of life.

Kronstadt and other rebellions were enough to persuade Lenin that military communism had failed. The regulatory policies were unwound, prohibitions on cash payment annulled and by the end of 1921, Lenin conceded that the time had not yet arrived when money could be abolished. Thus ended the boldest of all experiments in monetary policy.[64]

The retreat from military communism led along the route of the New Economic Policy. Launched in 1921, NEP, as it became known, restored many of the financial institutions that had been banned, including the central bank itself along with money-based trading. Indeed, after the end of the civil war in 1920, the Soviet government came to rely on the issue of money to supply seigniorage as the source of 80 per cent of revenues. Despite the fact that the bank had been reconstituted, the finance ministry would be responsible for a currency reform beginning with a redenomination – a replacement of notes with very high, but inflated denominational values, with notes of a lower denomination – which was launched in November 1921. A new note known as a state monetary token or *sovznak* with a face value of 1 ruble was to be equivalent to 10,000 rubles of previous issues of currency or credit notes alongside which they would circulate freely. Sovznak denominations ranging from 1 to 1,000 rubles were issued and would be legal tender.[65]

This redenomination and parallel currency exercise did not, however, result in the stabilisation of prices. In 1921, the supply of these finance ministry sovznak notes increased 1,500 per cent and prices, hardly surprisingly, rose 1,700 per cent. The price of a tram ticket in Moscow increased 25 per cent in the month of May 1922. So, the finance ministry responded in June 1922 to this and other price rises by introducing new high-denomination sovznak notes of 5,000 and 10,000 rubles. This series, known as the 1922 pattern, was to replace all other circulating notes including those of the old Tsarist design, Treasury and credit notes of Kerensky's provisional government and others, all of which were to be demonetised.[66] But these measures did not stem the tide of inflation. In 1922, the money supply increased by at least 11,000 per cent and prices by a staggering 7,400. In October of the same year yet another redenomination was launched, setting an exchange rate of 100 rubles of the 1922 pattern to 1 ruble of the 1923 pattern. The top denomination of the new series was to be 100 rubles, but by February of 1923, under the pressure of inflation, new denominations of 250, 500 and 1,000 rubles were introduced with a 5,000 ruble note announced in November 1923.[67]

Virtually in parallel with these issues, the reconstituted state bank was authorised to issue 'banknotes' with a unit value called *chervonets*. These notes were to be 'hard currency', the entire issue being backed by 25 per cent gold and the remaining 75 per cent covered by foreign currency, bills of exchange and commodities, or so it was claimed. Although an inscription on the notes promised that they were convertible to gold, that promise was caveated by a warning that the convertibility would only be authorised by a state decree, set at some indeterminate point in the future. In the event the Act was never passed. The chervonets notes were designed as a means of issuing loans to various enterprises and would eventually be repaid to the central bank. Gold chervonets coins were minted in 1923 to the same specification in weight and size as old Tsarist coins but were very much of a Soviet design. Designed for domestic as well as foreign trade, the chervonets coin ran foul of an embargo in 1925 by western powers on payments made with Soviet gold, a problem that the Soviet authorities addressed by sending all their coins back to be reminted according to the old Tsarist 10-ruble design that was exempt from the embargo.

By 1923, with the civil war over and the revolution beginning to consolidate its territorial gains, Russia had again succumbed to its habitual desire to issue a bewildering array of money substitutes. In addition to the sovznak monetary tokens of the finance ministry and the state bank's own notes, transportation certificates denominated in rubles issued by the ministry of communications and ministry of finance 'payment obligation' notes were circulating as currency.[68] The finance ministry's sovznak monetary tokens had a legal tender status that was not enjoyed by the chervonets; the finance ministry therefore continue to issue them as a means of payment for agricultural produce from the peasant class. Finance ministry sovznak monetary tokens also performed a useful function in smaller-scale transactions as a subsidiary currency.

The chervonets:sovznak monetary token exchange rate was floating and not fixed and, as the latter was favoured for smaller transactions, the chervonet was favoured for transactions of greater value. Because of this increase in its perceived value, the central bank's chervonets also began to replace foreign currency and even Tsarist-era gold coins as a preferred store of value as well as the unit of account. The difference in perceived value between the two parallel circulating currencies appears to be underlined by the fact that, while public confidence in the chervonets rose (despite the fact that it had originally no legal tender status), the finance ministry sovznak monetary tokens became subject to extreme depreciation and hyperinflation. (Given that one of its primary purposes was to pay for agricultural produce, we might speculate that the hyperinflation originated in the sale of essential agricultural produce). By running two parallel currencies that were not pegged to each other in this way, the government had decoupled hyperinflating small denomination finance ministry currency for lower transactions from the higher value central banknotes that held their value and performed the function of unit of account and store of value.

Why did this policy of competing currencies issued by two separate institutions, to all intents and purposes a part of the same government, work? One major and obvious factor is the special endorsement that the government had awarded the chervonets. The name had been chosen to evoke a gold coin of the era of Peter the Great. Inscriptions on the note pronounced its convertibility to gold and official announcements promised that the issue was backed by gold and foreign currency. The public bought the story just as, in 1923, the German public felt inclined to believe that the rentenmark, backed supposedly by land, would put an end to Germany's post-war hyperinflation.

It was not long, however, before the finance ministry's monetary token had depreciated to a point of worthlessness. Abandoning the original policy of a floating exchange rate between the two currencies, the government decreed a peg of 50,000 monetary tokens to the chervonets in March 1924 and began the process of retiring the sovznak from circulation at that rate. Three months later the game was up. In June 1924, the finance ministry stopped accepting its own paper money: always a sure sign that a currency had lost the confidence of its own issuing authority.[69]

In the meantime, the New Economic Policy reforms that reversed the military communism programme by freeing many industrial and smaller agricultural enterprises from central control had set Russia back on the road to recovery. The chervonets played its part by offering the population a stable store of value – or at least one that the public accepted was a stable store of value. It also rendered service to the government as a stable store of value in the payment of taxes, unlike the discarded monetary tokens now abandoned by the ministry of finance.

In due course a hard-line group emerged within the Bolshevik party, determined to turn the clock back on the reforms of the New Economic Policy. Among the targets this group selected was the convertible chervonets. Convertibility left too much choice in the hands of the public, offering a means of playing the currency markets and thereby challenging the rigorous central control of the economy by ideologues on the extreme left. Accordingly, in 1926 measures were introduced to prevent the export of the chervonets, cancel its promised convertibility and ban the import of foreign currencies.[70] If military communism was to be abandoned, the ultimate symbol of nineteenth-century capitalism, gold convertible paper, could not be allowed to prosper.

In the case of the revolution in Russia, as with those in America, France and Mexico, uncertainty of outcome and a collapse of public confidence caused the currency to collapse. But a determined revolutionary political leadership supported by military success was always able to weather the temporary nature of currency failure. The failure of a currency system comes about as a result of the failure of its host regime and, contrary to the view reputedly expressed by Lenin, rarely if ever has it been the root cause of the collapse of a political regime.

3

CIVIL WAR

'I will gladly break up the sacred images and melt them into coin for your war-chest.'

Laelius to Julius Caesar, Lucan's *Pharsalia*, Book One[1]

Rome

Laelius' solemn oath to Caesar in the opening scenes of Lucan's work sums up the depths to which the warring sides would be prepared to go during Caesar's civil war. Silver and gold were crucial for the payment of armies and thus to secure their loyalty and, in keeping with Laelius' oath, one of the earliest acts of Julius Caesar's troops on entering Rome during the civil war was the forcing open of the Temple of Saturn, which housed the public Treasury. With Caesar's approval and direction, they seized the wealth the state had accumulated as a result of wars with Carthage, Gaul and Epirus and the tribute of Crete, Cyprus and Asia Minor.[2] Civil war could force the warring sides to the most extreme acts of plunder. It will also lead to debasement and depreciation of currency and loss of revenues. Professor Forrest Capie has pointed out that a nation might be prepared to sustain higher taxes, increased national debt and a degree of inflation at times of war with another state, but that the immediate loss of tax revenues to a government during civil war has an immediate impact on budget deficits and public debt, driving significantly higher rates of inflation.[3]

Inflation is, moreover, aggravated during civil war as military defeat and loss of territory shrink the region in which the losing currency circulates.

The United States of America

The civil war in the United States of America was the result of fundamental differences of opinion on the question of slavery and the rights of states to pursue their own interests on the matter. Did the sovereignty of the state take precedence over the authority of the federal government, and did this give individual states the right to pursue their own preferred policies when other states and the federal government might be strongly opposed to those policies – above all, on the subject of slavery? Or was the unity of the country of such overriding importance and so compelling that the federal government would be justified in enforcing its authority over the individual state?

This tension between the authority of the centre and the independence of the states had a parallel in America's monetary history. Attempts to assert a federal authority over money had only partially succeeded at the foundation of the new state. A national bank of the United States – known as the first Bank of the United States – had been chartered by Congress in 1791, but the charter expired in 1811. Resistance to the first bank came from political elements that were opposed to any centralised authority above that of the individual state, and held banking in particular to be anathema to the agrarian ideal of Thomas Jefferson and others of the founding fathers. The second Bank of the United States, chartered in 1816, ran foul of the same political outlook and aroused the ire of President Andrew Jackson, who saw the bank's governors as politically motivated enemies, opposed to his own election in 1824 and then in 1828.

One of the tasks of the second Bank of the United States was to control the proliferation of paper currency issued by various banks, particularly in the south and west. Once Jackson had ensured that the bank's charter was not to be renewed in 1836, there was no brake on the issue of currency by a multiplicity of banks, a period of America's banking history known as the 'wildcat' or free banking era. One estimate suggests that more than 10,000 different types of notes were in circulation by the 1850s.[4] Thus, until the American Civil War of 1861–65 there was no national paper currency on issue (although the Federal Treasury was clearly the only authorised issuer of coinage, a right that had been specifically forbidden to the states in the constitution). The Civil War, during which both the opposing Union and Confederate governments issued banknotes, ultimately put an end to that situation.

Lincoln, the newly elected president, calculated the cost of winning the war would be at least $400 million. His Secretary to the Treasury, Salmon Chase, found that in the first three months of the new government, expenditure was running at $23.5 million, while revenues were a paltry $5.8 million. Proposals to address the long-term cost of the war were based on a division of $80 million through taxes and $240 million through loans, still short of the total sum Lincoln believed he needed, but enough to cover 80 per cent.

Chase's next move was the first step towards a Federal currency. Non-interest-bearing Treasury notes, convertible on demand to gold and acceptable in payment of taxes, were to all intents and purposes a national currency, differing from other currencies such as sterling only in that they were issued by a government ministry and not a bank. The commercial note-issuing banks obviously saw this operation as direct competition and threatened to present for conversion to gold any Treasury notes that they might accumulate.[5] This means of putting an issuing authority's reserves under extreme pressure to the point where it could trigger a 'run', so-called 'note-dueling', was not uncommon in the free banking era when one bank might suddenly present accumulated notes at the bank of origin in return for specie as a way of seriously damaging or sinking a competitor.

The rivalry between the Treasury and the banks continued, but eventually, in February 1862, a year after the war had broken out, Lincoln signed the bill creating an issue of inconvertible Federal notes with denominations down to and including $5 that were to be legal tender for all transactions, private and public, with a few exceptions. Although they were not convertible into specie, these notes could be exchanged for government bonds in the future. The first issue of such notes amounted to $150 million, but this sum was soon seen as inadequate and five months later, in July 1862, an Act for the issue of a further $150 million was signed.[6] Yet another $150 million issue was authorised eight months later in March 1863, the total issue of $450 million equating to a relatively modest 16 per cent of public debt. Further issues up to a maximum of $900 million were authorised. Much debate surrounded the question of whether these issues of inconvertible paper currency simply provided the fuel to stoke inflation, raising prices of goods that the Federal government needed to purchase and which, in turn, ensured that the national debt increased. Predictably, the value of the Federal dollar ascended and declined as confidence in a Union victory waxed and waned, but the annual rate of increase in prices only amounted to about 20 per cent, relatively modest, for instance, in comparison with other turbulent periods in modern history.[7]

Lincoln's legislation on currency, formalising the Federal government's control of currency issue, coming as it did against a history of some twenty-five years where there had been no centrally issued currency, much less a central bank, was seen by many as an unprecedented extension of Federal power.[8]

The challenges for the Confederate states were different – and more difficult. Following approval by the Confederate Congress in March 1861, the southern government based in Richmond set about issuing increasing volumes of Confederate currency as a desperate substitute for tax and public debt that the Confederate government struggled to raise. The Confederacy's economic woes were to some extent self-inflicted as a result of the decision to cease exporting cotton, a measure that the Confederates hoped would force Britain and other European states, dependent on American cotton for their textile industries, to intervene in the war. The only result of this ill-judged decision and of an effective blockade by the Union navy was to starve the South of its main source of revenue.

For as long as revenues from their agricultural produce were cut off by blockade, recourse to the printing of an inconvertible fiduciary currency was perhaps the only avenue available to the southern states in their attempts to finance the war. Some degree of credibility was vested in these notes by virtue of the fact that they could be used for the payment of taxes to the Confederate state. They were, moreover, supposed to be redeemable for specie, although in reality, all the banks in the southern states together held less gold and silver than the banks of New York City alone. Matters were made worse by the fact that the Federal blockade was also effective in starving the South of important paper, printing supplies and presses.

Those notes that the Confederate government were able to produce, however, were vulnerable to counterfeiting. Accurate images of the Confederate 'greyback' note were printed in northern illustrated newspapers, providing excellent specimens for enterprising northerners set on making some money, literally, out of the Confederate paper issue. One such entrepreneur, a former newspaper publisher called Samuel Upham who operated a general store in Philadelphia, acquired sets of the $5 and $10 plates from the newspaper publishers and began to sell replicas of the notes as souvenirs. That Upham's original intent was not to produce counterfeits as we know them is demonstrated by the fact that his first notes bore the word 'facsimile'. However, resourceful Union soldiers and civilians would buy up large numbers of the notes, cut the word 'facsimile' from the bottom margin of each one and pass them in Confederate areas or in areas on the boundary between Union- and Confederate-held territory.[9]

While Upham's venture was purely a case of private enterprise and not an instance of state-sponsored counterfeiting, the Union authorities did not make an effort to close down the operation. Indeed, Upham felt so confident of his position that he placed advertisements in newspapers promoting his Confederate dollar replicas as 'curiosities'. Perhaps unsurprisingly, Confederate authorities assumed that the Union authorities were at the very least condoning the operation.[10]

Upham's notes were so good and his promotional campaign so brazen that the southern authorities were enraged. Articles appeared in newspapers in the South denouncing him and his facsimiles, which, the Confederates obligingly confirmed, were so good as to be difficult to distinguish from the originals. To add insult to injury, Upham cited these denouncements in his own promotions as the ultimate endorsement of quality. Indeed, the success of Upham's operation attracted the sincerest form of flattery: his facsimiles were imitated by counterfeiters in New York and Philadelphia.[11]

The status and credibility of notes issued by both North and South reflected the credibility of their governments. It was vital that those notes be accepted by the populations of the two warring factions if both sides were to fight on. But the promise to redeem notes for gold opened the door to hoarders and speculators, and before long the Federal government's gold reserve was declining rapidly. The internal drain of gold (where gold is withdrawn from banks and circulation but does not leave the country) had to be stopped. In February 1862, therefore, the Union Congress passed a law pronouncing the Union's Treasury notes and United States bills to be legal tender, a departure from the long-held view that only gold and silver were real money.[12] This was true fiat money – authentic and valuable because the government said so, not because of its intrinsic value or because it was convertible to gold or silver on demand. This cartalist view of money sat comfortably with the side that asserted the central authority of government.

In the South, however, the monetary regime was looser, the Confederate constitution having waived the prohibition on states issuing money. Thus, the Confederacy's own currency was in competition with notes issued by its own constituent states and, as the Confederate Congress in the South had refused to pass legislation declaring the greyback (confederate treasury banknotes) legal tender, its status was less credible than that of the greenback. Matters were made worse when the shortage of coinage in the South obliged small traders to issue their own low-value paper tokens, just as factory owners in the United Kingdom during the Industrial Revolution would pay their workers in copper tokens when the supply of coins was insufficient.[13] In its decision-making on monetary matters, the Confederate side had made more than one rod for its own back by permitting states to issue notes and by failing to provide the greyback with legal tender status. The Federal side had pursued monetary policy in accordance with its own interventionist and centralising tenets. The Confederates had likewise conducted their monetary policy in accordance with their own permissive view of states' rights, but in doing so had seriously undermined their own economy.

On an operational level the Confederate issue of greybacks was further compromised by flaws in the sourcing of the notes themselves. The production of the greyback was based on the wet lithographic process, which printed from a stone rather than the steel-engraved plates used in the North, resulting in a poorer quality image. And given that note issue was one of the few means available to the South of financing the war, demand was great, necessitating note production by nine different printing companies. The potential for production errors was evidenced by the fact that there were no fewer than 229 different versions of the $20 note.[14]

In these circumstances counterfeiting could flourish. If 229 varieties of the official greyback $20 bill alone existed, and on top of that states were permitted to issue their own notes, the population could hardly be expected to spot a counterfeit. In Upham's own estimation, he had produced $15 million worth of facsimiles, the equivalent of 3 per cent of all the notes in circulation. Another estimate suggests that by the end of the war, counterfeits amounted to anywhere between a third and a half of all notes in circulation.

The Confederate government had no choice but to retire from circulation those notes that had been worst affected, taking some 3.5 million notes out of circulation and reaffirming for the public the deeply suspect nature of paper money issued by the southern government. In effect, the fragmented nature of Confederate politics, the weakness of its monetary constitution and the lack of any real revenues or specie reserve to back the greyback combined to destroy its credibility. The North need not embark on an official programme of counterfeiting the southern notes when the South had done so much to undermine its own currency.

The more notes were issued, the more they depreciated, the more were needed to pay the Confederacy's debts. One calculation suggests that the volume of banknotes circulating in the Confederate states increased by 82,600 per cent in the course of the war. Even if this is true, it is impossible to determine what proportion of the huge increase was down to Upham's counterfeits, unrestrained note production by the individual states and excessive private enterprise by commercial printers in the South. Depreciation accelerated whenever the South suffered military setbacks, prompting doubts that the notes would ever be redeemed for specie. Between 1 August 1862 and the end of December of that year, a period that saw military and political setbacks for the South, the greyback depreciated by 60 per cent.[15] The value of gold in terms of Confederate dollars shot up 500 per cent over a period of twelve months during which the Battle of Gettysburg in July 1863 marked another serious defeat for the South.[16] By the end of the war, the cost of living in the South was ninety-two times greater than it had been immediately before the war. In the four years between January 1861 and

December 1865, prices indexed at 100 rose to 9,211, a terrible increase, but nowhere near as bad as subsequent experiences in the twentieth and twenty-first centuries. [17]

The monetary disarray of the South, combined with the absence of an industrial base and self-imposed embargo on cotton exports, undermined its economy, constraining its ability to fight the war. And, although the contrasting monetary systems of North and South did not in themselves make the difference between victory and defeat, which would always be a result of military success, they did reflect the respective political philosophies of North and South: a centrally controlled currency system versus what was in effect a version of free banking. And it was the centralised system of the Federal North in money as well as in governance that prevailed and which foreshadowed the foundation of the US monetary as well as political system today.

The Russian Civil War

Civil war followed hard on the heels of the revolution of 1917 in Russia towards the end of the First World War. Bolshevik forces defending the revolution led by Lenin ranged against the 'Whites' who sought to overturn it. As in other cases of civil war, the country's monetary system was badly affected. Older, Tsarist notes continued to circulate, as did banknotes issued by the short-lived liberal government of Alexander Kerensky, while a multiplicity of rival notes were issued by the Whites and by the Bolsheviks. It is estimated that, throughout Russia at this time, 2,000 separate entities were issuing paper currencies. [18]

The White Counter-Revolution
It is misleading to think of a single united opposition to the Bolshevik forces in Russia immediately after the revolution. Beyond the relatively modest area controlled by the Soviets, opposition authorities established thirty-five different regional governments across some eighty-one provinces spanning eleven distinct time zones. Paper money was issued by military authorities, by civilian regional governments, by city administrations, district councils and commercial enterprises. [19]

In the south of Russia, largely controlled by the White Army opposition forces, hostilities in 1918 disrupted the transportation of money
from external sources of supply. Consequently, local currency production facilities of varying degrees of sophistication were established in
at least six towns. In the autumn of that year, the various military commands in the region agreed to centralise and harmonise their monetary
production, the various issues and monetary substitutes eventually being
withdrawn and replaced by currency based on that issued in the city
of Rostov-on-Don. The pacification of the southern region between
1918 and 1920 and a unified leadership of military forces under General
Anton Denikin created the right conditions for this regional currency
reform, although the priority allocation of money to military expenditure left insufficient for ordinary civilian use. In these circumstances,
notes of the Kerensky government were permitted to circulate.

When, in the winter of 1919–20, Denikin's forces were pushed
back by advancing Soviet forces, the currency production facilities in
Kiev, Odessa, Rostov and Novocherkassk were lost. The usual pattern
emerged: military defeat damaged public confidence in Denikin's currency. As the area under his control diminished, currency issued under
his authority was shifted to the shrinking areas under his control where
it could be spent. The ever-increasing volumes of notes circulating
among a population in the reduced area under Denikin's control could
only mean monetary inflation and depreciation. At the same time, the
printing press was becoming the principal economic resource of the
White forces under Denikin's control.[20]

As Denikin's command showed signs of faltering, Bolshevik successes
called for a change of opposition leadership. The dizzying numbers
of anti-Bolshevik authorities, including the southern armies led by
Denikin, eventually consolidated around the leadership of Admiral
Kolchak in 1919. Kolchak's leadership did not get off to a bad start.
Military successes convinced other opponents of the Bolsheviks
that this was a man who could lead them to victory over Lenin. This
political conviction would not have been diminished by the fact that
Kolchak had gained control of most of Russia's gold reserves, and yet,
as we shall see in the case of Spain, such control counted for little in
the face of an indomitable opponent. Pursuing a relatively open policy

of free movement for produce and people across the lines between the Bolsheviks and his own forces, Kolchak permitted food and other products to travel west from regions under his control while currency from the Soviet-controlled areas flowed east in payment.

With consolidation of political and military opposition to the Bolsheviks around Kolchak as the pre-eminent leader of the Whites came, naturally, an attempt to consolidate the multiplicity of currencies in circulation. A progressive programme of redemption began with the withdrawal of local and substitute moneys, which were to be exchanged for money issued by Kerensky's government. Once the former had been withdrawn from circulation, the Kerensky notes ('kerenkas') in circulation would be exchanged for Tsarist notes. The broad base of various currencies in circulation would therefore be progressively narrowed until, finally, the Tsarist notes would be replaced by a new series that had been commissioned from the American Banknote Company. However, this apparently straightforward progressive monetary reform ran up against various problems, including delays in the delivery of the American notes and an unpredictably large number of kerenkas being presented for exchange. Kolchak's government resorted to the issue of money substitutes in the form of short-term bonds.[21]

Military defeat of the White opposition forces, the capture and execution of Kolchak and the evacuation of White troops under the command of Denikin's successor, General Wrangel, from the Crimea, left western and southern Russia in the hands of Soviet authorities. Chaotic monetary arrangements on both sides of the conflict had, as far as can be seen, no influence on the eventual outcome of the civil war. Stability of the respective currency systems of Reds and Whites was an effect of military successes and never a cause.

Outside Intervention

The decision of the new, revolutionary, regime to withdraw from the First World War had been a major blow to its former allies France and Britain as it removed the threat of a second front in Germany's rear and consequently released more of the latter's forces for active service on the Western Front. The Allies deployed forces to northern Russia in July 1918 in support of the Whites with the ultimate aim of overthrowing the Bolshevik party and installing a government willing to resume the war against Germany.

To support the political and military operations of the British expeditionary force based in the north Russian port of Archangel and its White allies, British officials (notably J.M. Keynes) advised the White North Russian government on the establishment of a special currency-issuing authority, known as the *caisse d'emission*, based to some extent on the operations of Britain's colonial West African currency board. The currency board arrangement, which had already been pioneered in other parts of the British Empire in the nineteenth century, involved the strict fixing by law of exchange rates between the local currency and a reserve hard currency such as sterling, effectively vesting sterling with an equal importance in the currency system alongside the local currency.

The North Russian government's *caisse* issued coins and paper rubles at an exchange rate of 40 to the pound sterling. Rubles would only be issued in return for foreign currency. The British government undertook to buy 25,000,000 rubles worth of these currency notes to be used for procurement of provisions for the British troops in North Russia. For wider public consumption, the North Russian government announced that these rubles were guaranteed by its own property. In reality they were backed by a loan of sterling from the British government equivalent to 75 per cent of the total value of the ruble issue and held on deposit at the Bank of England. North Russian government bonds up to a maximum of the remaining 25 per cent of the value of the rubles on issue could be purchased by the *caisse d'emission*. These bonds, as well as the sterling loan on deposit at the Bank of England, yielded interest and therefore provided a profit to the *caisse* and to the North Russian government.

The population of the immediate area in which the *caisse d'emission* notes were to be used was thought to be 600,000. It was estimated by the senior British official attached to the expeditionary force that there were already 600 million rubles circulating in the region. Under the new arrangements, these older rubles were to be exchanged for the new *caisse d'emission* rubles at the rate of 48:40. But, older rubles depreciated and the rate of exchange offered by the *caisse d'emission* reflected that depreciation:

	40 *Caisse d'Emission* rubles exchange rates for old rubles
April 1919	48
Early May 1919	64
Mid–May 1919	72
Late June 1919	80

Source: Hanke, Steve, Jonung, Lars & Schuler, Kurt, *Russian Currency and Finance* (Routledge, 1993), p.148.

Under such circumstances where the *caisse d'emission* rubles held their value against the other available paper currency, it is hardly a surprise that *caisse* rubles were steadily becoming more popular, somewhat contrary to Gresham's law. Local estimates suggested that *caisse* rubles in circulation increased from zero rubles in November 1918 to nearly 53,000,000 rubles in July 1919. The value of old rubles in circulation, on the contrary, declined from about 600 million to about 300 million from October 1918 April 1919.[22] In constructing a currency board of this type with the ruble pegged at 40:1 to its backing reserve of sterling held at the Bank of England, Keynes had devised a scheme with dual benefits: its currency enjoyed the stability of sterling, but it accrued seigniorage – a profit for the Russian opposition based in Archangel.[23]

With the end of the First World War and Germany's defeat, the primary purpose of the expeditionary force and its monetary agency disappeared. All Allied troops had left North Russia by the end of September 1919. *Caisse* rubles continued to be redeemed for foreign exchange until the middle of October. Thereafter, some 13.5 million *caisse* rubles – also known as English rubles – remained in public circulation in North Russia. The *caisse d'emission* closed down its Russian operations and 55 million paper rubles held by the army were dumped at sea, with a book credit to that value credited to the army. Transferred to London, the remnant *caisse* operations were tasked with the settlement and redemption of this book credit for 55 million rubles.[24] In April 1920 the *caisse* and its note redemption operations ceased. The 13.5 million rubles in public possession issued by the *caisse* were rendered worthless.

The 'English' rubles, relatively stable and backed by sterling, were nothing without the military presence of the Allied forces, while the weaker and depreciating Bolshevik currency, backed by nothing more than the unstoppable advance of the Bolshevik forces, triumphed.

The Spanish Civil War 1936–39

The monetary dimension of the Spanish Civil War reflects the unique nature of that conflict. Led by the senior commanders of the Spanish military, particularly the officers commanding the army of Spain's colony in Morocco, the Nationalist side was an alliance that included social and political groups such as the major landowners and business-men, royalists, the church and fascists of the Falange party among others. Launching their revolt against an overwhelmingly left-wing govern-ment that similarly consisted of many different interests, the Nationalist campaign began in the colonies and moved on to gain a foothold in the southern agricultural regions of Spain. Despite the fact that a number of senior commanders and military formations remained loyal to the elected Republican government, the overwhelming majority of military officers were in favour of the Nationalist uprising and that strength was reinforced by direct intervention on the part of the fascist regimes of Germany and Italy. What the Nationalists did not control, however, were the industrial centres of the north – at least until June 1937 – as well as the Bank of Spain and its reserves – notably its gold reserves.

Republican parties of the left in the early years of the war had included communists, anarchists closely linked to the trade union movements and POUM, a Marxist party opposed to the dominance of the Soviet Union. The Republican coalition also included the regional government of the Catalan region and elements of the Basque country, both of which stood a better chance of autonomy under a left-wing government than they would under a Nationalist government bent on maintaining a unified Spain where Spanish would be the only accepted language. Although the Nationalist side consisted of parties of different persuasion, there was a high degree of cohesion based on an uncompromising central com-mand and control under the emerging leadership of General Franco.

Ideological and regional rivalries among the Republicans, however, seriously undermined the ability of the Republic's leadership to shape an effective opposition to the rebellion.

While the centralised command and control of the Nationalist military forces and the effective contribution of German and Italian military assets, together with a feeble demonstration of neutrality on the part of moderate Britain and France, were key elements in the eventual success of the Nationalist forces, the Republic's reliance on the Soviet Union for arms and some specialist military personnel served the government less well. The Nationalists' foreign supporters, Germany and Italy, supplied arms and men on soft terms, but in contrast the Soviet Union drove an exceptionally hard bargain with the Republican government.

Having taken a neutral position during the First World War, Spain had been able to benefit commercially from the conflict, accumulating what amounted to the fourth largest gold reserves in the world[25] – 635 tons valued at $715 million at the prevailing rate in 1936. According to some accounts, some 26 per cent of this total was shipped to France by 1937, initially in return for arms, but as France's neutrality kicked in, preventing arms shipments, the gold was converted to hard currency to be used by the Republican government in purchasing arms on the open market.[26] The Republic's finance minister, Juan Negrin, who was himself a communist, was also persuaded to establish a gold account in Moscow to be used for the purchase of armaments abroad. The balance of Spain's gold reserves – 510 tons of metal worth about $518 million at 1936 values – was to be sent to Moscow and left the country in September 1936, travelling to Moscow via the ports of Cartagena, Marseilles and Odessa. The Soviet Union was quick to submit its bills for 'fraternal support' – $51 million or 10 per cent of the value of the total Spanish gold reserves held in Moscow was promptly deducted to cover the support already rendered. Subsequent analysis has suggested that as the Soviets drew down on the Spanish gold in return for arms, they were vastly overcharging above market prices.[27]

Leaving aside the question of Soviet accounting for the value of arms and services provided, the public news of the transfer of gold reserves overseas had a clear and drastic impact on the value of the Republican peseta. Between November and December 1936 its value collapsed by

50 per cent on foreign exchanges, with predictably punishing results for the price of imports and the cost of living.[28] Between July 1936 and March 1937 prices in the Republican zone had doubled, and within two years of the start of the civil war the cost of living in such regions had tripled. By July 1937, the Nationalist peseta was worth three times more than the Republican version in terms of French francs and over the previous eight months prices in the Nationalist zone had increased by only 15 per cent. Throughout the course of the war, the Nationalist peseta had lost less than 28 per cent of its value.[29]

Why did the monetary system of the Nationalists survive the war in better condition than that of their Republican opponents? In what way did the two systems of management differ? Modern assessments have challenged the winning side's propaganda, according to which Franco's Nationalists had simply managed their resources more prudently. Both sides resorted equally to a wide range of means to finance their military campaigns: taxation, expropriation, asset sales, borrowing and a stop on payments all contributed, but both sides also depended on the creation of money.[30]

Collection of taxes in the Republican zone in 1937 is estimated at about 1,200 million pesetas – a little over 50 per cent of the 1935 pre-war budget of 2,140 million pesetas. Wartime revenue collections in Valencia and Catalonia, representing elements of the total Republican zone, were similarly much lower than they had been in 1935. So, revenue collection went in quite the wrong direction to support the vastly increased expenditure always resulting from war. Tax revenues in the Nationalist zone, in contrast, increased steadily between 1935 and 1938 to 847 million pesetas as they seized more of the industrial bases in the north of the country, although they still failed to reach the same level as in the Republican zone and amounted to only 38 per cent of the revenues collected in the pre-war Spain of 1935.[31]

Expropriation is considered to have been a significant factor in the raising of revenues, although concrete figures are not available. However, on the Republican side at least, the funds raised through confiscation in this way were not used to fund the war, but rather were set aside originally for reconstruction purposes. In the event, much of these funds were transferred overseas.[32]

Internal borrowing during a state of civil war was never likely to succeed for the same reason that trying to raise money on the international capital markets was not viable: possible lenders were simply not prepared to take the risk – particularly as both sides had at times suspended interest payments on loans.[33] External loans – from Germany and Italy to the Nationalists and from the Soviet Union to the Republican side – displayed a significant advantage to the Nationalists who obtained well over $700 million in this way, compared to only $70 million in loans to the Republicans. Altogether, the Republic's asset sale of its gold reserves plus loans from the Soviet Union amounted to nearly $770 million. The composition of the Nationalists' funding was quite the reverse: overwhelmingly consisting of loans, there was only a small amount of revenue achieved by the sale of assets.[34]

Money creation, however, remained the single largest source of funding for the two hostile parties. The calculations of Martin-Acena et al. ('Spanish Civil War Finances revisited', 2010) record Republican expenditure of 5.7 billion pesetas in 1936, of which 54 per cent was allocated to defence expenditure in 1937, rising to total expenditure of 21.3 billion pesetas in 1938, of which 67 per cent was dedicated to military expenditure. The total Republican expenditure through-out the war reached 40 billion pesetas of which, 24 billion pesetas or 60 per cent of expenditure was financed by credits and advances from the Bank of Spain.

In stark contrast to this level of expenditure on the Republican side, at least one calculation puts Nationalist expenditure throughout the duration of the war at no more than 11.9 billion pesetas – although admittedly the source of this calculation was a report produced by Franco's own finance minister in 1940 and it has subsequently been exposed as an underestimate. Nationalist reliance on its own rival Bank of Spain to provide credits – or at least to hold debit balances on the Nationalist government's account – covered 70 per cent of all expenditure. Moreover, the Nationalists' explanation of their expenditure was less than complete, since much of their military outlay was based on loans from Germany and Italy that they were not obliged to repay until after the war.[35]

Inflation also differed significantly between the Republican and Nationalist zones: 134 per cent in the nine months following July 1936 in the former, 12.5 per cent in the comparable period in the Nationalist zone.[36] The upward march of inflation in the Republican zone temporarily levelled out in June–July 1938, during the Battle of the Ebro when the Republic enjoyed military success. Thereafter, the Nationalists led by Franco regained the military advantage and the Republican peseta continued its decline until the end of the war. This is not to say, however, that the Nationalist peseta did not depreciate as well. Indeed, between July and December 1938 it fell by 33 per cent against the French franc and by 51 per cent against the US dollar.

A comparison of the increase in money stock in the two zones (Martin-Acena et al.) between 1936 and 1939 describes a four-fold growth of money stock per capita in the regions under Nationalist control, while a six-fold growth per capita was reached in the republican zone by the end of the war. The situation was, of course, aggravated by the fact that the proportion of the population in the Republican zone was diminishing as the Nationalist forces conquered more of the country, leaving a larger stock of money to be distributed among a smaller share of the population. The increasing amount of money per capita in circulation as well as worsening shortages of a range of food, goods and raw materials in the Republican zone were significant factors in driving up prices and depreciating the currency.

The Republican peseta's ability to command the confidence of the population was further damaged by the declaration of Franco's government that all banknotes issued by the Republicans after July 1936 would be illegal. Parts of the country closest to the Nationalist advance would therefore be most incentivised to part quickly with their Republican pesetas, increasing the stock of that currency in an ever-decreasing zone with a shrinking population. Runs on the banks in the Republican zone also added to the misery. As if these factors were not enough to accelerate depreciation, inflation and a general lack of confidence in the currency of the Republican government, things were made yet worse by the issue of currencies by regions and by revolutionary organisations. The Republican government only established centralised money issue in autumn 1937.[37]

During the civil war, two Central Banks operated, issuing two pesetas – a Nationalist one and a Republican one. Both sides imposed price and exchange controls. The Republicans started the war with a clear advantage in that it held the gold reserves, but credit lines from Germany and Italy made the difference in financial terms for the Nationalist side. In the end, though, it was military might rather than financial skill that secured victory for Franco and his generals.

Bosnia 1992–95

The civil war that tore Bosnia–Herzegovina apart in 1992–95 following the collapse of Yugoslavia involved the Muslim Bosniak community, ethnic Croats and Serbs all resident within the borders of the Republic of Bosnia–Herzegovina as principal protagonists. Although it is conventionally described as a civil war, the origins of this conflict were not purely a question of political principles as it had been in civil wars in England in the seventeenth century, in the United States in the nineteenth and in Spain and Russia during the twentieth. Instead, the opposing sides were ranged largely along ethnic lines, with the bitter rivalry between Serbs in the Republika Srpska region of Bosnia–Herzegovina and the Bosniak Muslims leading to the worst atrocities of the war. The nature of the conflict is nowhere better explained than in the fact that it was this war that made the phrase 'ethnic cleansing' internationally recognisable, even if the origins of the expression may be traced back earlier to Serb–Kosovar tensions in Kosovo.

While Yugoslavia, then comprising a federation of the countries of Serbia, Montenegro, Slovenia, Croatia, Macedonia and Bosnia–Herzegovina, was ruled by Tito, national interests were subsumed within the federal project and identity. Tito, who governed the federation from the end of the Second World War to his death in 1980, had discouraged nationalism among the constituent states and peoples. Following his death and the institution of a presidency that rotated among political leaders selected by national assemblies, these national interests began to surface, beginning with measures taken by the Serbian political leadership in 1990 to suppress the efforts of the autonomous region of Kosovo to achieve greater autonomy. Raising the stakes, Kosovo responded by unilaterally declaring itself a republic, the first in a series of steps taken by various countries of the federation towards independence. In the same year both Slovenia and Croatia gave signs of an intent to declare independence, at which point a Serbian minority announced its wish to secede from Croatia. When both Slovenia and Croatia formally announced their secession in 1991, Yugoslav People's Army units in Croatia attempted to support local Serb militias against their Croatian opponents. But in January 1992 the European Union recognised the independence of Croatia and Slovenia, encouraging Bosnia to follow suit. In March, the Bosniak majority in the Bosnian National Assembly voted for independence in the face of opposition from the substantial Serbian minority. The situation in Bosnia, where Serbian militias set about isolating the cities from the Serb-dominated countryside, escalated into a full-blown protracted conflict that drew in the United Nations, the European Union and NATO.[38]

The monetary stability of the constituent states of Yugoslavia was already teetering before the outbreak of hostilities in Bosnia. During this period of civil war – or rather inter-ethnic war – communities in Bosnia demonstrated their monetary loyalties through their preference for separate currencies. The Croatian dinar circulated among the Croatians of western Herzegovina, bordering Croatia; Serbian-dominated Yugoslavia's dinar was favoured in areas under Serb control; while the Muslim Bosniaks transacted, in part at least, by using their own Bosnian dinar, issued by the local central bank. Serbian communities in Croatia and Bosnia also issued their own local currencies, pegged to the Yugoslav dinar and to each other, a measure that in the course of the conflict simply acted as a transmission mechanism for hyperinflation from Yugoslavia to these other regions. Inflation, and in some cases *hyper*inflation, followed hard on the heels of political and ethnic fragmentation.

Only three months after Bosnia's declaration of independence, the country was locked into hyperinflation. In June 1992 a monthly inflation rate of 322 per cent was reached, with prices doubling every fourteen days. In 1992, the highest banknote denomination of the Bosnian currency was the 1,000 dinar; a year later it was the 100,000,000 dinar.

The supply lines of the capital, Sarajevo, surrounded by Serbian militias able to call down fire on the town from the hills that overlooked it, were choked, causing extremes of inflation as access to vital foodstuffs became increasingly difficult. Misha Glenny, a British journalist covering the Balkan wars in 1993, reported the impact on the population. While a salary – such as it was – might be as little as 2 to 5 deutschmarks (which had been adopted as a reliable currency) per month in Sarajevo, a single egg could cost as much as 4 deutschmarks. Only a few miles away prices in areas under Croatian control could be on average 75 per cent cheaper. In 1994 the Bosniak National Bank replaced the old, hyperinflated, dinar with a new dinar at the rate of 1 new dinar: 10,000 old dinar.

And in the Republika Srpska, the Serbian breakaway region of Bosnia–Herzegovina close to Sarajevo, the monthly hyperinflation rate of the local dinar issued by the Bank of the Republika Srpska reached a staggering 297 million per cent in January 1994. Although high levels of inflation or hyperinflation would have to be expected in the circumstances in which Republika Srpska found itself, the situation was clearly aggravated by a transfer of inflation from the Federal Republic of Yugoslavia, where hyperinflation in the same month of January 1994 reached a monthly rate of 313 million per cent. This state of affairs was no doubt generated by the fact that the National Bank of the Republika Srpska continued to see itself as a branch of the Yugoslav Central Bank in Belgrade, and indeed the electronic payments system for the Republika Srpska was fully integrated with the Yugoslav payment system. Moreover, the locally issued Republika Srpska currency was, as we have already noted, pegged to the Yugoslav dinar. The Yugoslav dinar and the dinar of the Republika Srpska were both wiped out in 1994 by this most extreme case of terminal inflation. Yugoslavia remonetised, introducing a new dinar in 1995. The Republika Srpska made no attempt to introduce a new locally issued currency after the 1994 collapse of its local currency, but rather took to issuing the new Yugoslav dinars in exchange for deutschmarks. In the calculations of Steve Hanke and Nicholas Krus, the currencies of Yugoslavia and the Republika Srpska issued until their complete collapse in 1994 hold the unenviable distinction of occupying the third and fourth places in the historic league table of extreme hyperinflation.[39]

Indicative of the extreme monetary instability in the Balkans at this time, US dollar exchange rate records between March 1992 and June 1998 do not record a rate for the Bosnian dinar, nor indeed does the Croatian dinar appear until the new currency, the kunar, was introduced in 1994, two years after Croatia had become independent.[40]

1 US Dollar =

	Croatian Dinar	Bosnian Dinar	Yugoslav Dinar
March 1992	Not Recorded	Not Recorded	177
June 1993	Not Recorded	Not Recorded	375,000
December 1993	Not Recorded	Not Recorded	21,943,000
September 1994	5.68*	Not recorded	20,869**
June 1995	4.97	Not Recorded	2.45***
March 1996	5.4	Not Recorded	4.9
March 1997	5.95	Not Recorded	6.1
September 1998	6.5	Not Recorded	11
September 1999	7.2	1.87****	14.8

* Kunar introduced

** Old dinar

*** New dinar introduced

**** Convertible mark introduced

The dire economic circumstances prevailing during the war and contributing to the collapse of the currency can be seen in the gross domestic product (GDP) figures for the period. In 1991, Bosnia's GDP amounted to $10.25 billion. By 1996 it had collapsed by more than 70 per cent to $2.78 billion.[41]

In these circumstances, where no single currency ruled and those that circulated were hopelessly weak, the population – especially those in areas under Bosniak control – elected to use the German deutschmark. It was a demonstration of the inverse of Gresham's law where, in a world of fiat rather than commodity currencies, a point of terminal inflation can be reached where good money must replace bad. There were parallels with the situation in Mexico in 1916 when conditions had so degenerated that gold coins, until then hoarded, returned to circulation, preferable to the worthless paper currency.

The December 1995 Dayton Accord that settled the civil war and provided a constitution for post-war Bosnia set out the simplest arrangements for a central bank. The constitution stipulated the creation of an executive board for the central bank that included as representatives of all three warring communities a governor from each ethnic group, with a foreign governor appointed by the International Monetary Fund presiding as a voting member of the board. Reflecting the politico-ethnic realities of the Republic of Bosnia–Herzegovina, the representatives were appointed from the two political 'entities' that lay within the boundaries of the Republic – the Bosniak and Croat coming together to form the Federation of Bosnia–Herzegovina and the Serb coming from Republika Srpska. As a means of neutralising political influence on the creation of money, the accord also stipulated that the 'bank' should operate a currency board system, legally locking in exchange rates to hard currency backing the issue of the new currency for the first six years of its existence, after which the Bosnian parliament would be able to authorise a change in its operations.

In mid 1996, a team of experts from the IMF began working in Bosnia on the detailed plans for the new currency system. Different options for the stabilisation of Bosnia's currency were considered: one option was the outright adoption of the deutschmark as the sole circulating currency, with its attendant problem of loss of seigniorage (the profit the central bank makes from the issue of currency), not to mention the constraining effect of imposing Europe's strongest currency on a country needing to recover from war and economic collapse. But the overwhelming consideration was the need to bring under control the extreme rate of hyperinflation in the country and if complete adoption of the deutschmark was going one step too far, a currency board arrangement, with all its rigorous constraints on the creation of money, seemed to be the right solution. The deutschmark was already circulating in Bosnia and the locally issued Bosnian dinar was, by 1996, already convertible to the deutschmark at a fixed rate (1 deutschmark = 100 Bosnian dinars).

A currency board arrangement, while stabilising the currency, would at least yield seigniorage to Bosnia and would introduce a local currency that, with all its symbolism, would support national identity and national cohesion. Given the currency board's limited range of operations, it had the additional merit of being easier to set up and less resource-intensive than a central bank. The third option – of different currency boards covering different regions of Bosnia – in other words, the Republika Srpska and the Federation of Bosnia–Herzegovina – would hardly enhance a sense of national cohesion. In the circumstances, a single 'bank' operating as a currency board for the entire republic emerged as a clear winner.[42]

Implementation required the replacement of both the National Bank of Bosnia–Herzegovina and the National Bank of the Republika Srpska with an entirely new Central Bank of Bosnia–Herzegovina. The National Bank of Bosnia–Herzegovina would transfer its monetary liabilities consisting of the notes, coins and securities in its vaults to the new Central Bank of Bosnia–Herzegovina and, consistent with the latter's new operational status as a currency board where currency issued had to be backed by the anchor currency, it would receive from the outgoing National Bank a sum of deutschmarks equivalent to the notes and coins already issued at the existing rate of 1 deutschmark: 100 (new, i.e. issue of 1994) Bosnian dinar. As the National Bank leadership had, to its credit, maintained a strong level of deutschmark backing for the new dinar from 1994, this requirement was not unrealistic. The Bosnian dinars already in circulation would be exchanged for a new currency as soon as the latter was ready. Balances held for commercial banks at the National Bank would be transferred to the new Central Bank at the established deutschmark rate.[43]

The same arrangement could not, however, apply to the National Bank of the Republika Srpska. As already reported, the bank acted to all intents and purposes as a branch of the Yugoslavian national bank, issuing Yugoslav dinars in exchange for deutschmarks, which in turn would be used to purchase dinars from the Yugoslavian national bank. The IMF team learned that the only dinars held in the vaults of the Republika Srpska bank had already been sold to the parent body in Belgrade but had not yet been transferred there. The team planning the transition accepted that the Serb republic had no assets or liabilities to transfer to the new Central Bank and required only that the National Bank of the Republic Srpska should be wound up in an orderly fashion.

The division of the country and its monetary system along ethnic lines had also had a direct and negative impact on the electronic payment system that had served Yugoslavia efficiently until the break-up of the federation. Each of the three communities – the Croats, Serbs and Bosniaks – had ended up with its own payment system designed to settle non-cash payments between bank accounts. The National Bank of Republika Srpska continued to use the system centred in Belgrade, Serbia, while the Croat and Bosniak communities each developed their own new systems that did not facilitate payments across all areas of the country. The reform of Bosnia's non-cash payment systems, the winding down of the payment bureaux that ran them and the establishment of a modern system facilitating payments across the entire country proved to be as contentious and complicated as the introduction of a new currency acceptable to all sides.[44]

Negotiations with representatives of the two political 'entities' were not entirely plain sailing. Both sides wanted to retain a degree of freedom of manoeuvre in case the Federation of Bosnia comprising the Bosniaks and the Croats on the one hand and the Republika Srpska were to separate after all. The residual hostility of the protagonists led to disagreements on the name of the currency and on designs. Eventually, in mid 1997, the bland but uncontroversial term 'convertible mark' was adopted, having the merits of linguistically linking the convertibility of the new local currency to the anchor currency, the deutschmark. Until the introduction of a single unified set of convertible mark designs could be implemented, the plan involved the introduction of 'coupons' as a temporary measure. Two sets of coupon designs would be issued, each separate set displaying symbols reflecting either the Republika Srpska or the Federation of Bosnia–Herzegovina. One set representing the Republika Srpska would show portraits of writers significant to Serbian history and culture and Serbian text in the Cyrillic script would be predominant. Another set, representing the Federation, would present symbols and writers' portraits chosen by the Croat and Bosniak representatives.

The question of the designs to be used was clearly a potential source of controversy, so, according to the Central Bank law, the coupon design of one 'entity' had to be acceptable to the other. This would assert the separate identity of the two sets of coupons and their sponsoring entity. However, there would also be shared design elements common to both sets emphasising the unification of the two entities in a single republic. The designs were eventually cleared through the UN's Office of the High Representative and in February 1998 presented to the joint presidency of three members, one Bosniak, one Croat and one Serb. In this way, the 'coupons' were to represent a transitional step, on the one hand acknowledging the two political entities within the state, on the other hand beginning the process of bringing the separate currencies together.[45]

In fact, and in spite of the provisions of the accord and assurances of some of the guaranteeing governments, the interim stage of coupon issue was circumvented. The dual Federation–Republika Srpska designs were never denominated as 'coupons' and these designs have essentially remained in circulation until the time of writing (2017) as the accepted two forms of a full-blown legal tender currency, the convertible mark, issued by a single authority. Care was taken to issue notes bearing the Federation designs (with text in Latin script) in the Bosniak–Croat area first, while notes bearing the Cyrillic script for the Republika Srpska were issued first in that part of the republic. After this initial issue, however, notes from either entity freely circulated in the area of the other 'entity'.[46]

A cynical observer might wonder whether the idea of the coupon had been from the very start merely a blind to overcome interminable wrangling over designs by representatives of both 'entities'. A less cynical view might hold that the original intention had indeed been to issue coupons as a temporary solution prior to the issue of banknotes, but that the international community had hit on the expediency of converting the coupon designs, which had been accepted by the two entities, into the final currency designs as that would be easier than trying to get both sides to agree on a single set of designs acceptable to all sides. Either way, the expediency seems to have worked and as a result, Bosnia possesses a circulating family of notes that is unique in the world in having two distinct sets of currency representing two entities issued by one authority. The only adjustment to this policy was the introduction in 2002 of a 200 convertible mark note that exists in only one design but is accepted by both entities. It seems likely that the passage of time and the acceptability of the notes already in circulation made it easier for both sides now to accept a single design.[47]

A deadline of 11 August 1997 had been set for the first stage of remonetisation, which would largely involve administrative and technical preparations for the changeover, but would also be the day on which the National Bank of Bosnia would hand over its functions, assets and liabilities to the new Central Bank. This phase would also include the conversion of bank deposits from Bosnian dinars to convertible marks, even though the latter would not be physically ready for exchange on that date. The existing rate of exchange of Bosnian dinar:deutschmark at 100:1 had been adopted as the basis for the Bosnian dinar:convertible mark rate. As the convertible mark was to be pegged to the deutschmark at 1:1, the Bosnian dinar:convertible mark rate was to be 100:1.

The Bosnian convertible mark was to remain convertible to the deutschmark at a rate of 1:1, until the deutschmark was replaced by the euro as the anchor currency. In the early period after the introduction of the convertible mark in June 1998 there was concern that some commercial banks were consistently using the new currency to buy deutschmarks, as was permitted by currency board arrangements. On the recommendation of one of the lead foreign advisers (Warren Coats of the IMF), the Central Bank continued to honour this fundamental principle of the currency board, thereby reinforcing confidence in the currency system and in the convertible mark.

The new convertible mark was introduced in June 1998, but deutschmarks, Croatian kunar and Yugoslavian dinar were still in circulation in 1999. The convertibility of the new currency to the anchor deutschmark in fact made it an attractive currency for the Republika Srpska. Although the latter entity had still been using the Yugoslav dinar from the end of the conflict until 1998, it progressively moved over to the convertible mark from July 1998 to 1999, increasing the proportion of public sector salaries paid in convertible marks until all wages were paid in that currency from early 1999 onwards.[48]

The history of the civil war in Bosnia and its effect on the currencies in circulation there is yet another demonstration of how easily complete collapse of a currency system can follow the outbreak of domestic conflict. But the post-war monetary arrangements prove equally effectively that wise stewardship can relatively quickly restore order to a country's ruined monetary system – provided the essential ingredient of peace has already been imposed.

4

MONEY SUPPLY AND THE FIRST WORLD WAR

'The Sinews of War are infinite Money.'

Marcus Tullius Cicero

Protagonists – The Opening Gambit

Britain

In a monetary world dominated and regulated by the gold stand-ard, where paper notes were readily convertible to gold and where a run on a currency might see a nation's gold reserves drain abroad, war threatened to shake the foundations of the global monetary system. The danger to Britain's monetary system had been recognised by London's commercial bankers as early as February 1914, in a memorandum warn-ing of the threat foreign powers could pose to the nation's gold reserve by demanding conversion to specie of the sterling notes they might hold as reserves for their own currencies. In some quarters it was publicly asserted that the ability of each protagonist to wage war would be deter-mined by the scale of their gold reserves. As developments in the Balkans in late July 1914 brought international tensions to a head, threatening war, there were runs on the gold stocks of commercial banks as people tried to convert their sterling banknotes into gold. Commercial banks began to withdraw gold from their accounts at the Bank of England and directed members of the public wishing to convert their sterling notes to gold to the Bank.

The difficulty was that the British denominational structure included a paper £5 note and higher values in paper, but there was no paper £1 note, smaller denominations being represented by a gold 'sovereign' coin worth a pound sterling and half sovereign worth 10 shillings. At the rate at which £5 notes were being presented for conversion, banks would soon run out of gold. The Bank's bullion reserves evaporated on 29 July and the following three days, dropping from $130 million to less than $50 million, and its stock of banknotes fell by 70 per cent.[1]

A system that geared banknote issue to the available gold reserves, and a system of convertibility to gold that had to be honoured ultimately by the central bank, threatened to collapse the money supply at precisely that time of national crisis when it was necessary for the public to have confidence in it. Even if the Bank of England, as national bank of issue, ultimately had the means of injecting more money into the economy to bolster public confidence, it was constrained by strict regulations on the minimum amount of gold that was needed to support the issue of paper banknotes. Moreover, the particular susceptibility of the British system to politically inspired panic is marked by this dramatic decline in gold reserves compared with those of Germany, which in a similar period lost only $25 million of gold from $500 million worth of gold reserves.

Representatives of the leading commercial banks proposed to the British government solutions to the problem of a constrained money supply threatened by hoarding. Either the Bank Act could be suspended, relaxing the rules restricting the issue of money, or the commercial banks could deposit gold and securities at the Bank that would enable it to conform to the regulations on reserves covering banknote issue and issue more notes.[2]

The option of suspending the convertibility of paper to gold and placing an embargo on the freedom to ship gold out of the country when desired had been discussed inconclusively prior to the war by the Committee of Imperial Defence. Free shipment of gold was considered by both the Bank of England and the City of London bankers as a fundamental plank of confidence in the City as an open economy. Should there be a ban on the export of gold, it would undermine confidence in Britain's credit, which for the banking capital of the world was unthinkable. Britain, never having been subject to a deliberate monetary attack on its economy as an instrument of war or political influence, had no reason to plan for the unthinkable – especially when the consequences for British financial hegemony could be so devastating, drawing with it a catastrophic range of secondary economic problems. Even though some experts had advised that planning for financial war was as vital as military and naval preparations, the received wisdom was that an embargo on the shipment of gold was to be avoided – practically at all costs. The Bank of England's first reaction, therefore, was to raise interest rates to a high of 10 per cent in order to attract deposits.[3]

On 31 July, however, a sub-committee of the Cabinet bowed to the inevitable, approving not only a suspension of the Bank Act, which constrained the government's ability to raise the amount of money issued, but also a series of other emergency measures. The proposal of the commercial banks to deposit gold and securities at the Bank of England in return for an exceptional issue of £45 million worth of notes was approved, as was suspension of conversion of paper notes to specie.[4]

A number of other emergency measures were taken, including the imposition of an extended bank holiday and the urgent printing and rapid issue of low-quality Treasury notes in the value of £1 and 10 shillings that could replace the sovereign and half sovereign, both as change instead of sovereigns for a £5 note, but also to facilitate transactions smaller than £5 that were proving a problem in the absence of hoarded coins. Exceptionally, these notes were Treasury, not Bank notes, a decision that aggravated Lord Cunliffe, the Governor of the Bank of England, who complained about the poor quality of the print work and the notes' vulnerability to forgery. The Treasury notes were to be convertible to gold at some point in the future to preserve confidence in them. When eventually the Treasury notes were taken out of circulation in 1928, the Bank of England took over responsibility for the issue of a £1 note.[5]

As a means of addressing the immediate problem of a gold drain, emergency note issues were a solution that most belligerents adopted, although the vast amounts involved contributed significantly to inflation later in the war.[6] While gold was withdrawn from day-to-day transactions due to the suspension of convertibility, it was required for the settlement of transactions with neutral countries such as the

Netherlands, Spain and, until 1917, the United States. Britain moved therefore to secure the output of gold mines in South Africa, Ghana and India exclusively and, to some extent, of those in Australia and New Zealand, building Britain's gold reserves to an unprecedented (according to Keynes) level of £73 million.[7]

The panic reached the further points of Empire in early August. The Canadian government responded to the early evidence of an internal gold drain by suspending convertibility; special Dominion notes were issued against cover of good-quality securities instead of gold. Notes issued by commercial banks that still held issuing rights were declared legal tender, permitting those banks to satisfy withdrawals by paying out their own notes rather than gold. Canada's response to the crisis echoed that of Britain and other countries closer to the epicentre of the crisis. [8]

Germany

Germany, on the other hand, had long before put in place arrangements to supplement its money in the event of war. As early as 1890, preparations had been made by which the Reichsbank would be permitted in the event of war to issue 2 billion marks above the normally permitted issue levels. A supplementary issue of notes called State Loan Currency Notes (Darlehnkassenschein), nominally backed by industrial assets and property, but not convertible to gold, would be issued by lending banks. Germany had also learned lessons from its confrontation with France during the Agadir incident of 1911, when France was believed to have orchestrated a run on Germany's banks and therefore on its gold reserves. In the three years from 1911 to 1914, therefore, Germany's gold reserves were increased from $200 million to $500 million. On top of that, a special 'war chest 'of 120 million gold marks from the French Indemnity paid at the end of the Franco–Prussian war was held in a tower in the Spandau district of Berlin until it was transferred to the Reichsbank to form part of the gold reserve. Nevertheless, public reaction to the news of possible hostilities prompted runs on commercial banks in Germany and Austria, where gold specie was withdrawn for the purposes of hoarding – a so-called internal drain where specie was withdrawn from circulation but did not leave the country.[9]

Although, in contrast to Britain, Germany foresaw some of the difficulties that would be thrown up by a banking panic induced by the threat of war, taking emergency measures such as the prior printing of small denomination notes, there was still a need to introduce emergency measures. Banks were instructed by the Reichsbank to limit the amount they would accept on deposit from foreigners. Convertibility of the mark to gold was suspended on 31 July and Treasury notes became acceptable as an alternative to gold as cover for the issue of increased volumes of notes.[10]

France

The policy of the Banque de France under Georges Pallain, its governor since 1897, was, like that of the Reichsbank, one of preparation for conflict. The Banque was not keen to convert notes tendered by the public into gold. In November 1912 the first Balkan War, involving an alliance of various Balkan states against Ottoman Turkey, was reaching a critical state, increasing tensions among European governments. Gold fetched a premium during that month in Germany, Austria, Belgium, Russia and France and the Banque de France showed itself very reluctant to convert notes for gold, which was only provided under the most urgent demand and then only up to a maximum of 300 francs per head.[11] This kind of prudence meant that by July 1914 its gold reserves were valued at more than $800 million.

Despite the size of France's reserves, it was no less susceptible to an internal drain of gold than was Britain. It became apparent that gold was being hoarded, with the result that it was impossible to get change for 50-and 100-franc notes.[12] Cafes and shops stopped accepting banknotes. Commercial banks struggled to cope with their customers' demands for coin. On 29 July, crowds formed outside the Banque de France to convert notes into gold. However, Pallain had foreseen the dangers of such a run and had previously issued secret sealed instructions to all Banque de France branches, commanding them to cease converting notes to gold in the event of a war. Accordingly, convertibility to gold was suspended on 1 August on the day of France's general mobilisation. The upper limit for banknote issue was raised from 6.8 to 12 billion francs. On 18 August, as

German troops moved into Belgium and then France, orders were given to transport the entire French gold reserve to various locations in southern and central France.[13]

Austria

As the belligerent responsible for the outbreak of war beginning with an ultimatum to Serbia, Austria's Hapsburg government knew, before any other state, that war was imminent. (As the market panic started before the ultimatum was submitted, it is surmised that the news of imminent war had been leaked.) It is therefore hardly surprising that it was the Austrian banking system that first experienced a series of runs as the population rushed to withdraw specie from the banks. A limit on the value of specie that any individual might withdraw was one of a number of measures introduced to contain the panic. Interest rates were raised. The requirement for currency on issue to be covered by 40 per cent of its value in gold was suspended on 4 August and, as with France and Britain, the value of currency in note form to be issued was increased dramatically.[14]

Development

The Protagonists
Britain

As far as Prime Minister Lloyd George was concerned, Britain's monetary system was in a parlous state by 1917. Although sterling had been disengaged from gold convertibility within the UK, payments to neutral creditor countries such as the US were still made by shipping gold to them. To assist in the trade between the US and Britain – and in particular to avoid regular gold transfers across the Atlantic, which was subject to the menace of submarine warfare – a gold depository was established at the finance ministry in Ottawa, Canada. Anyone depositing gold at this facility would in return obtain a credit that could be used to settle obligations in London. In a period of four months, this facility accepted deposits worth £21 million. In 1917 the Governor of the Bank of England, Lord Cunliffe, a notoriously difficult and forceful character who had felt his authority challenged by government policies, instructed the government of Canada not to accept instructions from the Treasury in London. Failure to settle accounts with the US, among other creditor nations, would have had serious implications for Britain's war effort. This unwise move brought down upon Cunliffe's head the wrath of Lloyd George, who by then was Prime Minister. Cunliffe was forced to retract and subsequently his tenure of office was not renewed.

By 28 June, the investment bank of J.P. Morgan, the official British financial agents in America, had only sufficient financial resources to maintain the official sterling:dollar exchange rate of $4.76:£1 for one more day. The very real prospect of a collapse of the sterling:dollar exchange rate would be a fatal blow to the international credibility of Britain's financial system. Balfour, the Foreign Secretary, observed that Britain stood on the 'edge of a financial disaster which would be worse than a defeat on the field', a view more or less shared by J.M. Keynes.[15] In the event, the US had already entered the war on the side of the Allies in April 1917 and its administration agreed that some of the financial support now being provided to Britain could be used in defence of the pound.

The year 1917 was one of monetary crisis elsewhere in the Empire. International controls on the export of silver and consequent increases in the metal's price led to its scarcity in India by the end of 1916. As the price of silver rose, the government of India foresaw the prospect of silver being hoarded or melted down as the value of the silver content exceeded the face value of the coin. It looked as though the convertibility of the rupee would have to be suspended, just as gold convertibility had been suspended in Britain at the start of the war. Germany played on these fears, circulating rumours to the effect that the rupee would soon cease to be convertible.[16]

This situation dragged on into 1918. By June of that year, India's silver reserve stood at less than 25 per cent of what was considered to be the absolute minimum to cover notes in circulation. The prospect of the suspension of convertibility raised a range of concerns: bank runs, a general loss of confidence in the rupee and in Britain's ability to prosecute the war. Although the suspension of convertibility in Britain had passed off without a general collapse of confidence in this way, India was different. Sections of the population and the educated classes already sought the end of British rule and there was less reason to assume the solidarity of the population with the prosecution of the war. A breakdown in confidence in the monetary system in India added to the government's woes. The rupee was saved, as was the pound sterling, when America came to the rescue: in April 1918 the US Pitman Act authorised the melting of up to 350 million silver dollars, of which 200 million ounces of silver were sold to the government of India, resulting in the production of 438 million silver rupees.[17]

France

Even the winners lost out in the parallel war of monetary attrition: six times more French francs were on issue at the end of the war than had been circulating before it, but the franc declined somewhat less than the Italian lire. By the end of the war it was less than two-thirds of its pre-war value. In line with Italy's position, France might have expected greater depreciation proportionate to the increase in money supply, but, as Keynes explains it, she was able to pay for necessary imports on the back of loans from the US and Britain. This meant that, for the time being, France was not drained of money leaving the country to settle transactions. The true impact of the war and the expansion of currency supply had effectively been concealed for the time being by borrowing. Although this appeared to spare France some of the pain, in reality it really did little more than defer the problem as France, of all the Allies, was by far the greatest borrower. By the end of the war it owed $5 billion to the US and the United Kingdom, a sum more than four times greater than the indemnity it had been obliged to pay Germany at the end of the war of 1871.[18]

Italy

Italy, in contrast, was more dependent on the import of raw materials, and sources of revenue such as remittances from the Italian diaspora and tourism were disrupted by the war.[19] Italy's money issue was five to six times its pre-war level and the lire lost half of its value in the course of the war. This was worse than France but nowhere near as disastrous as the situation among the central powers of Germany and Austria.

Germany

Unable to secure loans in the main capital markets of London, Paris and New York, Germany was consequently forced to pay for imports from its own gold reserves.

By the end of the war, when Germany's gold reserves were practically exhausted, neutral states supplying Germany with necessities would insist on payment, for example, in goods and raw materials. In this way, Denmark, Norway and Switzerland took payment in coal for shipments of foodstuffs. Between 1913 and 1917 the money in circulation had increased five times, and between 1914 and 1918 the value of the mark on international exchanges halved, and then halved again in nine months after the end of the war.[20]

In the calculations of J.M. Keynes,[21] the note circulation of Germany was as much as ten times its pre-war levels and the mark consequently fell to one-eighth of its pre-war value, although the five-fold rise in prices was much less than the increase that Keynes would have expected. Between November 1918 and November 1920 the value of marks in circulation had risen from 27 billion to 77 billion By the end of 1920 – a year or more after Keynes had resigned from the peace talks – prices in Germany had risen to ten times their pre-war level.[22]

Austria

The economic impact of the war and its effect on monetary stability and inflation was, if anything, worse during the war years in Austria than it was in Germany. In 1914, £1 sterling was worth 25 kronen. At the end of the war it was worth 35,000 kronen. Prices in Austria soared. By the end of the war a kilogram of poor-quality ersatz flour in Vienna was fifty times more expensive than the high-quality flour available at the start of the war. Notes with a face value of 10,000 kronen were issued.[23]

As a result of the vastly increased money supply, the currencies of some belligerents were practically worthless at exchange abroad. This was true of the currencies of Austria–Hungary and Russia. The bigger the political and military fall, the worse it was for a country's currency.

The Ottoman Empire

The monetary and economic panic in Turkey on the outbreak of war began, appropriately enough, with a run on the Istanbul branch of an Austrian bank, which promptly closed its doors. In response, the Ottoman government initiated a set of emergency measures including a stop on the payment of debts and an embargo on the export of gold. This merely accelerated the run on a number of other banks. Entirely in line with the responses of other belligerent states, convertibility of notes to gold was suspended and smaller denomination notes were issued, as in Britain, France and Germany.[24]

The government of the Ottoman Empire attempted a significant currency reform in 1916, in the middle of the First World War. Coins that had been in circulation before 1844 were withdrawn from circulation. The standard rate of 100 silver kuruş to 1 gold lira was re-established and varying exchange rates in the provinces for different coins in circulation were abolished.

Within a year, however, the irresistible dynamics of war took over and the government began the process of issuing large volumes of paper money denominated as kaime, including very low denominations that were used for daily transactions, driving out of circulation the silver coinage in accordance with Gresham's law. Although volumes of kaime in circulation did not reach the same extraordinary proportions of the middle of the nineteenth century, they were still increasing at a rate certain to accelerate depreciation:

	Kaime volumes in circulation
Beginning 1917	50 million
End 1917	100 million
Late 1918	161 million[25]

The consequence of a wartime over-production of banknotes and consequent depreciation was spiralling inflation, particularly during the period 1916–18. The cost of living throughout the period of the First World War increased eighteen-fold.[26]

Romanov Russia

Unsurprising parallels with the dire collapse of Turkey's currency during the First World War are to be found in the impact of that same war on the Russian monetary system. Russia had only adopted the gold standard in 1897 and silver continued to circulate both as full-bodied coins (where the value of the coin reflected the value of the silver itself) and lower denomination tokens alongside paper money convertible to gold until the war began. Convertibility was soon suspended. Silver rubles ceased to be minted in 1915, while some of the lower denomination tokens continued to be produced. Gold in private hands was hoarded and by late 1916 and early 1917 even copper coins were disappearing from circulation.

As in Turkey, paper money usurped the place of metal coins, although the government made efforts to purchase nickel coins from Japan, which in the event never entered circulation. In desperation, small denomination notes were issued based on the etched designs used to produce stamps in 1913.[27]

In the three years between the start of the war and Russia's revolutionary collapse, paper money was issued in such volumes that the gold reserves backing paper (even though it was inconvertible) sank from 101 per cent cover to less than 40 per cent, drawing with it the inevitable inflation. According to some calculations, Russia's money supply increased a staggering twelve times during the war, compared to that of France, Germany and Britain, each of which had increased six times, while the money supply of Japan had more or less doubled. The purchasing power of the ruble after three years of war was 14 per cent of what it had been at the start of the conflict.[28]

	1914	1915	1916	1917
Credit ruble notes on issue by value (billions)	1665	2,947	5,617	9,101
Level of gold cover backing credit ruble notes	101.8 per cent	58.8 per cent	40.2 per cent	39.7 per cent

Source: Bokarev et al., *Monetary Circulation of Russia* (1984), p.223.[29]

The decline in the value of the ruble on foreign exchanges was accelerated by an aggressive currency attack mounted by the German government. All the ruble notes held in Germany and in occupied territories were gathered and dumped on the currency market in Stockholm, depressing the value of the ruble, but also securing useful currencies of neutral countries with which Germany traded for vital food supplies.[30]

The overthrow of the Romanov dynasty in February 1917 merely accelerated the issue of wartime paper rubles by the new Russian provisional government. By October 1917 the volume of paper rubles on issue reached 16.5 billion rubles. Towards the end of the Tsar's reign, notes were being issued so rapidly that they lacked individual serial numbers. Rubles issued by the provisional government followed suit.[31] Prices soared, fast outpacing the issue of money.

The provisional government had lost control; failure to issue enough currency would starve the armies of provisions and other supplies. The presses rolled ever faster to try to catch up with inflation. While some modern Russian analysts (Bokarev et al., p.232) believe that the monetary situation could have been recovered by radical reversals in military and political policy, this approach loses sight of the reality that economic imperatives take second place against the existential challenges of war.

Compared to the rate of inflation under the provisional government, inflation under the Tsar was relatively modest, but probably only because the economic downturn had not reached full speed. For a time, money issued by the old regime was perceived to be more reliable and was hoarded by the population as a store of value while provisional government rubles were used for day-to-day transactions. Notes issued during the leadership of Alexander Kerensky until the Bolshevik's October Revolution were offered at a discount of 15–20 per cent in exchange for Tsarist rubles. Quite naturally, the population looked back favourably to a currency that seemed to lose its value less rapidly and less obviously than that issued more recently.

Neutrals

Some neutral states gained enormously as suppliers of produce and raw materials to the belligerents. As gold remained the means of settling international transaction, a flow of gold to neutral states became quite significant. Spain's gold reserves tripled during the First World War.

But even the neutral states suffered bank runs in the days immediately before the outbreak of hostilities. Their non-belligerent status yielded no greater public confidence in their monetary systems than was the case with the countries that were at war. Their imports and exports suffered in the early months of the war as shipping lanes were disrupted, credit lines were closed down and the export of gold in settlement of transactions was banned by many, although not by all countries.

The consequences of the war and a run on banks in the belligerent states prompted those banks – particularly British ones – to call in loans to other countries, including neutrals. The crisis rippled out across Latin America as far as Chile and Peru on the Pacific seaboard. Emergency measures including suspension of convertibility (or delay in the planned move to convertibility), a ban on the export of gold and the issue of emergency notes were adopted there as they were in Europe.[32]

The United States

The First World War marked the United States' emergence on to the world stage as a – perhaps *the* – monetary power, having by the end of the war benefited from massive inflows of gold from the Allied powers. But, before that point was reached, America, like the European belligerents, had suffered a near collapse of its economic system in the week or so before the war began. The stock market was closed to prevent European creditors from dumping US securities and Midwestern banks withdrew cash from banks in the east of the country. In the ensuing panic, citizens rushed to convert banknotes into gold. However, as some of the wiser countries had chosen to do, America had a pre-printed currency ready for issue in cases of emergency to neutralise the possibility of any internal drain of gold. This emergency issue, approved in law by the Aldrich-Vreeland Act of 1908, provided for a total of $500 million, a portion of which was promptly released into circulation and by end of August had added a further $200 million to the currency in circulation.[33]

That had addressed the problem of an internal drain, but just as great a problem was posed by the threat of an external drain. Prior to the war America had been a debtor country, living on loans, most of which had come from the great European banking houses. In settling its international transactions, the US had exported $100 million in gold in 1914 and by the autumn still had a further $300 million net in obligations to settle with Britain. With the country's gold stocks rapidly declining, the government feared a run on the banks and a lack of enough gold in the country to support its continuing adherence to the gold standard. A partial solution, somewhat akin to the proposal of British bankers to pay a large sum of gold into the Bank of England to support the gold-convertible sterling, was put forward by American bankers who wanted to establish a gold pool to settle US transactions abroad. In fact, the concern that America might come off the gold standard prompted Britain to consider ways and means of preventing that from happening. Should America withdraw from the gold standard, its inability and unwillingness to ship gold overseas to settle its bills would have seriously affected Britain's access to gold. They need not have worried too much on this point.[34]

The financial cost to the European belligerents had been enormous, amounting to some $200 billion in expenditure, roughly equivalent to half of their pre-war gross domestic product. As the war progressed the Allied powers of France, Britain and Italy turned to America as an apparently inexhaustible source of agricultural produce and materiel, settling transactions in gold and thereby more than doubling America's bullion reserves from a little under $2 billion to $4 billion. As the US was still on the gold standard, the effect was to double the currency supply in circulation, threatening a surge of inflation. Federal Reserve Governor Benjamin Strong wisely took the pre-emptive step of holding back on the issue of notes proportionate to the volume of gold held, thereby effectively breaching a convention of the gold standard. Moreover, far from being a consumer of European finance, America became the principal source of finance to the Allies, lending $2 billion or so annually to Britain and France. Although America's own participation in the war was financed by fiat money issue from January 1917 to January 1919 as monthly expenditure rose more than twenty-four-fold, it had managed to attract so much gold that by the end of the war America held the world's greatest gold reserves. Neutrality between 1914 and 1917 had paid well.[35]

The First World War marked the beginning of the dollar's rise to global pre-eminence not only because of the change in America's debtor/creditor status vis-à-vis the European powers, but also because it had become the preferred medium of exchange for other countries' transactions. As sterling's rate against gold had begun to fluctuate wildly from 1915, other countries, notably in Latin America and Asia, came to prefer the dollar, which was still on a convertible gold standard. While America's industrial power, which had surpassed that of Britain a generation earlier, would have resulted in the dollar mounting a serious challenge to the pound before too long, the war accelerated the process and enabled it to overtake the pound faster than it probably would have done. By 1924 the dollar already occupied first place in the foreign reserves of countries around the world, having pushed sterling into second place, although the relative positions were again temporarily reversed in 1931.[36]

The Netherlands

While all other European states with gold standard monetary systems elected to suspend convertibility at the outbreak of war, Holland delayed.[37] Silver circulating coinage began to be hoarded and there was a run on the banks towards the end of July. The Netherlands Bank reserve of silver and copper was reduced by 50 per cent in a few days. A 10-guilder note was worth only 8 silver guilder coins. The disappearance of lower denomination coins made it impossible to pay for small purchases with anything other than the larger denomination paper notes.[38]

The panic spread from the commercial banks to the Central Bank, which, it was feared, would suspend convertibility and, just as many cafes and restaurants in France refused to accept banknotes at the height of the panic, paper money was shunned in payment for transactions in Holland. The usual series of emergency measures as practised elsewhere in belligerent states now found some rapid application in neutral Holland: the strict ratio of gold cover to paper issue was suspended. When England experienced an internal drain of gold sovereigns and half sovereigns, it responded by issuing notes worth £1 and 10 shillings to fulfil the requirement for those coins. In the Netherlands, the silver coinage drain was addressed by the issue of small silver certificates known as silverbons, which carried a state guarantee, and by the issue of additional silver coins. After the initial panic and the threat of invasion subsided, the prospect of a currency collapse faded. The country settled into a comfortable, commercially beneficial relationship with both sets of protagonists.

Holland's neutral status and border with Germany made it a natural destination for goods smuggled into and out of Germany. The movement of coinage between the two countries was also evident. German marks were observed to circulate in Limburg, almost certainly exchanged for low-denomination Dutch copper coins. As copper was a controlled metal, restrictions were imposed on the export of Dutch coins to Germany. The export of gold was also prohibited.[39]

As the war progressed, the Dutch economy benefited from the country's neutrality and its geographical location between Germany and Britain. Dutch banks provided loans to both sides. Dollar-denominated securities held by German and Austrian investors found their way to the Netherlands to be rebadged as Dutch assets and then shipped on to America for liquidation. Belligerents bought produce and goods from the Netherlands and settled in gold. Bullion and specie cover for banknote issue in the Netherlands reached 75 per cent.

Iran

While the government of Iran had not come out in favour of one side or the other at the outset of the war, the hostile powers were not willing to grant it the luxury of neutrality. The country's strategic location between Russia's central Asian territories and British India had always ensured that each of the two imperial powers would seek to exercise influence at the expense of the other during the late nineteenth century, the rivalry extending to the field of banking. Russia had already established a military presence in northern Persia in 1912, exciting concern in London. But, in the immediate run up to the First World War, with Russia and England in alliance against an increasingly assertive Germany, tensions between the two imperial powers on a governmental level had subsided.[40] In direct reaction to the outbreak of war, Britain took measures in the south to secure access to the country's oil, forming a regiment of Iranian soldiers officered by Britons.

Imagined threats took a very real form when, in November 1914, the Ottoman government declared a jihad against the Russian and British Empires, resulting in Turkish incursions into Iranian territory. Although an early attempt in 1915 by Ottoman troops to seize Azerbaijan was beaten back by Russian troops, German agents were able to foster revolt among tribes in the south and west of Iran, with German influence peaking in 1915.

The Iranian government was not impelled in the same way to issue vast amounts of paper money to cover war expenditure, and in fact the population, faced with a period of economic uncertainty if not outright war, elected to use silver coins rather than notes, in a reversal of normal behaviour under Gresham's law. The uncertain military outlook in 1915, with Britain's position threatened by successful German activity in Iran, exacerbated the general trend towards coin and away from paper:

City	Period	Notes in circulation
Tabriz	March 1915	651,000 tomans
	September 1915	155,000 tomans
Hamadan	March 1915	324,812 tomans
	September 1915	42,000 tomans
Tehran	April 1915	2,201,176 tomans
	June 1915	673,261 tomans

Source: Matthee, Floor & Clawson, *The Monetary History of Iran* (I.B. Tauris, 2013), p.256.

The End Game

Defeat in 1918 spelt not only great loss of life to no purpose, but also humiliation and economic disaster for Germany and its allies. The terms of the Paris peace treaties that were eventually forced on the vanquished left no room for reconstruction or for rehabilitation of the economy. Germany, for one, was deprived of its overseas colonies and therefore a major source of raw materials; it lost its entire merchant marine fleet, was obliged to hand over railway rolling stock to the

Allies, and lost control of its coal mines in the Saarland. On top of this, the Allies sought to seize private German property as well as public German assets. They also imposed unreasonably high demands for monetary reparations that Germany, having had so many of its assets seized, could not hope to fulfil.

The Austro-Hungarian Empire was dismantled, leaving Vienna as capital of a country with little hinterland and Hungary with reduced territory. The monetary systems of both countries suffered drastically.

While political and territorial issues of the post-war settlement were to be in the hands of the League of Nations, financial and economic matters would be settled by the Reparations Commission, to be based in Paris. The Paris peace treaty did not concern itself with the long-term sustainability and success of the economies of either the victors or the vanquished. This was all the more true of the council of four, the heads of government of Britain, France, the United States and Italy – Lloyd George, Clemenceau, Woodrow Wilson and Orlando – who approached the issue of reparations through the prism of international affairs, domestic politics or moral philosophy, but not from the point of view of economic common sense.

The Reparations Commission would address and resolve a wide range of economic issues including the German reparations, the administration of Germany's debt and the liquidation of the Central Bank of the Austro-Hungarian Empire, as well as the introduction of a new currency for Austria.[41]

Among the early matters to settle was the restitution of cash deposits seized from the National Bank of Belgium and gold paid to Germany by Russia under the Treaty of Brest-Litovsk. In the latter case, Russia, suing Germany for peace, had agreed under the treaty to pay some 245,000kg of gold as well as large amounts of cash in ruble notes to settle an indemnity of 6 billion marks. The 1918 Armistice agreement provided for Germany's surrender of the Russian gold.[42]

The cost of war, the loans extended from one ally to another, the unhitching of paper currency from its gold anchor and the consequent unchecked production of money, reparations levied on Russia by Germany, by the Allies on Germany, and the general breakdown of the currency systems of the central powers would offer fertile ground for a range of classic monetary ills. Hyperinflation, currency smuggling, politically motivated counterfeiting, unchecked issue of private moneys: practically every monetary pathogen was observed during the decade after the peace.[43]

The monetary question uppermost in central bankers' minds after the war, however, was that of a return to the gold standard. For so long had gold been accepted as the foundation of a solid economy that the idea of money free of the restraint imposed by convertibility to the precious metal was inconceivable. The question was not whether, but rather when and under what conditions European states would return to the gold standard. The essence of the problem was the vast amount of inconvertible money in circulation issued by the belligerents.

THE NEW WORLD MONETARY DISORDER

Germany's Monetary Catastrophe

At the end of the war, the question of overwhelming importance for Germany was the scale of the Allies' demands for reparations. While a mark had been worth 24 cents in 1914, by 1920 it was only worth 1.5 cents and prices rose nine-fold over the same period. Against this backdrop, the Allies' demands were not only punitive in the extreme, but were simply unrealistic. As well as Germany's rail rolling stock, merchant marine fleet, the coal mines of the Saar region and raw materials that were to be surrendered, the Allies demanded payment in gold and foreign securities that were all counted as immediately transferable wealth. The Reichsbank's gold reserve, confirmed as having a value of more than $577 million, had been expanded by general appeals to the public to surrender gold in all forms as well as in coin. A much smaller sum of $5 million in silver was also held in the Reichsbank's vaults. Of this reserve, $250 million – a little under half of the entire precious metal reserve –was transferred to the Allies in payment for food alone during the first half of 1919.

Further transfers of gold had to be made to Germany's neutral creditors and were duly sanctioned by the Allies' supreme economic council for fear that Germany's failure to pay would further undermine confidence in its currency. As a result of these and the food payments, the total precious metal reserve in the Reichsbank was valued in September 1919 down from $577 million to $275 million.[1] The Allies' claims on the remaining amount, however, had to be tempered by the realisation that the effect of removing all of Germany's gold reserve would destroy the mark's remaining value in exchange for other currencies. This, of course, would have been a very undesirable development for Belgium and also for France, where large volumes of marks remained in the hands of the population. Keynes warned against forcing the Reichsbank to hand over anything other than a small proportion of the gold towards the first required instalment of reparations in the amount of $5 billion.[2]

Even though there was an eighteen-month period of stabilisation in 1920–21 when confidence was such that $2 billion worth of foreign investment was attracted to Germany, it did not last beyond political shocks in the middle of 1921, notably a series of assassinations by right-wing groups and France's long-running opposition to any relaxation of the reparations programme. The exchange rate of the mark during the post-war period fell in reaction to all manner of political events. The mere arrival of Allied representatives – the Committee of Guarantees – in Berlin in September 1921 to oversee the levies on Germany's import and export duties as part of the reparations arrangement caused the mark's fall from 350 to 650 to the pound. A temporary stability since April 1922 was overturned in June of that year by the assassination of Walter Rathenau, the Foreign Minister and arch proponent of compliance with reparations demands, by right-wing students. In a week the value of the mark fell from 1,300 to 1,600 to the pound. The arrival in Berlin of the Reparations Commission would be enough to cause a further drop. Another visit by the Committee of Guarantees in the summer of 1922 drove the mark down again from 1,800 to 2,400 to the pound.[3]

Prices rose forty-fold in 1922. People began to use foreign currencies in preference to the depreciating mark and so the government banned their use for domestic pricing and transactions in October 1922.[4]

The rate of issue of banknotes accelerated. In 1922, government expenditure exceeded revenues by three to one. A year later the gap reached ten to one, as the government printed vast quantities of money to support the workers in the Ruhr who were carrying out a campaign of passive resistance to occupation by France and Belgium. To cope with budget shortfalls the government ordered ever more banknotes printed. As the printing presses struggled to keep up, a law was passed in

July 1922 permitting regional and municipal authorities, as well as some industrial enterprises, to produce their own emergency money substitutes. Although this was conditional upon the deposit of assets, in reality emergency note issue by the regions and cities as well as by industry was no more controlled than was the Reichsbank note issue, and by November 1922 there were a total of forty issuing authorities operating in the occupied areas. Throughout 1922, a total of 1 trillion marks was issued. In September–October 1922 a litre of milk almost doubled in price, and butter, which in April was 50 marks per pound, reached 800 marks per pound in November.

In January 1923, France and Belgium invaded the Ruhr on the grounds that Germany was failing to fulfil its reparations obligations. British Prime Minister David Lloyd George interpreted this move as part of a ploy to create a Rhineland buffer state between Germany and France. Germany reacted by deploying the nation's entire banknote production capacity. In the first six months of 1923, the value of currency issued reached 17 trillion marks, employing 30 paper mills and 133 banknote-printing factories. In addition to the municipal and state authorities and the private enterprises permitted to issue money since the emergency legislation of the previous year, private banks that had a right to issue a limited amount of currency lobbied to have that limit increased. The tail of inflation was wagging the dog of economic prudence and the decision-makers and opinion-formers in government and the press failed to recognise it.

French methods used to suppress German passive resistance to the occupation included an embargo in the first half of August 1923 on the import of money. In the month of August 1923 alone, the mark fell from 1.3 million to the dollar to 5 million to the dollar. The first 100 million mark note was issued on 22 August and less than two weeks later it was followed by a note with the face value of 500 million marks. As is so often the case when a paper currency reaches the end of its life as a credible medium of exchange, farmers were refusing to accept it in return for produce. Ultimately, the buck – good or bad – stops at the farmer. The extraordinary combination of hyperinflation and the absence of adequate volumes of currency was leading to strikes, riots and violent demonstrations as passive resistance threatened to tip over into something altogether more threatening.[5]

In October 1923, France ramped up the pressure on the German government and the local authorities in the Rhineland by openly supporting the idea of a separate Rhenish state together with its own separate currency, as Lloyd George had foreseen. A declaration of independence on 21 October by the aspiring statelet centred in Aachen in the Belgian-controlled zone was followed by other such declarations in towns such as Bonn and Mainz. French authorities also encouraged separatist ambitions in the Palatinate area and Bavaria. These multiple, apparently disconnected, moves might point less towards a plan for a buffer state and more towards a French policy of stimulating the complete fragmentation of Germany back into its constituent parts prior to the unification of 1870. Whether the objective was a single buffer state between Germany or the complete break-up of the Empire, neither was achieved. Nor did the separate Rhineland currency come to pass. Only a month later the downward inflationary spiral of the German mark was arrested, providing much-needed monetary stability and thereby re-establishing public confidence in the mark and, by extension, in the government. Local coups continued to plague the central Weimar government, however: communist-led attempts to establish breakaway governments in Hamburg and Saxony, in October and November respectively, were suppressed with military force, while a right-wing coup attempt by Hitler was similarly put down by means of martial law in November 1923.[6]

The highest denomination notes now bore a face value of 100 billion marks, but a single kilo of butter cost 250 billion marks. In the last three weeks of October 1923 prices doubled every couple of days. The value of savings and investments was wiped out. Von Haverstein, governor of the Reichsbank, was swept along by the seemingly uncontrollable power of depreciation and inflation. To confront the problem by stopping the presses would have meant depriving the government of its means of fulfilling budget obligations, paying civil servants and even the much-reduced armed forces. The population at large would similarly have been deprived of their albeit vastly depreciated money with no guarantee that the hyperinflation would abate. A very real possibility of civil disorder or revolution existed, all the more credible for the recent memory of the Spartacist uprising in 1919 that had threatened to install Soviet-style government in Germany. Von Haverstein was not the man to take that risk.[7]

With a monthly inflation rate peaking in October 1923 alone at 29,500 per cent and prices doubling every three to four days, people began to react in ways that have characterised human behaviour during previous bouts of inflationary monetary collapse.[8] Farmers stopped taking their produce to market. Goods rather than money were demanded in exchange for other goods. Credit dried up. Confronted with this economic catastrophe, many central bankers would have quailed at the task of rescuing the nation's monetary system from complete collapse. Not so Hjalmar Schacht, who had been appointed currency commissioner by the German Chancellor Gustav Stresemann in November 1923. Of all the unusual characters who were the leading central bankers of the first half of the twentieth century, it would be fair to say that Schacht's personality and career were the most remarkable. Having initially supported Hitler's rise to power between the 1930s and 1945, acting first as governor of his Reichsbank and then Minister of Economics, he subsequently opposed Nazi policies on Jews. Schacht's differences of opinions with the Nazis and suspicions of his involvement with the resistance movement that attempted to assassinate Hitler in July 1944 led to his transportation to no fewer than three death camps including Ravensbrück and Dachau, which, miraculously, he survived. Schacht's fall from grace under the Nazis and the time he spent in Dachau did not, however, exempt him from arrest and trial by the Allies at the end of the war. Again, he survived, having been acquitted of the charges brought against him of planning and waging wars of aggression. There was throughout Schacht's life seemingly a knack for coming through crises. But most of these were in the future. In 1923, his task was to prevent the total collapse of the reichsmark.

Schacht set about his task with few resources but a belief in his own authority. The introduction in November 1923 of the rentenmark, not legal tender and not convertible to gold but supposedly backed by a mortgage – an annual 5 per cent tax on all German agricultural and industrial land – was the first step. One rentenmark could be exchanged for 1 trillion reichsmarks; 4.2 rentenmarks was worth $1, the pre-war exchange rate.[9] Although the rentenmark was not convertible, a gold reserve was nevertheless required to render it believable. The only problem was that the gold reserve needed to be restored after the majority of it had been wiped out during the war and the immediate post-war period. From just under $1 billion before the war the gold reserve had declined to less than $150 million worth of gold at the end of the war. Foreign loans, including the American Dawes loan of 1924, enabled Germany to recreate a reserve of gold and foreign exchange amounting to the legally required 40 per cent of all notes on issue. Using international loans as a means of creating a gold reserve was not in itself unprecedented. Precisely this approach had been used by Japan to supplement gold obtained as a result of its war indemnity from China in 1895, both at the initial creation of its gold standard in the late nineteenth century and subsequently.[10]

In addition to these measures, Schacht ensured that there was a legal cap on the amount of rentenmarks issued into circulation, making them relatively scarce and consequently more valuable. New issues of emergency money issued by industrial enterprises were also banned – or rather, Schacht announced they would not be redeemed by the Reichsbank. All attempts to persuade Schacht to breach the ceiling were successfully resisted. The Reichsbank stopped issuing currency and the Rentenbank took over that function, a measure that brought a halt to the seemingly limitless production of the reichsmark.

The fixing of the rentenmark to an exchange rate against gold and against the dollar also worked to create confidence in the new notes. The exchange rate of reichsmark to rentenmark was only fixed at 1 trillion:1 after Schacht permitted a seemingly bottomless collapse of the reichsmark from 630 billion to the dollar on 12 November 1923 to 4.2 trillion in eight days. The nadir was reached in late November at an astonishing 11 trillion to the dollar and two weeks later prices were stable. Although the introduction of the rentenmark is widely seen as a confidence trick since it was based on no firmer a footing than the reichsmark, its success was remarkable. As the complete failure of a currency is marked by an absence of food in cities when farmers refuse to supply it against worthless notes, the reverse is true: a successful rescue currency will release agricultural produce to the cities, and that is what happened in response to the rentenmark's introduction. Meat, vegetables, dairy products and cereals reappeared in November and December 1923. As the new currency was perceived to be worth something, the population held on to it as a store of value. Although the transition was not without its problems, Schacht's success resulted in him being appointed President of the Reichsbank in December 1923.[11]

Schacht went on to consolidate and reinforce the foundations of the German monetary system. A law of 1924 required a 40 per cent cover for all notes issued, of which 75 per cent was to be in gold and the remainder in foreign exchange. For Schacht this was not good enough. He set about replacing the foreign exchange element with gold; from 1924 to the end of 1928, gold reserves at the Reichsbank rose from 37 per cent to 84 per cent of all reserves.[12] Schacht's policy discredited the so-called gold exchange standard by which gold in national reserves could be replaced by gold-convertible currencies. And while Germany moved towards a predominantly gold-based reserve, France also announced its commitment to a gold-only reserve by its Monetary Law of 1928. Conditions in the mid-to-late 1920s echoed the race for gold in the 1870s, a significant contributing factor in both cases to the subsequent deflation as there was insufficient gold to go around all the competing economies.

For eight years from the point at which Schacht arrested the hyperinflation to the onset of the Great Depression in 1931, the cloud hanging over the German economy was the question of reparations. The possibility that the Allies would take punitive action against any default – as had already happened at the time of the occupation of the Ruhr by France and Belgium – the sheer scale of the demands in cash and in kind and the potential impact on Germany's reserve that had been foreseen by Keynes – added up to an unmanageable degree of uncertainty. Schacht made it his business to argue against the sheer excess of the reparations on speaking tours abroad. Right-wing movements in Germany raged against the Allies and their demands. At their peak, the reparations demanded by the Allies amounted to $32 billion. As the years passed, they slowly came to terms with the fact that Germany was in no position to make payments of that magnitude. When at last it stopped paying altogether in 1931, Germany had paid only $4 billion.[13]

A lasting consequence of the reparations issue was the establishment of a bank that would manage the transactions between central banks, and in particular the reparations to be paid by Germany. The Bank for International Settlements, the original idea for which had been proposed by Schacht, would hold gold and currency deposits of various central banks and would enable transactions to be made simply by the agreed transfer of assets from one central bank's account to that of another central bank held at this new bank based in Switzerland. The bank's charter, enshrined in The Hague convention signed in January 1930 by the UK, France, Germany, Belgium, Italy, Japan and Switzerland, established the immunity from seizure of the deposits at the bank at any time, including during periods of war. The fact that the bank was to be established in neutral Switzerland reinforced this immunity.[14] In a way that had not been foreseen at the bank's foundation in 1930, this simple transfer arrangement would be exploited unscrupulously by Germany at the beginning of the next European war.

Germany's hyperinflation during the post-war period has been the subject of countless books and reports. Although it was far from being the most extreme example ever of hyperinflation, it is nonetheless held up as the worst example of the nightmare that is uncontrolled money supply. Circumstances created by the war – the blockade, unreasonable reparations that destroyed Germany's real economy, reduction of the gold reserves that backed its currency, excessive and reckless issue of currency by the Reichsbank and vast quantities of privately issued notes in circulation – threatened to create conditions that the Weimar government and its central bank would never be able to reverse. Foreign military intervention by France and Belgium, the prospect of national fragmentation and coups and counter-coups by left and right magnified the perception of a country out of control and have provided a marvellous storyline for countless books. All of these conditions combined to create what is for most people the paradigm of hyperinflation, even though more extreme cases have been recorded since in Yugoslavia, Zimbabwe and Hungary.[15]

Austria

The consequences of the Great War for Austria were even more devastating than they were for Germany. Austria's eastern-facing empire was comprehensively dismantled in a way that the continental German empire was not, resulting in the creation of a number of new countries in Europe. All that remained of the Hapsburg Empire was the heartland of Austria operating a shattered monetary system. For a short time the currency of the dual Austro-Hungarian Empire continued to circulate in the former constituent states of the empire that were now independent. This widespread tolerance of a legacy currency did not, however, survive unwise policies on the part of the Austrian state, which put pressure on the Austro-Hungarian bank to issue more currency with the purpose of financing Austria's debts. Fearful of the prospect of inflation imported from Austria, Romania, Hungary, Bosnia, Croatia and Slovenia chose to differentiate their currency by overstamping the original Austro-Hungarian notes as an emergency measure until they could introduce their own independent currencies. (In the case of Czechoslovakia, this use of overstamping was reprised during the so-called Velvet Divorce of 1993 when the union of the Czech and Slovak republics was dissolved.) Notes that, for whatever reason, had not been stamped returned to Austria in large volumes, obliging the government in Vienna to start stamping its own notes.[16]

Between May 1921 and May 1922, the krone collapsed from 2,000 to 35,000 to the pound sterling. By the end of August, following the rejection by the entente powers of a requested loan to the Austrian government, the krone hit a new low of 350,000 to the pound. By 1922 the krone, costing sixty times more to print than its own face value, was so depreciated that the banknotes were being used as scrap paper by office clerks. A monthly inflation rate of 129 per cent was recorded in August 1922 alone, with prices doubling every twenty-five and a half days. The country teetered on the edge of general collapse and mutiny by the disaffected army was feared. Although an edict required the population to accept Austrian notes, the same edict permitted the use of foreign currencies and, inevitably, the population turned where they could to US dollars, Swiss francs and (irony of ironies) Czech crowns, as a stable alternative to the Austrian krone. The country was on the verge of collapse. In these circumstances, Austrian politicians were so demoralised that the idea of union with Germany seemed to offer the best prospect of survival, an idea that had already been vetoed by the Allies in 1919.[17] On this occasion, the Allies forestalled the need for union by pumping emergency funding into Austria, but the prospect of an Austrian–German union was to be a recurring nightmare for France in the inter-war years.

Difficult as it is for us now to imagine it, one possibility was the merger of Austria into Italy, or at the very least Austria's designation as an Italian protectorate. To pre-empt this possibility and to prevent the complete collapse of Austria, entente powers agreed to a major loan and from September 1922 the exchange rate and prices started to improve.

Occupied Belgium

Belgium, invaded by Germany in 1914 in breach of its internationally recognised neutrality and occupied until the Armistice of 1918, was a microcosm of Europe-wide currency problems. Convertibility to gold was suspended on the outbreak of war, a special emergency series of notes was issued and the National Bank shipped its official banknote and gold reserves to London for safety. The occupying power, infuriated by this pre-emptive strike, removed the right of the National Bank to issue Belgium's currency and transferred that right to the Société Générale. Belgian occupation francs, a currency system organised by Hjalmar Schacht – subsequently a major force, as we have seen, in Germany's economy as President of the Reichsbank in the post-war period – could be bought with German marks at an exchange rate very favourable to the mark. More than 800 municipalities added to the confusion by issuing local private currencies until, to impose some form of monetary order on the country, the occupying authorities imposed the German mark as legal tender. Banknote circulation doubled over the course of the war, inevitably leading to inflation.[18]

Belgium's monetary woes did not end with the withdrawal of German troops at the Armistice. About 6 billion German marks were held by the population and to withdraw them from circulation,

Belgian authorities offered an exchange rate of 1 mark:1.2 francs when, by 1919, the real exchange rate was 3 marks:1 franc. As J.M. Keynes explains in *The Economic Consequences of the Peace* (p.123), the Belgian government had hoped that marks circulating in Belgium would be redeemed in gold by the German government as one of its first priorities under the terms of the post-war settlement. It therefore seemed to be in the Belgian government's interests to gather up as many occupation marks as possible by using a rate attractive to anyone who had a stock of marks to dispense with. This assumption was to lead to disappointment, however, when the Paris peace conference concluded that genuine reparations claims would take precedence over this attempted state-led currency speculation. In fact, the outcome was worse than expected as, with such an exchange rate favourable to those wanting to exchange their marks for francs, this was an irresistible temptation to smuggle more marks into Belgium from Germany.

France

The flow of gold from Europe to America – $300 million worth in 1930 – continued as the Depression began to bite. But even more remarkable was the flow of gold to France, where the Banque de France had maintained a policy of keeping the franc at a lower rate of exchange than, for instance, sterling. French exports flourished while those of Britain suffered, disadvantaged by the decision to put sterling on its old parity of $4.86, too high a rate for competition in the international markets. The new franc exchange rate was beneficial to the economy. More gold – $500 million worth – moved to France in 1930 than had transferred to America. Indeed, after 1930, America's share of the world's gold reserves slipped while those of France soared. Churchill had spoken of a gold reserve of £150 million – approximately $724 million at the exchange rate of the time – to back sterling in the 1925 budget speech in which he announced the return to gold. But much of that had disappeared abroad in the period to 1930. France on the other hand had accumulated a gold reserve of $2 billion by 1930, and two years later had increased the reserve to $3 billion. [19]

This twentieth-century bullionism (the long-held view that only accumulations of precious metals were an indicator of national wealth) guaranteed an imbalance of gold reserves among the developed economies of Europe, America and the British Empire. With diminishing stocks of gold, many countries were unable to support the existing money supply in a gold-based monetary system. As 1931 proceeded, America's industrial giants failed and the fragility of the German banking system became clear as one bank after another collapsed. Banks also failed in Eastern Europe.

Britain

Silver's role as the basis for a token money subordinate to gold in Britain was further reinforced after the First World War when the price of silver rose significantly as a result of rising wartime demand for the metal in China and India. At higher prices, procurement of silver bullion for minting became more expensive and, compared to the face value of those silver coins in England, the cost of minting was prohibitively expensive. The only solution was to reduce the amount of silver used in the subsidiary coinage from 92 per cent of the total metal content to 50 per cent. This new arrangement was due to come into force in March 1920, and the advance notice of the debasement caused the price of silver to peak in London, followed by a general global trend downwards in silver prices.[20]

But for post-war England there was a bigger issue to address than its subsidiary silver coinage: could Britain afford to return to the gold standard post-bellum as it had after the end of the Napoleonic wars? The war had not erased the general view of gold as the benchmark by which economies were judged to be developed or otherwise. Britain, which had been on a gold standard de facto for 200 years and de jure for nearly 100, had more to lose in reputation than most. Up to the beginning of the war it had been the wealthiest country in the world and the global financial capital. If Britain were to withdraw from the gold standard it would signal its demotion from the summit of international capital. There was a widespread view that the clock needed to be turned 'back to 1914'.[21]

Another perspective was presented by the harsh realities of the British economy. There had been no hasty return to the gold standard at the end of the war. The pound had been allowed to float, unemployment was high and prices were far above those, for instance, of the US.[22] While some economists felt that a deliberate deflationary policy would bring prices down and the obvious way of achieving that would be by returning to the gold standard at the old pre-war parity, which would fix it to the dollar at $4.86, others foresaw only further misery as a result. If the pound was valued at too high a level compared to the dollar and other currencies, exports would be inhibited, jobs cut and the ability of the economy to grow would be constrained.

As Britain's policy-makers dithered over the questions of when and at what parity to return to gold, a number of European states including Germany, Austria and Hungary – all of which had good reason to cling to the stability of gold, having experienced unprecedented hyperinflation immediately after the war – had already taken the plunge. Britain's overseas dominions Canada, New Zealand and Australia were also making plans to return to the gold standard, leaving London, the centre of the Empire and of the historic gold standard, trailing indecisively. When received wisdom held that fixed exchange rates, stability and convertibility to gold were the foundation for all reliable currencies, the pound was starting to look a less reliable global currency than the German mark. London's place as the world's financial centre was under threat.

Few policy-makers in Britain opposed a return to the gold standard after the war. Philip Snowden, a socialist who became the Labour Party's first Chancellor of the Exchequer in 1924, was in favour of it. At the other end of the political spectrum, Winston Churchill, appointed Chancellor (finance minister) later that same year in the Conservative government led by Stanley Baldwin, also concluded, after lengthy consultations with Treasury experts, the Bank of England and other economists, that a resumption of the gold standard was for the best. In his budget speech of 28 April 1925[23] he announced the decision to return to gold that day.

The resumption of the gold standard, however, would not mean a complete return to the habitual arrangements of free convertibility of paper notes to gold coins that existed before the First World War. Churchill urged all to use paper notes as the primary form of circulating cash. Gold coins would not be issued at the demand of anyone submitting notes for redemption, no doubt because Britain's gold reserves were barely able to support a policy of resumption that entailed convertibility of all notes. The Bank of England would choose whether to convert paper to coins. A sterling:gold parity was fixed and the volume of notes to be allowed to circulate would be limited to an amount that would be covered by a portion of the gold reserve set at £150 million. This gold reserve and the bank interest rate would be used to defend the sterling:gold parity. Churchill also made it clear that the government had coordinated its return to the gold standard with Australia, New Zealand, the Netherlands and the Dutch colony of the East Indies, all of which would resume the gold standard on the same day.

With Britain now heavily in debt to the US and still reliant on imports of food and raw material, it was inevitable that there would be a net outflow of gold, particularly to America. Over the summer of 1929 and through to September of that year, $145 million worth of Britain's gold reserves out of a total of $800 million left the country for America, but also for France, where a monetary law of June 1928 laid down the requirement that all of France's reserves should be held in gold, rather than foreign currency. France's preoccupation with gold reserves had previously found expression in statements by Emile Moreau, Governor of the Banque de France, according to whom, Britain's sterling was not acceptable as a reserve currency because it was insufficiently backed with gold in comparison with US dollars.[24] As a result of the 1928 law, and consistent with this view of sterling, France converted substantial sterling holdings into gold, much of which was transferred from the UK's account to the accounts of France within the Bank of England. Between 1926 and 1932, France's holdings of gold grew from 8 to 28 per cent of the entire world stock of that metal.[25] India also absorbed much of the gold produced globally: up to 10 per cent of all gold ever produced may have reached India by the 1920s, although by 1931 the flow reversed and India exported much of its gold holdings, becoming a net exporter.[26]

Notwithstanding the relative weakness of Britain's gold reserves in comparison with those of France and America, Britain's economy was not in the worst position. Although 2 million people were out of work in 1929 in Britain, more than double that number were out of work in Germany and even more in America. Industrial production in both those countries fell substantially more than it had done in Britain in the same year. Elsewhere, economies were stagnating and even Australia (among others), which had returned to the gold standard before Britain, had already withdrawn from it.[27]

Britain's economic plight was aggravated by a severe budget deficit that the government proposed to tackle by means of deep cuts in government expenditure, tax hikes and further borrowing from America, none of which achieved the task of stabilising the economy. Worse still, the French government, having lent large sums to Britain, began to have doubts about the Bank of England's risky lending to German and Austrian banks. It began calling in its deposits from the Bank of England.[28]

With intolerable pressure mounting on the country's economy, the Invergordon Mutiny served to push the government into the inescapable withdrawal from the gold standard on 21 September 1931. Foreign investors who held large amounts of sterling found themselves unable to redeem their notes for gold. Moreover, released from its link to gold, sterling depreciated, adding to the woes experienced by foreigners holding British currency. By December 1931, having been allowed to float, the pound lost 30 per cent of its value. The Banque de France had held $350 million worth of sterling deposits; indeed the Governor of the Banque de France, tellingly, had said as early as 1927 that the Banque could force Britain off the gold standard by converting its massive holdings of sterling to gold.[29] When at last Britain came off the gold standard, France was left holding an excess of sterling and lost $125 million of the gold value of its sterling holdings as the value plummeted. Other European central banks suffered losses of a similar magnitude. A further twenty-five countries followed Britain off the gold standard in the next few months.

For the man in the street, however, Britain's abandonment of the gold standard did not result in the collapse of his world. Prices stabilised and deflation was replaced by modest inflation. The banking system held together and food continued to reach the population.[30] There could be life beyond the gold standard.

America: Last Man Standing

But if the impact was less catastrophic for Britain than anyone had expected, the consequences for America of the collapse of the gold standard could hardly have been foreseen. America had been one of two principal beneficiaries of gold leaving Britain during the First World War, and during the late 1920s, when so many countries had returned to the gold standard, in reality only America had sufficient gold to permit gold coins to circulate.[31] But following Britain's withdrawal from the gold standard the flow moved back across the Atlantic. European central banks that had been burnt by sterling's withdrawal from the gold standard feared that America would go the same way. They rapidly converted their dollar deposits into gold and withdrew them from the US. The panic was not confined to foreign central banks. Depositors withdrew half a billion dollars out of the banking system in gold and hoarded it. Many US banks collapsed as a result. A lack of confidence in the banking system and the withdrawal of money from banks for the purpose of hoarding inevitably created the right conditions for deflation. Production fell 25 per cent, bankruptcies rose and unemployment exceeded the 10 million mark. A Great Depression had set in.

Japan

At some time or other during the First World War, almost all countries had suspended gold convertibility, releasing the constraints on banknote production.[32] In the case of Japan, an outflow of gold to India in return for imported goods and raw materials had been the norm for some time. In its trade relationship with China, however, Japan had enjoyed a positive balance of trade since their war of 1894–95 and one might have imagined the flow of specie would be inbound to Japan. In fact, much was shipped back out to China in the form of loans to reinforce Japan's position as the creditor in the relationship. When the US placed an embargo on the export of gold during the First World War, Japan was cut off from the main source of specie to backfill the gold lost to China and India. Japan therefore followed suit and like all other belligerents placed an embargo on the export of gold.[33]

Following the First World War, the opposing conservative Seiyūkai and liberal Dōshikai parties wrestled not only with questions of military expenditure but also with fundamental monetary policies. The conservative Seiyūkai party's finance minister sought to maintain the embargo on the export of gold from Japan except where that could be used for massive loans to finance infrastructure and administrative projects in China with a view to Japanese economic domination.[34] He also advocated the repatriation of Japan's overseas gold reserve, fearing that holding it abroad would make it a hostage to fortune in the event of another global catastrophe. Consequently, much of Japan's overseas specie reserve was indeed repatriated.[35]

Inoue Junnosuke, Governor of the Bank of Japan and subsequently Minister of Finance of the liberal Minseitō party (a successor to the Dōshikai party) held, unsurprisingly, different views. Inoue's attitude towards gold was based on the belief that, in relaxing the embargo on the export of gold to settle transactions with foreign importers to Japan, the country's money supply would necessarily dwindle, causing deflation in domestic prices. With prices of Japanese goods in decline, exports would be stimulated and there would be a corresponding inflow of gold. By lifting the embargo, Inoue reckoned that gold would act as a safety valve to regulate prices. An initial outflow would be replaced at some point by an inflow. This approach was maintained by later liberal governments led by one liberal party or another in subsequent years. Thus, the liberal (or Constitutional) Kenseikai government of 1926–29 was shipping gold overseas once or twice a month with a view to shrinking the money supply.[36] On the matter of monetary policy, particularly on gold convertibility, the liberal and conservative parties formed up against each other along much clearer lines than they did on matters of public sector expenditure.

Deflationary measures were also adopted by a short-lived government headed by Kato Tomosaburo, an admiral of the Imperial Japanese Navy who, remarkably, had attracted the anger of senior officers in his own service when he signed Japan up to the Washington Conference limitations on naval expansion. Tomasaburo had as a result been appointed as an independent and non-party Prime Minister. Under pressure from Japan's Chambers of Commerce to lower prices as a step towards the lowering of wages with the aim of increasing export competitiveness, Kato's government launched a set of deflationary policies. Among these policies was a decision to exclude Japan's overseas specie holdings from the reserve used to back Japan's yen banknotes. Reducing the size of the reserve in this arbitrary fashion would limit the ability of the Bank of Japan to issue convertible yen notes just as effectively as Inoue's policy of shipping gold overseas in settlement of international transactions, achieving the depression of prices, but with the added benefit that this policy would at least preserve Japan's gold in the country's ownership. Japan's gold held overseas would effectively be quarantined from the currency system. Takahashi Korekiyo, finance finister of Seiyūkai, which had taken office in 1918, had in any case adopted a policy of repatriating the gold reserves held overseas. Taken together, Takahashi's policy of gold repatriation and Tomasaburo's policy of ruling out the use of Japan's overseas reserve for the purposes of banknote issue meant that its gold exchange system settled on London was over.[37]

While methods of achieving the desired deflation differed according to party affiliation, both conservative and liberal sides shared a common view of what was happening to the international economic order after the First World War. The conservative Takahashi and the liberal Inoue both believed that an era of armed conflict had given way to an age of economic hostility. By April 1929, even the Seiyūkai party had announced a deflationary plan based on the export of gold, giving in to the international trend of a return to the gold standard. As a point of difference between constitutional conservative and liberal parties, the shipping of gold overseas no longer seemed of significance.

As had been anticipated − and desired by the liberal party − the transfer of gold to foreign creditors reduced the number of banknotes in circulation. Domestic prices dropped as anticipated, but so also did economic activity. As gold increased in value relative to silver, Japan's exports to China, which was still on the silver standard, dwindled as China's population struggled to pay the higher prices. On a domestic level, price deflation for grain particularly hit the poorer farmers, who would be heavily indebted for the cost of seed and unable to recoup their costs in the marketplace. Unrest over the deflating economy together with anger at the naval shipbuilding limits imposed by the London treaty provoked violent action on the part of radical elements on the right. In November 1930, Prime Minister Hamaguchi of the Minseitō party was shot and wounded in Tokyo. He died nine months later.[38]

Inoue was next to fall victim to the extremists. In January 1932 he was shot by a young right-wing extremist. The tide of politics in Japan was turning against liberalism. The following month Inoue's Minseitō party was soundly defeated during general elections by the conservative Seiyūkai party. Foreign exchange controls followed.[39] Takahashi Koreyiko, who had resigned from the Seiyūkai party in 1925 and then gone on to serve as finance minister in successive governments, fell victim to military extremists in the 26 February incident, an attempted military coup in 1936.

It would be unrealistic to claim that Hamaguchi, Inoue and Takahashi were assassinated because of their attitude towards the gold standard. Right-wing extremists and radicalised military elements were strongly motivated by hatred of those politicians of both liberal and centre-right persuasion who had supported the London naval treaty and reined in military spending. Takahashi and Inoue held diametrically opposed views in respect of the use of gold to set the domestic and international value of the yen, but both held in common a belief in reduced defence expenditure. This was, in the eyes of violent men on the right, grounds enough for their assassination.

6

POLITICAL COUNTERFEITING

We are familiar with the common criminal activity of counterfeiting, but we are much less familiar with instances of counterfeiting carried out by one state against the currency of another. And yet it goes back many centuries. During the fifth century, when the Merovingians in the north of Gaul and the Visigoths in the south took control of the Roman mints in Western Europe, they produced coins, among them gold solidi, still bearing the names of the emperors of Rome. Similarly, the Lombards who invaded Italy in the mid-sixth century continued to mint coins bearing the name of Emperor Justinian.[1] And again, the pennies of the English King Aethelred I were duplicated by Boguslav of Poland, to the extent that the name of the English monarch and his moneyer (mint master) were replicated on the Polish version.[2] Sterling silver pennies were also counterfeited in the late thirteenth century by the rulers of Brabant, Flanders, Holland and Luxembourg, among others.

Europeans did not confine their counterfeiting to the currency of other European states. The high quality of gold coins circulating in the Muslim states bordering the Mediterranean ensured that those coins were copied in northern Spain and southern Italy in the eleventh to the thirteenth centuries, with modifications only to the inscriptions in the case of the former. Counterfeiting was encouraged and indeed per-petrated by the authorities of Genoa as well as by individual Genoan trading houses in the thirteenth century that produced imitations of milares, the distinctive square silver coins of the Islamic rulers of North Africa and southern Spain. Milares were also counterfeited in seignioral mins in France and by no less than the counts of Poitiers and Anjou, brothers of the king, St Louis.[3]

Why would these foreigners replicate the coinage of late imperial Roman or Muslim rulers, rather than introduce their own currency and designs in a bid to reinforce their own power? It is unlikely to have been an attempt to 'debauch' the currency of the existing power, since there is no evidence that the imitation, or counterfeit, coins were of debased gold or silver. If not subversive, then it would seem likely that the purpose was to vest the coins with the authority and therefore trustworthiness and, most importantly, the value of easily recognisable images. The motive was not to undermine the currency being replicated, but rather to enhance the credibility of the currency being issued in Genoa or the other states where counterfeiting was conducted.

Further evidence of the importance of familiar images in public acceptance of currency may be seen in the imitation of coins of the Tartar Golden Horde by Russian principalities for circulation in those principalities in the fourteenth century. Silver coins issued by this north-western-most Khanate of the Mongol empire circulated widely in neighbouring Russian lands by the middle of that century. In 1359 the Khanate was plunged into violent internal rivalries and its coins stopped entering these Russian domains. The Russian princes made up for the loss of this supply by minting coins imitating the older coins of the Horde dating back to the 1330s and 1340s that had become so familiar to their subjects in the first half of the century.[4] The natural conservatism of consumers vested greater confidence in these foreign coins. When, towards the end of the fourteenth century, the Golden Horde was overwhelmed by the armies of Tamerlane and its stores of bullion and specie were looted and sent to the East, coining ceased and deprived neighbouring Russian lands for the second time of its main source of money. Coins of the Horde were once again imitated as a convenient solution, but the independent princes at about the same time began to mint their own coins, presumably having concluded that the vanquished Horde was no longer a reliable source of coined money and that self-sufficiency was the best course of action.[5] In the Middle Ages, when currencies crossed many (if not all) borders freely, countries in both southern Europe and Russia did not see the circulation of currencies with foreign symbols as a threat to national identity. The counterfeiting of those coins was carried out, not to undermine the currencies of those other countries in a pre-meditated act of hostility, but to provide a reliable medium of exchange at a time when national sentiments and the origin of a currency were not interdependent.

Changes in the silver:gold exchange rate flowing between Europe and the Middle East caused silver at one time to be plentiful and then rare in the Levant and in Asia Minor. In the latter half of the fourteenth century, gold was more plentiful in the Mediterranean region to the extent that mints operated by the Ottoman Turks and the City State of Genoa in the eastern Mediterranean took to minting imitations of gold Venetian ducats, which by this period had become the common trading currency of the region.[6] The operation of the Ottoman mints producing counterfeit ducats was auctioned off to private businessmen, albeit under strict supervision by the state.

British Counterfeiting of US Continental Dollars

Counterfeiting of specie in precious metals for domestic consumption, providing the coins were of the same quality, was somehow not counterfeiting as we understand it now. If the worth of a coin was vested in the quality of its metal rather than any 'cartalist' or state-decreed value, unauthorised replicas with a gold or silver content every bit as good as the originals might be just as acceptable to an undiscriminating population. Fiat paper currencies that were not convertible to gold presented quite a different opportunity, especially for those wishing to counterfeit the currencies of hostile countries.

Britain's organised counterfeiting of the US continental dollars issued by the United States Congress to finance the costs of the American War of Independence (1775–83) is perhaps the first instance of counterfeiting designed to undermine the value of an enemy's currency, a concept made possible by the cheapness of counterfeiting a paper fiat currency rather than coined precious metal. A campaign was mounted to counterfeit the rebellious colonies' currency, an operation carried out on board a British warship in New York harbour. Tories – those elements in the American colonies remaining loyal to Britain – were encouraged to act as a channel to pass counterfeit bills in the rebelling states, and public announcements were made on the excellent quality of British counterfeits, further undermining confidence in the continentals. The operation was ultimately successful in aggravating the depreciation of the 'continentals', although the high volumes of notes of genuine issue and the circumstances of civil war and domestic and international doubts as to the likely victory of the rebel states would have in any case driven significant depreciation. The precarious condition of the continental dollar was recognised by Washington himself when he wrote that 'a wagon-load of money will scarcely purchase a wagon-load of provisions'. By 1781, a total of $200 million in notes issued between 1775 and 1779 by Congress were worthless and were never redeemed.[7]

One refined aspect of the public announcements issued by the British authorities that cast doubt on the paper money in circulation was the suggestion that the counterfeits were so good as to be indistinguishable from the real thing. Indeed, preserved samples of the British counterfeits that were printed using the engraved copper plates or Intaglio method, rather than the more basic letterpress or typeset method of the Congressional printers, are of better quality than the genuine continentals. Benjamin Franklin, a printer by training who had been active on the issue of paper currency for the American colonies many years before and who had been tasked by Congress with the production of continentals, himself commented on the fact that it was impossible to distinguish the genuine from the counterfeit continentals. (However, as a printer, he should have been able to tell the difference between notes printed in letterpress and those printed in copper plate. Was the anecdote apocryphal?)[8]

Various instances of the interception of counterfeit money in the possession of British troops and of the seizure of British dispatches relating to the counterfeiting campaign are cited, including correspondence from George Washington himself on the subject. Thomas Paine, the former British customs officer and libertarian writer who had emigrated to the American colonies shortly before the outbreak of the revolutionary war, condemned the British General William Howe in an open letter for his role in overseeing the operation. The congressional Board of Treasury

concluded that the only way of dealing with this menace was by recalling the banknote issues most subject to counterfeiting, rather than by
publicising for the benefit of the population the errors in the counterfeits, as this latter measure would simply help the British to correct the
flaws in their forgeries.[9]

A plethora of currencies issued not by Congress but by the individual states and cities simply added to the confusion. Accordingly,
Washington issued an instruction to the effect that only continental, and
not state-issued money was to be used. The House of Representatives
of Massachusetts also acknowledged in a leaflet of December 1777 that
counterfeits of currency issued by that and neighbouring states had contributed seriously to the vast increase of the money in circulation and
had prompted an increase 'of all commodities to an extravagant price'.[10]
Congress itself appealed to the people of the colonies, proposing that the
various legislatures 'sink their respective emissions, that so, there being
but one kind of bills, there may be less danger of counterfeits'.[11] In other
words, the more variety there was in the type of currency on issue, the
more susceptible the population was to confusion over what was genuine and what was not.

Some eyewitness participants in the War of Independence were convinced that it was as a result of British counterfeiting that the continental
dollars were, by the end of the war, worthless and repudiated. Eyewitness
perceptions are no doubt valid, but are not definitive evidence that counterfeiting rather than wider public and international lack of confidence
in the colonists' chances of success was responsible for the complete collapse of the continental dollar. At the very least, though, we must assume
that state-sponsored counterfeiting contributed to that collapse.

British Counterfeiting of French Assignats

Britain's counterfeiting of continental dollars, while not perhaps as
successful as some might have thought, was certainly seen as a useful
instrument in the struggle against the revolutionary forces in the
American colonies. It was a recent memory at the outbreak of the
French Revolution in 1789 and no doubt someone suggested the ploy

should be deployed again, this time against revolutionary French currency known as the assignat.

State-sponsored counterfeiting of French revolutionary assignats in England under the protection of William Pitt's government is cited as one of the main reasons for the collapse of that paper currency. The extent and official sanction of this operation was for some time concealed from public knowledge, but first appears to have come to light during a court case heard in England's Court of King's Bench. In this case, the English engraver of a plate used to forge assignats lodged a case to recover the value of a promissory note with which he had been paid for his efforts, but which the individual who had commissioned the plate had refused to honour. The engraver had defended his agreement to supply a plate for the purpose of counterfeiting, claiming that the work had been done ultimately at the requirement of the English government. It was suggested that the counterfeiting operation therefore was not an illegal act in England.[12] The judge hearing this case, Lord Kenyon, upheld this position, affirming that in a state of war it was legitimate to 'distress an enemy' by counterfeiting his currency.

According to one source, paper for the operation was made at a mill in North Tyne, Northumberland, and the notes were printed in the same region and supplied to the Duke of York's army operating on the continent against France's revolutionary armies. Other sources suggest that the counterfeiting operation had become a cottage industry, with seventeen printing facilities and 400 men involved in the London area alone, resulting in 12–15 billion francs worth of forgeries circulating in France by May 1795 – perhaps the same amount again as the assignats that had been officially issued by the government of France.[13]

The Catholic clergy in France, highly motivated to overturn the assignat because of the expropriation of church lands that were being mortgaged by means of the new paper currency, played a key role in the conspiracy to distribute the forged versions. The distribution operation was conducted under the control of the Comte D'Artois, brother of Louis XVI and afterwards Charles X of France.[14] Some members of the clergy in exile were going further than merely distributing the counterfeits: they were producing the counterfeits themselves. A team of émigré priests, coordinated by the relatives of the king's last finance minister,

Calonne, were engaged in a counterfeiting operation based in Sloane Square in London.[15]

Assignats were not only counterfeited in England. The production of counterfeit assignats in the émigré centre of Coblenz was no secret: in 1792 one member of France's revolutionary battalions was convinced that he and his comrades should march on Koblenz to deal with the counterfeiting operation.[16] The production of counterfeit assignats by French émigrés was reported in the same year by Goethe, the German romantic poet and minister of the State of Weimar who played an active part in that state's wartime alliance against revolutionary France. Following the Battle of Valmy in 1792, at which the French revolutionary forces repelled the Austrian–Prussian alliance, Goethe and his employer, the Duke of Saxe-Weimar, together with other allied forces withdrew through modern day Belgium towards the German border. At the small town of Arlon, Goethe stumbled across some strange wagons that appeared to be larger than others belonging to the retreating forces. These wagons, he learnt, contained a mobile factory used by French émigrés to counterfeit assignats during the campaign to invade France and overturn the revolutionary powers.

As a high official of the anti-revolutionary alliance, Goethe might have been inclined to approve of an operation designed to undermine the economy of his enemies. Quite to the contrary, he seems to have sympathised with the smaller tradespeople and general population of the region who had had problems enough with the extreme depreciation of the real assignats but were now suffering from a glut of notes that, despite the quality of the counterfeiting, were widely suspected as fake. Unsurprisingly, confidence in the assignats fell most severely in the east and south of the country, notably in the Rhone Valley and along the Rhine, the regions where military operations created the conditions least conducive to confidence in the paper currency. But suspicions about the authenticity of assignats spread far and wide – even undermining the confidence of the émigrés themselves.[17]

Although rumours of counterfeit assignats circulated in the markets, those rumours were denied by the revolutionary authorities that, of course, had no interest in a general collapse of public confidence in the new currency. With fakes flooding the economy from large numbers of cottage industry counterfeiting operations in Britain, among émigré priests and aristocrats in England and in exile on the continent, and even a mobile counterfeiting operation accompanying the invasion of France, denials would have fallen on deaf ears. The exact impact of counterfeiting on the value of the assignat is impossible to calculate and even if it alone was not responsible for the failure of the assignats and mandats, it would be naïve to imagine that it did not play a significant role.

French Counterfeiting of Russian Assignats

Britain may have been a leader in state sponsorship of political counterfeiting, but others soon adopted the idea. Napoleon Bonaparte, ever open to creative methods of waging war, is believed to have ordered the counterfeiting of British and Austrian notes. He is also credited with ordering the counterfeiting of Russian assignats, which are believed to have appeared prior to France's invasion of Russia in 1812.

Based on the condition of the surviving counterfeits, which were discernible from genuine rubles on the basis of typographical errors among other points (French counterfeiters being unfamiliar with the Cyrillic alphabet), it seems unlikely that they had spent much time in circulation. Bonaparte's intentions in launching this series of counterfeits appear to have been directed towards the financing of his army's operations in Russia by duping the population into supplying goods in return for false assignats. In this way it differed from the primary purpose of Britain's operations to undermine America's continental dollars and revolutionary France's assignats by expanding the money supply to the point where those currencies would become worthless.

Philippe, Comte de Segur, a contemporary of Napoleon favoured by the latter with senior appointments until he voted for the emperor's deposition in 1814, described the case in his history of Napoleon's expedition to Russia. In de Segur's account, the counterfeits had been produced illicitly by a printer whose work had been discovered by a police raid. Segur reported that the emperor found the production of counterfeits 'repugnant' and ordered their destruction. Russian historical accounts take a less sympathetic position. During the retreat from Russia, the emperor gave orders that the reserve of counterfeit assignats should be destroyed, apparently to prevent Russian authorities from discovering them. This would also point towards a purpose other than monetary sabotage. Had economic warfare been Bonaparte's intention he might have broadcast news of large numbers of counterfeits in circulation, just as Britain had during the American War of Independence. The fact that the exchange rate of Russian assignats in 1812 remained the same as before – again in contrast to the British operations against America and France – points towards a covert financial deception employing relatively low numbers of counterfeits rather than an attempt to sew panic among the Russian population.[18]

The Case of the Hungarian Francs

In some cases, political counterfeiting is designed overtly to ruin a country's monetary system and to be blatant about it. In other cases its purpose is to raise funds covertly without (indeed, preferably not) destroying the value. In the case of the French francs counterfeited in Hungary that came to light in 1925, there were multiple purposes. It was hoped that the counterfeits would undermine the stability of France's currency, an act of revenge for France's leading role in the imposition of the Treaty of Trianon on Hungary, creating a landlocked state reduced in size and in population following the First World War. But the plot was also planned to raise funds for covert political activities by the plotters.

As is often the case, a banknote, apparently genuine to the eye in all other respects, was detected by a person whose daily business involved the handling and scrutiny of notes. In this case the manager of a private bank in The Hague, Netherlands, first detected the counterfeits on the grounds that they did not feel quite right. By coincidence, the manager concerned also happened to be an expert on counterfeits and an adviser to the police on them. The individual who had passed the note turned out to be a courier of the Hungarian Foreign Ministry, travelling on a diplomatic passport. The courier was followed to a hotel by two detectives who, notwithstanding his apparent diplomatic status, were able to get access to his room for long enough to find large numbers of

1,000-franc banknotes, one of which they were able somehow to identify as a counterfeit. When the courier demanded to see the Hungarian
ambassador to The Hague, the issue developed into a full-blown diplomatic incident. Insisting on his right to see the ambassador, the courier
revealed to the Hungarian consul that he had been tasked with 'special
activities' by the chief of the Hungarian National Police. The detectives
at this point passed the case over to the Dutch Foreign Ministry.

It subsequently became clear that the 'courier' was in fact a colonel of
the Hungarian general staff and that two accomplices who had also been
arrested in The Hague for attempting to pass fake 1,000-franc notes at
bureaux de change also turned out to be serving Hungarian military
officers. The courier's claim was confirmed to the Hungarian embassy
in The Hague by the Foreign Ministry in Budapest and Hungary's chief
of police confirmed to his superiors, the Ministers of the Interior and
of Justice, that he had indeed issued documentation to the conspirators that provided them with diplomatic cover. The newspapers of the
Netherlands, Hungary, France and of Canada and Australia all published
reports on the conspiracy, which became an international cause célèbre
and in the view of contemporaries almost forced Hungary out of the
League of Nations.[19] Senior figures in Hungary's political establishment
were implicated in the plot, the origins of which were subsequently
shown to have emanated from Germany.

The 1923 occupation of the Ruhr region by France and Belgium
in response to Germany's failure to fulfil one of its reparations
commitments had added insult to the injury of defeat in 1918.
German industrialists backed a planned counter-strike involving the
mass counterfeiting of the French franc, but were unable to complete
their operation before a rescheduling of Germany's reparations was
agreed. The American-led rescheduling – the Dawes Plan of 1924
– together with British and American pressure on France to find an
accommodation with Germany succeeded in reducing the tension.
Rather than waste a perfectly good counterfeiting operation, the idea
and the means to execute it were offered by the former quartermaster
general of the German general staff Erich von Ludendorff to the
former Austro-Hungarian minister Prince Windisch-Grätz. Following
the defeat of Germany, Ludendorff, who as the real brains behind

Germany's wartime strategy had fallen further than most, reacted in bitterness by siding with right-wing elements. His contact with Windisch-Grätz is thus interpreted by some as the first clear indication of Hungary's inclination to ally itself with German fascism. Windisch-Grätz mobilised support in Budapest for the proposal.

Printing presses and special paper were freighted from Germany to Hungary. Army officers in charge of Hungary's National Cartographic Office were implicated in the plot, no doubt chosen for the printing capabilities of their organisation. According to one source, even the chief chaplain of the Hungarian Army was drawn into the conspiracy when he agreed to the counterfeit notes being stored in his residence. Members of the Hungarian armed forces, operating under diplomatic cover, would distribute the counterfeit notes by changing them at private banks in the Netherlands, Sweden, Italy and Belgium, but not directly in France. The genuine notes obtained by the process of exchanging the counterfeit notes would be transferred to Hungary through diplomatic pouches. The Hungarian ambassadors in the relevant states were remain uninformed until the operation had reached near completion.

When Windisch-Grätz was brought to court in Hungary to answer charges of leading the plot, he revealed that the operation was designed to raise funds to support pro-Hungarian political activities in Slovakia and elsewhere abroad and to finance political operations at home. It also emerged from the trial that Istvan Bethlen, Prime Minister of Hungary, had received a report on the counterfeiting operation from the Deputy Foreign Minister in late 1925; the Prime Minister was then shown to have had prior knowledge of the plot. The principal plotters were convicted and sentenced to terms of imprisonment of various lengths, although the court found that the patriotic motives of the conspirators offered extenuating circumstances and all sentences were either reduced or the convicted were allowed to enjoy a particularly lenient imprisonment. Although Prime Minister Bethlen offered his resignation to the Regent of Hungary, Admiral Horthy, it was not accepted and the government did not fall.[20]

To add a further twist to the already convoluted direction of central European politics, Windisch-Grätz subsequently claimed that the plot had originated not with the right-wing Ludendorff, but, implausibly, with

Gustav Stresemann, moderate Foreign Minister of the Weimar Republic who had been known for a policy of reconciliation with France.[21]

Although the Hungarian plot was an abject failure, it was perhaps the most important of all counterfeiting cases in that it directly led to the 1929–31 Geneva Convention on the Suppression of Counterfeiting Banknotes and to the establishment of the principle that any individual counterfeiting the currency of one country in a second country should be prosecuted in the latter or extradited for prosecution.

Stalin's Russia Counterfeits US Dollars

Napoleon had counterfeited Russian assignats not to destabilise the Russian economy, but to provide funding for his invasion of that country. In the late 1920s, Russia's state intelligence service launched an operation to counterfeit US dollars, with a similar view to covertly create illicit funding – in this case to provide the finance for equipment that Russia needed to deliver the Soviet Union's first five-year plan, due to begin in 1928. The onset of the Great Depression in 1929 and the collapse of commodity markets dealt a blow to the Soviet Union's primary source of revenue: the export of produce such as wheat. There was then an added imperative to produce increasing volumes of counterfeit dollars and distribute them covertly in various countries.

From May 1928 to 1934, very high-quality fake $100 bills were being passed in various locations from China to Latin America, including Mexico, the United States, Romania, Austria, Poland, Bulgaria, Switzerland and Germany. In Cuba large volumes of fake notes were passed in the casinos for which Havana was famous. The first suggestion that the origin of these notes was Russia's state intelligence service emerged in Warsaw following the arrest of a Polish communist official found to be in possession of counterfeit American $100 and $20 notes. The Polish investigation pointed towards Russia and Germany as the origin of the notes.

In Germany the 'route to market' for the fake notes was the Berlin branch of a small private bank, Sass and Martini, which had been sold off by the original owners and ended up with some delightful irony in the hands of a Berlin communist. During a court case in Germany in January 1930, it was alleged that a phenomenal $2.5 billion worth of counterfeit notes were issued to a rebel warlord in China and to the Soviet Far Eastern Army.

The quality of the counterfeit notes concerned pointed towards a high-quality operation. Cotton rag-based paper was used and the engraved work exhibited very few errors. Nevertheless, investigations by the US Secret Service and by the German and Polish police revealed the scale of the operation. Statements by an American Communist Party official during a US congressional hearing and the 1939 memoirs of General Walter Krivitsky, the former head of Soviet Military Intelligence for Western Europe who had defected, confirmed details of the operation and revealed that the printing was carried out in Berlin, not in Russia.

Despite the quality of the product, the failure of the operation to pass the counterfeits posed serious possibilities for embarrassing Soviet military intelligence and the Soviet leadership. Krivitsky was tasked with closing down the operation and, although some apparent private enterprise kept the operation going until 1934 in America, by 1936 the counterfeiting scam was over.[22]

Operation Bernhard

The Nazi plan to counterfeit British sterling during the Second World War is now the best known of all instances of state counterfeiting. According to some, Operation Bernhard was the brainchild of Reinhard Heydrich, head of Germany's combined secret police and security service, while others attribute the idea to SS Major Bernhard Krueger, after whom it has been named and who ran the counterfeiting operation in the Sachsenhausen concentration camp. Yet another view is that it had been conceived by the SS officer Alfred Naujocks, who has also been credited with both the Gleiwitz incident, the initial incursion into Polish territory seen as the opening scene of the Second World War, and the Venlo incident in which two British intelligence officers were kidnapped from the Dutch town on the border with Germany in 1939.

Whoever it was among these three committed Nazis who came up with the scheme, association of these extraordinary and sinister characters with the plan only adds to the drama.

Originally the plot had been designed to produce vast quantities of perfect counterfeits that, when delivered to the British economy in sufficiently large quantities, would cause massive inflation. The primary objective, then, was to disrupt and undermine the target economy rather than to raise covert funds. To achieve this objective, the notes would have to be indistinguishable from the real thing, making it impossible for the authorities and the population in the United Kingdom to identify and weed out the counterfeits as they entered circulation. The preferred means of delivery was to be the simplest and most direct method available: the notes would be dropped from aircraft overflying British airspace. But as the project only began in 1942, by which time Germany had already lost its main chance of air superiority over British airspace, the principal route to market was unavailable. As an attempt to wreck the monetary system of a hostile state, Operation Bernhard was, from the start, a failure.

Accepting these circumstances, Germany's secret service adapted to events, altering its primary objective. The counterfeits were to be used as a means of financing its operations and of buying materials in neutral states. Attempts were made to distribute the fake sterling notes in occupied lands, including France and Greece. However, the policy of Germany's Finance Ministry and Minister Walter Funk was, wherever possible, to stabilise the currencies of occupied states, even if the immediate interests of Germany might perhaps have been to see a series of weak currencies in occupied Europe with the exception of the reichsmark. On the assumption that Germany would win the war, Funk and other leading economic politicians did not want to be saddled with a group of wrecked economies. He therefore forbade the secret service from distributing fake currencies in most occupied states, although Russia and other parts of the Soviet Union were exceptions to the rule.[23]

Germany was not alone in counterfeiting currency during the Second World War. During the campaign in the Horn of Africa, where Britain sought to liberate Ethiopia from Italian occupation, the only currency accepted by the local population was the long-established trading currency, the Maria Teresa dollar, originally minted in Austria. Britain therefore resorted to its duplication based on counterfeited dies. However, like the crusader regimes that counterfeited the gold coinage of the Middle East at the same standards of fineness as the genuine article, achieving high-quality duplication, the British Maria Teresa dollars were of standard .833 fineness of silver, that is to say 833 parts out of 1,000 were silver, precisely the same silver content as the original coins from the Austrian mint.[24] The objective in this case was neither to undermine the local currency, nor to produce counterfeits that could be used to buy local produce at little cost, but rather to supply Allied forces with adequate volumes of a commodity specie that would be accepted locally precisely because its precious metal content was demonstrably good.

The Superdollar and Operation Mali

Fiat paper currency continues to provide a target for state counterfeiters, even when the currency concerned includes some level of printed security in the form of anti-counterfeiting features. Figures published by the Board of Governors of the Federal Reserve System in 2005 state that some US $760 billion worth of all denominations were at that time in circulation globally, of which $545 billion were in $100 bills.[25] By 2015, figures published on the Federal Reserve Bank website show that the total value of dollars in circulation amounted to more than $1.3 trillion, of which more than a trillion dollars were in the form of $100 bills – nearly six times the total face value of all $20 bills, the next most common note.[26] It is not difficult to understand why the $100 bill might present an attractive target for counterfeiters – whether criminal or state-sponsored.

Since 1989, high-quality counterfeit $100 bills – so-called 'super-dollars' – have been appearing around the world, initially in the Far East and then further afield. Informed opinion in the United States now points towards North Korea as the origin of these counterfeits, but the network of participants in the passing of these counterfeits stretched around the world.

In 2002 the Irish press reported that US Secret Service investigations had identified a link to the Workers' Party of Ireland that had arranged the transfer of superdollars to Britain. There the police's Operation Mali had picked up the conspiracy to pass the counterfeit dollars and drawn it to the attention of the secret service, which, it transpired, had already been investigating the same plot that was believed initially to be connected to the Chinese Communist Party.[27]

According to a television report by the BBC in 2004 on the so-called superdollar, a primary point for the transfer of the counterfeits to the Irish Workers' Party was the North Korean embassy in Moscow. The same programme reported that North Korea's objective was two-fold: to finance the Pyongyang regime, but also to undermine the US economy.[28]

A Federal Reserve press release on a joint Treasury, Federal Reserve and secret service report of 2006 asserts that counterfeits accounted at that time for no more than 1 in 10,000 notes, still a significant number given the overall volume of US dollars in circulation. The September 2006 joint report to Congress describes the supernote counterfeits as a 'strategic case with national security implications' for the United States and confirms that the US Secret Service had conducted a long-term study of the specific threat since 1989. The report categorically states the view of the US Secret Service that the supernotes were produced and distributed 'with the full consent and control of the North Korean government'. It also noted that in June 2006 Interpol issued an alert about attempts by North Korea to obtain items that would help to produce US currency. Finally, the report noted: 'Over the course of this sixteen-year investigation, approximately $22 million in supernotes has been passed to the public, and approximately $50 million in supernotes has been seized by the US Secret Service.'[29] Interpol's own annual 2006 report did indeed record the issue of an 'orange' notice[30] alert on the production of supernotes but, more circumspectly, noted that the supernotes were *'allegedly* produced in the Democratic Republic of Korea (North Korea)'.

Leaked correspondence published subsequently on the internet showed that, earlier in that same year, American authorities had liaised with German officials to prevent the export to North Korea of an intaglio printing press made in Germany which would be capable of producing counterfeit US dollars. German authorities confirmed their readiness to block any such export. Again in 2006, US officials were tasked to request British government support to ensure no equipment or materials would be exported from the UK which might be used by North Korea to counterfeit US currency.

From coins bearing the images of late Roman emperors produced in Roman mints by the Visigoth invaders in Gaul, to fake notes of the US dollar, today's international medium of exchange and store of value, currencies over the past 1,500 years have been susceptible to counterfeiting, usually for criminal purposes, but also for political and military purposes. As new forms of transactions are presented – notably today's online and digital transactions – there is no reason to think they will not at some time be attacked for the same military and political objectives, not using coining dies or printing plates, but the computers and software of the twenty-first century.

Confederate states 5 dollar bill: The poor quality of printing hints at the Confederate states' weak policies on currency issue.

Mexico 1915: 50-centavos note issued by General Serrano's Army of the north-east. During the Mexican Revolution various military entities issued their own currency, often of low value and low quality, such as this note.

Mexico 1916: 1 national gold peso. In May 1916 new currency was introduced to replace the many different notes issued by banks, military units and regional governments. This note, issued by the state of Yucatan, was printed by the Parsons Trading Company of New York and is clearly of a higher quality. However, the reform attempt was unsuccessful and by December 1916 the new notes had depreciated to only 5 per cent of their value at issue.

Russia 1919: *caisse d'emission* **1-ruble note.** In July 1918, following the outbreak of revolution, Allied troops were deployed to the north of Russia in an attempt to keep that country in the war against Germany. To support Allied operations and the local anti-Bolshevik authorities, *caisse d'emission* ruble notes were issued with a fixed exchange rate to sterling. The inscription in the central panel of this note reads: 'The State Caisse D'Emission will exchange this credit note for Pounds Sterling in any amount at the rate of 40 rubles = 1 pound sterling.'

Germany, November 1923: 2-billion-mark note issued by the Reichsbank. This month represented the low point in Germany's hyperinflation in the period following the First World War.

Germany 1923: When inflation reached its worst point in Germany in November 1923, currency commissioner Hjalmar Schacht launched the rentenmark, pictured here, which brought the collapse of the reichsmark to an end.

Japan invasion money of the Second World War, Oceania: 1-shilling note. As Japan's empire expanded rapidly during the war, the government issued occupation notes denominated not in yen but in local currencies. The objective was to prevent the circulation of yen in conquered territories and the possibility that notes denominated in the currency would be returned to Japan, stimulating inflation at the centre of the empire. This note was for circulation in Papua New Guinea and the Pacific Islands.

Japanese invasion money, Oceania: 1-pound note. This was also issued for use in Papua New Guinea and the Pacific Islands.

Japanese invasion money, Malaysia: 10-dollar note. The design of this and other notes for Japanese-occupied Malaysia and elsewhere gave the currency its disparaging nickname of 'banana money'.

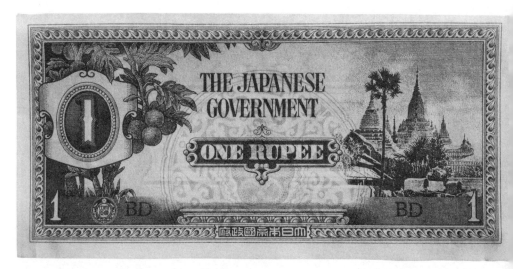

Japanese invasion money, Burma: 1-rupee note. The redemption of these Japanese-issued notes by returning British authorities in 1945 presented a policy conundrum.

German occupation currency, Kreditkassenscheine: 20-reichsmark note. Germany also issued a separate currency for occupied territories. However, the Reich authorities made the mistake of denominating the currency in reichsmarks for all occupied countries, which encouraged German troops to move large volumes of the currency around various countries in Europe. To prevent this large-scale transfer of currency around the Reich, the Nazis began to withdraw this type of note from circulation in 1943.

Germany 1945: Allied military marks, 1,000-mark note. These notes were designed in the US and printed by the Forbes Company of Boston for the Allied forces occupying Germany. When the Soviet authorities insisted on having duplicate plates for their own unlimited publication of these marks, the initial objections of some American officials were overcome by US Treasury official Harry Dexter White.

Germany 1946: US military payment certificates. US authorities introduced the MPC to counter a black market in allied military marks, which could be converted into US dollars and then remitted to America.

Hungary 1946: 1-billion pengo note. The highest rate of inflation ever recorded was that of Hungary under Soviet occupation at the end of the Second World War.

Yugoslavia 1990s: 5-billion-dinar note. In January 1994, Yugoslavia was fighting wars in Croatia and Bosnia and, under UN sanctions. In that month hyperinflation in Yugoslavia reached a daily rate of 64 per cent, with prices doubling every 1.4 days. It is the third worst inflation rate on record (Hanke–Krus Hyperinflation Table).

Republika Srpska, Bosnia: 50-million-dinar note. The Serb Republic area of Bosnia produced its own banknotes but pegged the currency to that of the Yugoslav dinar. Moreover, Republika Srpska's electronic payments system was fully integrated with that of Yugoslavia. Under these circumstances it is hardly surprising that Yugoslavia's inflation was transmitted to Republika Srpska. In January 1994, inflation there peaked at a daily rate of 64.3 per cent – only a shade below that of Yugoslavia. This note was issued in 1992, well before the peak of inflation, but already pointing towards a general currency collapse.

CURRENCY AND THE SECOND WORLD WAR

The Asian–Pacific War

Japan's invasion of China in 1931 was the opening shot in the Second World War. Two years before Hitler came to power in Germany and four years before Italy under Mussolini invaded Ethiopia, senior Japanese officers fabricated a pretext (the so-called Mukden Incident) for the invasion of northern China and the seizure of Manchuria. Japan's military operations in China went on until the end of the war in 1945.

Although the war until 1937 was relatively limited in scale, currency attacks by Japan on China's silver-based system soon became a major concern for the Chinese government. Currency policies instigated by other countries also resulted in unintended consequences for the Chinese monetary system. Thus, the decision by the government of Franklin Delano Roosevelt in the United States in 1934 to purchase silver in response to lobbying by senior politicians from silver-producing states boosted the market price. The Chinese population, prey to the fear and uncertainties of war, behaved quite sensibly: they converted banknotes to silver and, with the profits obtained from silver at a high price, bought gold. The Chinese government had little choice but to take China off the silver standard and introduce a non-convertible paper-based currency.

Reserves were sold to sustain an exchange rate of the paper money to the US dollar and sterling based on recent historical figures. In 1935, for instance, the Chinese government approached the US government with a proposal that the latter buy 100–200 million ounces of China's reserve of silver. Although agreement was not reached on the terms of this large-scale deal, the US did immediately buy 20 million ounces, providing China with US dollars that could in turn be sold to maintain the value of China's own paper currency. When Japan's Yokohama specie bank took steps to undermine China's currency by means of propaganda, America responded by purchasing a further 50 million ounces at a premium to the market price. When Japanese banks repeated their aggressive attacks on China's currency, America carried out a series of silver purchases starting in April 1936 through to 1937. American payments would be held in New York and used exclusively for the stabilisation of China's currency.[1]

Despite the repeated American silver purchases, the Chinese government was still left with a great deal of silver in its reserve threatened by the onward march of Japanese military and monetary operations. In 1937 the conflict went up another gear when Japanese troops extended the area of their operations in China. America responded again by purchasing Chinese silver on the premise that the stability of its currency was at least as important as the success of its arms in defending the country. In the eighteen months from November 1935, America had spent $67 million in purchasing Chinese silver. But, to put this in context, China had spent US $42 million in market interventions in support of its currency in only five weeks after the widening of hostilities between China and Japan.

As China fought to protect the integrity of its currency, Japan took measures to undermine its monetary independence. New banks of issue were established by Japanese authorities across China between 1932 and 1941: the Federated Reserve Bank of China in the north and later the Central Reserve Bank of Nanking issuing in the south, as well as the Mengchiang Bank in Inner Mongolia and the Central Bank of Manchukuo. Local notes would be issued, backed by yen notes, which were replacing sterling and US dollars as the foundation of China's currency system while China's own notes were ousted from circulation and with them its authority diminished. But it took some time before this foreign fiat currency was accepted and Japanese authorities had to force its acceptability by placing a tight stranglehold on various territories, imposing currency controls to prevent Chinese nationalist currency entering zones under their control. The new Japanese currencies were endowed with practical legitimacy when they became the only legal means of paying local taxes and conducting a range of everyday transactions. Having the power to print money at will in this way allowed the occupying authorities to finance their operations at the expense of the local population.[2]

As part of this policy of replacing the national currency system with its own puppet monetary issues, Japan made efforts in December 1938 to persuade Britain and France to accept as the legitimate currency of China the dollars issued by its Federated Reserve Bank of China. Both Britain and France refused to accept the demand, adding to a sense of growing confrontation.[3] A good three years before the Japanese invasions of Malaya and Hong Kong and the attack on Pearl Harbor, the major protagonists in the Asia–Pacific war were already forming up against each other in the monetary arena.

When stocks of silver became depleted, Britain took steps in 1939 to support China's currency stabilisation directly. In March 1939, a fund was launched by the British and Chinese governments with financial support from four major commercial banks providing £10 million for foreign exchange operations that would be conducted through the same four participating commercial banks. By mid-July, however, the £10 million stabilisation fund had been completely drawn down and within a month the value of the Chinese dollar in exchange for other currencies had collapsed by 50 per cent. The Chinese finance minister saw Japan's attacks on China's monetary system as at least as dangerous as its military advances.[4]

With tensions ramping up in July 1939, Japan again demanded that Britain recognise the Japanese-issued currency as the only legal tender for China and cease to recognise the currency issued by the Chinese authorities themselves. The British response – stating that it was impossible to cease to recognise the currency of a recognised government – might have been the first occasion on which such a principle had been expressed and would have contributed to the growing hostility of Japan towards Britain. A further disagreement arose when Japan insisted Britain surrender the ownership of Chinese silver deposited with British institutions, a move that echoed Germany's seizure of Austria's gold in spring 1938 and German moves to seize Czech gold in March 1939. Britain also rejected this demand out of hand.[5]

Only the outbreak of the European war in September reversed the decline in the exchange rate of the Chinese dollar to most other European currencies. By April 1941, America had also signed up to participate in currency stabilisation operations, making $50 million available in credits for that purpose.[6]

American currency operations in defence of China's monetary system and in direct competition with the operations of Japan's own attacks must have been interpreted by the Japanese authorities as further proof that America was the main obstacle to their expansionist drive. Indeed, America was providing large volumes of silver to the government of India on the basis of secret loans in 1940, the year before America's entry into the war.[7] One step short of war, monetary operations of this nature were as vital a commitment to support of the Allies as the Lend-Lease programme.

The Chinese nationalist government took further steps to protect its own currency. In March 1939 – that is, when the stabilisation fund was in preparation – Dr Kung, the Finance Minister, reached an agreement with the British banknote printing company De La Rue, as a result of which a note-printing operation was established in the international settlement area of Shanghai with a contingency site in Rangoon, Burma, to be engaged in the event that Shanghai should fall to Japanese troops, who were already surrounding the city. The contract underpinning this agreement was based on the supply by De La Rue of 2 billion banknotes, with the necessary materials being smuggled into Shanghai and the completed notes being smuggled out in dustcarts. Although this operation was quietly and quickly wound down when it became apparent that Japanese troops were about to move on the international settlements, De La Rue continued to support the Chinese government's currency requirements and produced the 1,000-yuan note issued by the Central Bank of China in 1942.[8]

Japan's currency had already shown signs of severe weakening before the wider world war began. Resorting to measures recognisable to any government seeking to debase the intrinsic value of its currency, Japan issued aluminium coins that initially were valued at one sen (one one-hundredth of a yen), but were then revalued at one yen.[9]

Although during the early years of war Japan clung to the pretence of a fully gold-convertible yen, the reality was that this position was unsustainable. By 1942 the yen had already lost 50 per cent of its value against the dollar. In that year the government saw the way things were going and took new measures permitting reserves required to cover banknote issue to be based on the Bank of Japan's holdings of government bonds and on the loans it had extended to the Japanese government. Even then, the volume of notes that the Bank of Japan might issue was determined by the Ministry of Finance. One estimate suggests that during the later years of the war, the issue of money accounted for anywhere between half and three-quarters of all government revenue. Japan's money had gone the way of all currencies during war since the introduction of fiduciary currencies: detached from its anchor of gold, subject only to the demands made by government needing to finance war, the yen settled into a declining depreciation.[10]

Japan's Military Currencies

As Japan's conquests reached beyond China, across East Asia and the South Pacific in the early years of the war, their occupying military authorities issued their own local currency (military scrip) denominated not in yen but in the local currency: in pesos for the Philippines, guilders for the Dutch East Indies and the straits dollar for Singapore. The Yokohama Specie Bank, succeeded by the Southeast Regions Development Bank, took over issue for South East Asia while the Bank of Taiwan took over responsibility for the issue of scrip in the Philippines. Foreign and pre-war currencies also continued to circulate, but in time disappeared out of circulation as they were hoarded and as the military scrip, as the less credible paper, was used increasingly as the medium of exchange. In Thailand and Indo-China a different arrangement operated. Local currencies were supplied to the Yokohama Specie Bank in those countries by the Bank of Siam and Banque de l'Indochine in return for credits to their accounts at the Bank of Japan. This arrangement, which imposed at least some form of responsibility in issue (if only nominal), together with the fact that in those two countries the currency looked just as it had done before the war, seems to have made a difference. The increase in money supply and the increase in prices in these two countries compared to those in Malaya, Burma, Indonesia and the Philippines over the duration of the war was astonishingly low.

The production of notes for the Dutch East Indies was ordered in April 1941, long before the Japanese invaded in March 1942, giving clear evidence of the preparedness of the Japanese military machine. Exchange rates were reset by the occupying powers to overvalue the yen against the local currencies, in all cases setting one yen to one peso or one guilder and in both situations more than doubling the purchasing power of the yen and giving purchasing power advantage to Japan whenever it needed to import valuable commodities.[11]

In issuing military scrip instead of using yen throughout the empire, the government was insulating Japan itself from any excessive issue of national currency in the conquered territories and the possibility that this currency would return to Japan, stimulating inflation. At the edges of Japan's military power, the soundness of this money would be seen as less reliable. Consequently, Japanese locally issued currency often resulted in inflation, which was worse the further away from the centre it appeared and weakened further as Japanese forces lost ground in the later stages of the war. The only exception to this simple rule of thumb was the situation in the Philippines, where the monthly rise in prices during the last year of occupation proved higher than in Burma and other more remote occupied countries. In Malaya, however, the most extreme of all cases, prices were an astonishing 11,000 times greater than they had been at the start of the war.[12]

There was, though, one apparent exception to the policy of avoiding a yen-based currency in occupied territories. When Japan invaded Hong Kong in December 1941, it seized and issued more than HK $120 million notes from various banks in the territory. But this was only an interim measure until military yen scrip could be issued as the only legal tender, Hong Kong dollars having then been prohibited. Despite this prohibition, however, there was still a demand for the currency as there was a widespread assumption that the Japanese and their military scrip would in due course be ousted and the Hong Kong dollar restored. As elsewhere, the value of the Hong Kong military yen declined rapidly the more likely it seemed that Japan would lose the war. When the military yen scrip was introduced, an exchange rate of four to the dollar was imposed. When British troops at last retook Hong Kong in 1945, military yen were converted to Hong Kong dollars at a rate of 100:1, up to a limit of 500 yen.[13] We might wonder why, of all the territories seized by Japan during the war, Hong Kong was the only one where military scrip denominated in yen was introduced. The simple answer would seem to be that Japan saw Hong Kong only as an extension of mainland China, where Japan had already imposed a yen-based scrip.

Japan's issue of large volumes of military scrip in countries such as the Philippines, Indonesia and Burma created legacy problems for colonial powers re-entering those countries. Perhaps the biggest single problem for those powers was whether to give any value to the Japanese scrip in circulation. Burma, which Japanese forces had invaded in January 1942, constituted the furthest reach of Japanese conquest. A currency vacuum had been created there by British authorities, who instructed retreating officials and troops to destroy or repatriate to India the official notes and coins, including notes produced by the Government of India and the Reserve Bank of India that circulated in Burma.[14]

Indian silver rupee coins, however, were favoured in Burma, particularly by the hill tribes who generally remained loyal to the British authorities. Large volumes of coins were hoarded and sometimes used for private transactions but only between trusted parties, as Japanese authorities always assumed possession of rupee coins to be an indication of pro-British sympathies.

In the absence of a legacy circulating currency and with produce and other vital goods becoming scarcer throughout 1943, the Japanese occupying troops would have had no option but to issue large volumes of their own currency, even if that had not been part of their intended policy. One estimate suggests that the Japanese issue of military scrip amounted to sixteen times the value of British notes in circulation in Burma prior to the arrival of the invading forces.[15]

In the two and a half years from the start of the invasion to the summer of 1944, the high volume of issue was reflected in the depreciation of the Burmese military scrip issued by Japan, a drop in value estimated at somewhere between 60 and 75 per cent. Responsible for the issue of these notes was the Yokohama Specie Bank. At the same time, volumes of currency in circulation were further increased by the introduction of counterfeit notes produced by the British under the code name Grenville, and of genuine silver rupee coins by British forces operating behind Japanese lines. A million Japanese scrip 10-rupee notes were counterfeited in Britain in this way and covertly supplied to Burma by British special forces. When Japanese authorities returned the compliment by counterfeiting the British Indian 10-rupee notes, the Reserve Bank of India upgraded the security of the genuine notes by incorporating a new watermark. When further counterfeits of the 100-rupee note were discovered in May 1944, the security was further upgraded by the Reserve Bank of India by including an embedded security thread of the type introduced in the British sterling notes during the war. The counterfeiting of Japanese military scrip applied not only to that of Burma, but also to the other scrip issued in other occupied territories including the Philippines and Dutch East Indies.[16]

As British troops gradually reasserted control of Burma in the course of 1945, Japanese currency depreciated. From an artificially set exchange rate of 1:1 at the beginning of their occupation, Japanese troops found that twenty of their military rupees were now worth only one British rupee. A notional agreement to allow a Burmese puppet regime full control over their own currency had never come to fruition. Military scrip there was never replaced by notes issued by a Burmese central bank, probably because Japanese military control of Burma never consolidated to the extent that would allow trust in a Burmese national government.[17]

And as Britain reasserted its position in Burma, decisions had to be taken regarding the replacement of Japanese military scrip and in particular whether the withdrawn Japanese notes would be purchased from the population with new notes or would simply be cancelled without compensation. The principles applied in Burma, the first British territory to be reoccupied, would inevitably form the basis for currency replacement in other British territories regained from the Japanese. The solution involved Japanese military scrip being replaced by British Military Administration notes, which in turn would be backed by sterling.

But there were two immediate concerns: first, that large volumes of British notes would have to be issued to cover the excessive volumes of depreciated Japanese notes in circulation, prolonging the inflation. Worse still, a second concern was that unreliable elements prepared to collaborate with the Japanese would accept Japanese notes, knowing that they could then exchange them for British notes. In this way, recognition of some value in the Japanese notes might prolong Japanese resistance. Moreover, and in the longer term, there was scepticism that Britain would be able to recover value for any Japanese rupees in reparations from the Japanese government at the end of the war.[18] An opposing body of opinion held that too wide a community would be ruined by refusing to exchange Japanese issued notes for British Military Administration notes.

A policy was eventually formulated according to which Japanese-issued notes in small sums would be accepted for emergency relief supplies and to settle debts to the British administration, but large-denomination notes would not be accepted because it was believed that they were mainly held by black marketeers or those who had collaborated with the Japanese.[19] In essence, Japanese military scrip was to be demonetised without anything more than marginal monetary compensation. In the event, relief supplies were distributed to the Burmese population without charge by one of the British armies re-entering Burma, so that there was no occasion or need for the Japanese military scrip to be exchanged for food in the north of the country. In the south, however, another British army was indeed exchanging supplies to the local population in exchange for Japanese-issued rupees.

A formal declaration by British authorities in May 1945 officially demonetised Japanese-issued rupees. Unscrupulous individuals sought to get shot of their holdings of those rupees by using them to buy up valuable produce and goods in the countryside, where the population was unaware that they were no longer legal tender. Although Japanese-issued rupee notes were still used in parts of Burma after it was reoccupied by the British, their value had declined from the 1:1 set down at the launch of Japanese military scrip in the country to 100 Japanese rupees to one British rupee. At the same time, hoarded British coins and notes that had not circulated during the Japanese occupation now started to reappear – particularly in the north of the country.[20]

British Military Administration notes remained in circulation in Burma until 1947, although in June 1946 the Burmese government decided to issue its own notes, finally severing the monetary connection with the government and the Reserve Bank of India. In 1947 the Burma currency board was created, free of influence from India, but with one of its five members nominated by the Bank of England. Burmese rupees were to be backed by sterling. As Burmese notes printed in England were issued into circulation, British Military Administration notes were withdrawn.[21]

An identical policy was adopted by American authorities as they displaced Japanese forces in the Philippines, although this was formulated independently and without coordination with British authorities.[22]

Between 1939 and 1945, the value of notes in circulation in Japan had increased ten-fold. Following Japan's defeat and occupation, American authorities had planned to issue their own military scrip for Japan, but other than several series of notes issued in Okinawa, the occupying authorities accepted that Bank of Japan notes would be a perfectly acceptable form of payment. A yen:dollar exchange rate of 15:1 (in contrast to the pre-war rate of 4.23:1) was set in September 1945, but the yen continued to depreciate.[23] New yen valued at 1/350 of the pre-war yen led to inflation, which at least enabled the Japanese government to inflate away its debts. The newly devalued currency also provided a competitive monetary basis for Japan's future export success.[24] But by 1949 the inflation – and near hyperinflation – needed to be brought under control. Consequently, the US authorities insisted on a deflationary stage of relative stability in 1949 based on a US dollar standard.[25]

Currency Systems of the Third Reich

Nazi Germany's need to import vast quantities of materials in preparation for its war effort had already led during the pre-war period to the design of a system that would permit it to import those materials without having to transfer gold or hard currency to other countries in return. A system to regulate trade between European states had already been developed in Germany in the 1930s to circumvent the need to settle international transactions by cash or gold transfers. In the inter-war era, when the shipping of gold in settlement of foreign debts had the effect of reducing the amount of money in circulation, some countries sought to reduce the amount of gold leaving their borders. The idea had first been used by Switzerland and Hungary to settle their bilateral transactions and had then been adopted by other countries, including Sweden. The Nazi regime latched on to it and took it a stage further. The system – bilateral or multilateral exchange clearing – was used by them as the basis for trade in raw materials from, for instance, Balkan states, in return for Germany's finished goods, reducing vastly the amount of cash or gold that had to cross borders.

When Germany needed to import materials such as chrome from the Balkans it would credit an account held in Germany with the payment; when eventually the country selling chrome agreed to buy something from Germany – almost always a finished product – that same account was debited. No money crossed borders in these transactions. The value of an export to one country or another was simply set against the value held in that country's account in Germany. This process not only conserved Germany's gold reserves, but also locked other countries into its market for exports.

The wartime development of this system, set out by Hitler's Finance Minister Walter Funk in 1940, involved the fixing of exchange rates between the currencies of occupied European states and that of Germany with a central clearing house in Berlin managing transactions between countries. Such a system, imposed without choice on Germany's vassal states, simply bypassed the need for gold as an intermediating mechanism to fix exchange rates.[26]

Moreover, the recognition that paper had been released from the constraints of gold allowed governments to issue military scrip or occupation currencies on a scale never seen before. Occupying troops could force the population of an occupied country to accept military scrip in payment for provisions and services and there was no pretence that it would ever be converted into gold. Moreover, the imposition of military scrip at bayonet point was even more compelling for an intimidated population than any abstract concept of legal tender. Monetary policy was not, however, so straightforward as to be only a matter of brute force. The occupier ultimately recognised that there was little advantage in destroying the monetary stability of its empire. As Germany was going to win the war (so it believed), it would be desirable for the occupied states to be stable in monetary terms. Military scrip would, therefore, not be allowed to reach hyperinflationary levels. Germany's monetary policies in Europe would vary according to whether a country was seen as neutral, occupied or friendly, reflecting the realities and recognising that no single monetary system would suit the Reich and wider Europe.[27]

In the first few years of the war, Germany took draconian steps to bolster its own currency. Gold reserves of occupied territories were confiscated, beginning with those of Austria at that country's Anschluss with the Reich in March and April 1938. The Austrian National Bank's gold reserves and its 4,000 shares in the Bank for International Settlements (BIS) were transferred to the Reichsbank with no obstruction from the senior management of BIS. As Austrian reserves and banking assets were transferred wholesale to the Reichsbank, the operation was more straightforward than the transfer of the banking assets of the Sudetenland, a slice of Czechoslovak territory ceded to Germany in September 1938. Local bank branches there were severed from their head offices in Czechoslovakia and were obliged to convert their cash holdings into reichsmarks. Adding insult to injury, in February 1939 Germany demanded Czechoslovakia transfer some 14.5 metric tonnes of gold (about 14.5 per cent of the national gold reserves) to back the German currency now circulating in the Sudetenland, although the German occupation in the following month made the demand obsolete.[28]

The invasion of Czechoslovakia itself in March 1939 resulted in one of the best-reported instances of central bank plunder during the Second World War. Czechoslovakia had reacted to Germany's annexation of the Sudetenland by transferring 94 tonnes of its gold to two accounts at the Bank of England, one account for the National Bank of Czechoslovakia and one for its sub-account in the name of the Bank for International Settlements. Only 6 tonnes, or 6 per cent, of the national gold reserves remained in Czechoslovakia. Reich officials now forced officials of the

National Bank of Czechoslovakia to request the BIS to arrange the transfer of just over 23 tonnes of gold from the BIS' sub-account for Czechoslovakia at the Bank of England to the Reichsbank's account also at the Bank of England. This gold was eventually transferred via the Dutch and Belgian national banks to Berlin.

Although a second instruction to transfer 27 tonnes of gold in the same way was blocked, nearly a quarter of Czechoslovakia's national gold reserve had already been siphoned out of the Bank of England with the agreement of the leading central bankers in Switzerland, Britain and France. The fact that these instructions were delivered via the Bank for International Settlements lent them a veneer of legitimacy in central banking terms.[29]

France, which had moved its gold reserves during the First World War to the south of France away from advancing German troops, now moved a substantial part of it to America and much of the remainder to its colonies in Africa. In this way, France's monetary manoeuvres signalled its political and military hostility to the Reich. Consequently, when German troops marched into Paris in 1940, the occupiers established a special team, the Devisenschutzkommando, or currency protection team, with powers to demand declarations of gold and foreign currency holdings from French banks. A German official was appointed overseer of the Bank of France with regulatory powers. Other states that were to be occupied – Holland, Norway and Belgium – had also evacuated their gold reserves abroad. Some 200 tonnes of Belgium's gold was transferred to French custody and was relocated to Senegal, until the collaborationist Vichy government later bowed to German demands that the Belgian gold be transferred to the Reichsbank. Determined to reap the advantages of occupation, Germany levied massive indemnities on occupied states, equivalent to 40 per cent of Germany's own taxation, of which nearly half came from France.[30]

In all, Germany seized more than $600 million worth of gold, some $480 million of which was expropriated from the central banks of occupied states.[31] As the number of conquered territories increased, the currencies of the occupied states were fixed to the reichsmark, which in turn was fixed to gold or to the dollar, which had not detached from gold. It was, in effect, a form of occupation gold exchange standard.

As the war wound on, however, it became more difficult to access sufficient dollars to support this system. Gold reserves that Germany did hold were needed to settle accounts with neutral territories, transactions that were usually processed through Switzerland as a neutral channel to other non-participating states. In the finest tradition of neutral countries, Portugal acquired gold from the Reichsbank in return for escudos, enabling Germany to buy vital products such as tungsten on the Portuguese economy.[32] An indication of the wartime profits available to neutral countries is well illustrated in the Bank for International Settlements 14th annual report published after the end of the war. Latin American countries were shown to have had increases in monetary reserves of gold and foreign currency and a consequent increase in their money supply of between 100 and 300 per cent.[33]

The pegging of the reichsmark to gold or dollars was therefore discarded in 1941, ten years after much of the rest of the world had cut loose. Nevertheless, this did not mean that the mark was free to float against other currencies and vice versa. As the dominant force in Europe, Germany was able to impose exchange rates between the mark and the local currencies in occupied territories and even the currencies of friendly states such as Bulgaria and Hungary. It is hardly surprising that the exchange rates were set to overvalue the mark. For example, in France at the start of the war the mark was worth 10 or 12 French francs, while under occupation, the exchange rate was increased to 1 mark: 20 francs. In Belgium, the mark was worth 7 or 8 Belgian francs at the pre-war rate, but was set at 12.5 Belgian francs to the mark under occupation.[34]

Reichsmark-denominated military scrip was distributed by a net-work of banks (the Reichskreditkassen) established throughout occupied lands. Between 1939 and 1941, that military scrip (known as Reichskreditkassenscheine) was distributed in Poland, Denmark, Norway, Holland, Belgium, France, the Balkans and Russia. A different series of military scrip – the Military Promissory note – circulated in Germany.[35]

Germany, like Japan, had taken the precaution of issuing military scrip detached from the national currency to prevent excessive inflation in the homeland should the military scrip be returned to Germany for conversion into reichsmarks. However, the Nazi government had omitted to forbid the repatriation of military scrip by returning troops. When excessive amounts were returned to Germany in this way it had a negative effect on the money supply there, causing inflation in precisely that country where it was intended not to.[36]

At the same time, it remained a liability on the German government and as the German authorities avoided the trap of issuing too much of it, local populations favoured it and hoarded it; its circulation in various countries of Europe also made it an attractive instrument for smuggling and black-market operations.[37] Moreover, different rates of inflation in the occupied countries producing different prices for identical goods in different countries meant that the mark-denominated military scrip had greater purchasing power in some countries than in others. Consequently, Reichskreditkassenscheine military scrip found its way in greater volumes to those countries where it enjoyed greater purchasing power. Such was the case with Reichskreditkassenscheine issued in the Balkans that were transferred by German troops to France, where they enjoyed a better exchange rate and purchasing power.[38]

Recognising the long-term disadvantage of allowing the occupied states to accumulate large volumes of military scrip that Germany would at some point have to honour, steps were taken to retire them from circulation. As, eventually, the scrip came to rest in the central banks of those countries, they were repatriated to Germany and their value was added to the cumulative debt owed by Germany, one of the factors contributing to the expansion of Reich debt from 31 billion marks in 1939 to 380 billion by the end of the war. In Western Europe, this exercise was completed by the end of 1943, after which the local governments supplied local currency for the troops' use. On transfer to any other country German troops were not permitted to exchange the currency of one occupied state for that of another.[39]

Unsurprisingly, the impact of the war on the monetary systems of the losing Axis powers and their closest allies was, with only a few exceptions, worse than it was on the Allies. The value of notes in circulation in Japan increased more than ten-fold; in Italy, almost twenty times, and in Bulgaria, more than fourteen times. Among the Allies, in contrast, the impact was comparatively modest: the value of notes in circulation in Britain increased by a little over two and a half times, and in the United States less than four-fold. Note issue in France – at something like three and a half times the value issued at the start of the war – was greater under occupation but not as bad as in the Axis powers. The country worst afflicted, however, was Yugoslavia. Here seven different currencies from Bulgaria, Hungary, Italy, Serbia and Croatia as well as two different issues from Albania circulated, further aggravating the conditions of monetary disarray. Notes in circulation in Yugoslavia increased in value a staggering twenty-six-fold. Even in tiny Iceland, the result of vastly expanded military activity by Britain and the United States led to the value of notes in circulation increasing nearly fourteen times. It is difficult to come to any conclusion other than that the belief that there would be no return to gold convertibility after the Second World War led countries to issue paper currency more freely than they would do during the First World War.[40] If this assessment is true, fiat issue in any major future conflict might be even more extravagant.

Britain's Monetary Empire at War – The Sterling Bloc

On the outbreak of war, Britain, which had been off the gold standard since 1931, mobilised the monetary resources of its empire. Reserves of individual colonies were pooled and exchange controls imposed. Despite these measures, Britain's assets were badly eroded by the war and its liabilities inflated. Reserves in 1938 were valued at £864 million, reached a low point of £74 million in 1940, and ten years later had risen to £369 million. Liabilities in the form of sterling balances held in Britain by foreigners grew nearly four-fold over the same period, from £760 million to £2,700 million.[41] Those foreign entities – mostly British colonies such as India or countries such as Egypt that were not formally British colonies but were administratively run by Britain and were members of the sterling zone – had accumulated sums of sterling mostly by supplying Britain with produce and war materiel. Of Britain's nearly £3 billion in liabilities, just over half were owed to Egypt and India for precisely those reasons.

To try to conserve foreign exchange for the purposes of pursuing war objectives, the sterling bloc came into existence. In 1944, an official order set out the membership of the sterling bloc, ranging from the dominions such as Australia and New Zealand, through other colonies, to territories such as Palestine that Britain administered under a League of Nations mandate. Even territories over which Britain's authority was at best a temporary wartime emergency measure – Iceland and the Faroe Isles – were officially embraced within the sterling zone. When members of the sterling bloc earned foreign exchange revenues, they would sell that foreign exchange in London and convert it to sterling. Where foreign exchange was required by members of the sterling bloc to buy imports from countries outside the bloc, the necessary foreign exchange was purchased in London.

These sums could either be used to purchase products from Britain (which in wartime were few and far between) or would be held in London in blocked accounts, by which it was meant that money owed to other countries would not be allowed to leave Britain while the accounts remained blocked under wartime emergency measures. Towards the end of the war this arrangement would lead to significant tensions between Britain and its colonial creditors. By 1944, those same creditors were much keener to hold gold or dollars with which they could purchase products from America, which seemed to have an abundance of products to sell. However, under the blocked account arrangements, sterling balances were not convertible to gold or dollars until several years after the end of the war.

Trade agreements signed by Britain at the end of the war with other, non-sterling bloc countries also included terms favourable to Britain as centre of the sterling bloc, as was the case with the Anglo–Turkish Trade and Payments Agreement of May 1945. According to this agreement, whenever Turkey needed to buy the local currency of a country within the sterling bloc in order to make payments in that local currency (for example, dinars for transactions with neighbouring Iraq, which operated a sterling currency board) it would be purchased at the Bank of England with sterling. By this means, some proportion of Turkey's payments would always be coming back to the Bank of England thanks to the sterling bloc arrangement.[42]

Early Success – Ethiopia

Of all the territories liberated by the Allies throughout the course of the war, Ethiopia was one of the first, fittingly in view of the early significance of Italy's seizure of the country in defiance of the League of Nations. Freeing the country in 1941 from Italy's relatively short-lived administration of six years, British forces introduced the East African shilling as the currency of convenience to support British troop operations there. As the British authorities declared that the shilling would be freely convertible to Maria Teresa dollars, long the preferred currency for Ethiopia, and fixed the rate at which they could be exchanged, there was little local resistance to use of the shilling. Moreover, the Maria Teresa dollar and the East African shilling, by a decree of 1942, were declared the only legal tender currencies for Ethiopia, depriving the Italian lire of full legal tender status. Thus, the acceptability of this new and untried currency, the shilling, was guaranteed by its convertibility. The lire, on the other hand, as a result of this decree was no longer a legal tender currency and traders therefore would be less inclined to accept payments in it. While the convertibility to Maria Teresa dollars bought acceptability for the East African shilling, it could not confer on it quite the same approbation that the silver dollar enjoyed among farmers. Thus, although the shilling had originally been fixed to the dollar at a specific exchange rate, it was not long before farmers undermined that exchange rate by demanding payment only in silver dollars. As in other instances of extreme distress for any currency system, it was again the agricultural producers who enjoyed greatest leverage. Forced to change increasing amounts of shillings on the market into silver dollars, British troops soon found the exchange rate tilting against them and in favour of the silver dollar.[43]

Britain's authority in monetary matters relating to Ethiopia in fact seemed to some an indication of more sinister intentions, perhaps of a design to incorporate Ethiopia into the British Empire. Indeed, the Anglo–Ethiopian agreement that formed the basis of the administration of the country in the immediate period after the expulsion of Italian troops contained the following clause, which seemed to support such suspicions:

Article IV (d) In order to facilitate the absorption into Ethiopian economy of the funds to be provided ... and to promote the early resumption of trade between Ethiopia and the surrounding territories, His Majesty the Emperor [of Ethiopia] agrees that in all matters relating to currency in Ethiopia the Government of the United Kingdom shall be consulted and that arrangements concerning it shall be made only with the concurrence of that Government.[44]

Taking this a step further, British military authorities sought to persuade the emperor that, rather than a full-blown central bank, a currency board tying a new Ethiopian pound to the East African pound and not to the Maria Teresa dollar would be a more appropriate mechanism for the operation of the country's monetary system.

Other aspects of the currency board proposal for Ethiopia, such as the location of its headquarters in London and the insistence on a sterling-denominated reserve to back it, were equally disagreeable to the emperor and the Ethiopian government. In monetary terms it must have seemed as though the country had been liberated only to see its monetary system dictated not by one set of foreigners, the Italians, but by another set, the British.

Whether these were, as some American observers felt, preliminary steps to absorb Ethiopia into the British Empire or not, it was certainly forceful, but perhaps understandably so given Britain's precarious military position in 1941, prior to America's entry into the war. In the absence of any evidence to suggest this was anything other than an emergency wartime measure, it is impossible to infer that it was part of a wider, longer-term aggrandisement. Nevertheless, the emperor and his government were determined to exercise greater independence in their own monetary affairs and turned to a third party that appeared to have no interest in any long-term power in the region: America.

Confidential discussions between US officials and bankers resulted after all in the creation of a central bank in Addis Ababa – the State Bank – and a silver-based currency system, quite contrary to the British proposal for a sterling-backed currency board based in London. To secure the independence of this new institution, an American banker was invited to head the State Bank and the silver to be minted into the new coins would come from the US under the lend-lease programme. A new family of banknotes was to be printed in America.

The new American currency was issued in Ethiopia in 1945. Although American influence in Addis Ababa waned after the war, its ability to supplant Britain as the lead partner for Ethiopia in these matters between 1942 and 1945 was an indication of the way the wind was blowing in the wider world, a change of wind that would lead to America's domination of the post-war global economy and monetary architecture.

Allied Monetary Measures in North Africa

The simple expedient of overvaluing an occupier's currency against that of the occupied was adopted by both sides. As Britain overwhelmed Italian forces during the early phase of the North African campaign, local lire were permitted to circulate, but at a rate of exchange to sterling very disadvantageous to the lire. Any advantage this may have bestowed on the occupiers was soon balanced out by the inflationary pressures it induced. When British Military Authority currency – military scrip – was introduced in what is now Libya in 1943 as the German campaign there collapsed, the lowest denomination was a 1-shilling note, too high a value for the local economy, adding to the inflation caused by the overvalued exchange rate. And, as the British military scrip was worth even more in other areas such as British-controlled Egypt and Tunisia, it naturally shifted in those directions, trafficked by British troops. Efforts to regulate and monitor this trafficking may have had only limited success.[45]

In the same theatre of war, US troops who had participated in Operation Torch, the liberation of north-west Africa from collaborationist Vichy French forces in November 1942, were issued with so-called yellow seal dollars. These notes were based on silver certificates – notes that to all intents and purposes looked like US dollar bills, but had been originally issued after the 1873 US Act ending the coinage of silver in the US. The original issue of silver certificates was to some extent a concession to the lobbying of silver-producing states, as a result of which the Treasury undertook to purchase between $2 and $4 million of silver per month.

Silver certificates were accepted in payment of US customs and taxes but were not strictly speaking legal tender for private transactions. Most significantly, silver certificates were not convertible to the US' gold.

The silver certificates issued to US troops in North Africa and subsequently in Sicily bore a yellow seal to enable easy identification, should Axis forces manage to seize large quantities in active operational theatres of war. The yellow seal on the silver certificates would thus clearly set them aside from standard US dollars and prevent any attempt to flood the monetary system with captured yellow seal bills. In this respect, they paralleled the purpose of Reichskreditkassenscheine: notes to be used only in occupied or operational theatres so as to quarantine them from the monetary system of the homeland. (This was a feature not only of the European theatre of war, but also of Japan's military monetary policy in the Asia–Pacific region.) On the other hand, the eventual and controlled repatriation of yellow seal silver certificates to the US would not fall foul of regulations relating to the export and import of standard US dollars.[46]

These were the perceived advantages. But this system of military scrip brought with it problems as much as did Germany's Reichskreditkassenscheine system. Yellow seal or 'spearhead' currency was seen as more stable and more valuable than the existing local currency: it was associated with the winning side and therefore was likely to be a surer store of value. Currency issued by the losing side in any conflict was always bound to lose value and at some point would be withdrawn from circulation. These perceptions encouraged hoarding of spearhead currency and its exploitation by US troops for black-market activities, yielding profits that were repatriated to the US. Moreover, the preference for silver certificates to be hoarded by the local population weakened and destabilised the local currency, while at the same time creating a claim on the US economy. The monetary asset was passing into the hands of foreign populations, leaving the US burdened with a growing liability. Another way of looking at it was that the US was paying for the liberation of occupied territories through this monetary arrangement while the local administrations of those territories were contributing next to nothing in monetary terms. The disadvantages might well seem starker than the benefits.[47]

As Allied forces consolidated their control of North Africa, US and British authorities considered the options for a locally issued currency to replace the spearhead currency. While the Americans were ready to print and issue a local franc currency on their own authority, the British insisted that North Africa had been liberated, not occupied by Allied forces, notwithstanding the fact that it was, until Operation Torch, under control of the collaborationist Vichy regime. In the British view, therefore, the new currency should be issued by the Free French national liberation committee. A careful compromise was reached involving notes printed in America that would bear the inscription 'Allied Military' but would be issued by banks under control of the National Liberation Committee. As would be seen later in the war, de Gaulle's insistence that France should control currency issue in French territories reflected his uncompromising position on French sovereignty and on France's equal status with the US and Britain as an ally. These notes replaced the local notes circulating under the Vichy regime prior to Operation Torch.

Having resolved by compromise the question of who would produce and issue the currency, the next problem to tackle was that of exchange rates. Here again, the British approach appeared to be somewhat more accommodating to French sensitivities and interests than that of Roosevelt's government. French authorities wanted an exchange rate of 49 francs to the dollar. Churchill's government proposed that the exchange rate would be 200 francs to the pound sterling or 50 to the US dollar. The US government on the other hand set the exchange rate at 300 to the pound or 75 to the dollar, overvaluing the pound, but more importantly from the point of view of US interests, overvaluing the dollar. To a large extent this was to ensure that US troops enjoyed favourable purchasing power when serving overseas on operations.[48] More cynically, a rate unfavourable to the French population and government in North Africa reflected Roosevelt's antipathy towards de Gaulle and a certain lack of interest in reviving the economies of countries that at some point had collaborated with the Nazis. The American position softened in the face of French opposition and the exchange rate of 200 francs to the pound and 50 to the dollar was finally accepted at the Casablanca conference in 1943. Southard, the American official close to these events, suggested in his post-war analysis that the French insistence on a stronger exchange rate of 50 rather than 75 francs to the dollar was to some extent due to a belief that there would be a strong inflationary effect after liberation and that a stronger exchange rate for the franc to the dollar would help to counter this inflationary trend.[49]

Currency, Power and Influence in Occupied Italy

US attitudes towards the question of currency in Italy were if anything less compromising than they had been in North Africa. The official War Department position from at least 1940 was that the primary purpose of military government was to achieve military objectives, and not the welfare of the civilian population of the occupied country.[50]

The idea of issuing Allied military lire (subsequently known as AM lire and consequently mistaken for American lire) originated with Assistant Secretary of the US Treasury Harry Dexter White, whose subsequent exposure as a Soviet spy (or at least a Soviet collaborator to some extent or other) now casts a long shadow over his motives. White presented proposals in February 1943 to the Monetary and Fiscal Affairs Committee of the Combined Chiefs of Staff organisation. His presentation and explanations somehow persuaded the committee that the introduction of large volumes of lire issued by the Allies would not induce high inflation. The Allied military lire would be legal tender at par with existing Italian lire and would be at the service of all Allied troops in Italy. Furthermore, White's plan noted, responsibility for AM lire – its redemption for Bank of Italy notes and its withdrawal from circulation – would eventually fall to an Italian, rather than to the US government. This indeed was the position maintained after the war by people such as Southard, who held that the issue of these notes under military government in emergency conditions was forced on the Allies by the inability of the local authorities to provide enough local currency for Allied use. In this view, eventual redemption of the military lire would indeed be the responsibility of the Italian government.[51]

The question of the exchange rate set by the Allies for the Italian lire in the latter stages of the war was a controversial one in the post-war period. In the pre-war period, the lire had been set by Mussolini's government at an exchange rate of 19 to the dollar, or 92 to the pound sterling. But, from the point when Italy invaded Ethiopia to the collapse of Mussolini's government in 1943, the country's foreign reserves had been drained and the monetary system was under acute pressure. The economic reality and historical experiences – for instance, during the First World War – indicated that heavy depreciation of the lire must have taken place.

A proposal to set a relatively benign exchange rate of 60 lire to the US dollar was rejected by White as insufficiently generous towards American troops and too generous to Italian fascists. Persuaded by White's arguments, the committee tasked with setting the rate opted for 100 lire to the dollar – five times weaker than its pre-war rate. The economic historian Kindleberger, who was closely involved in wartime and post-war monetary planning for the occupied territories and had worked with White in Washington, felt that even 100 lire to the dollar overvalued the lire. Nevertheless, this distorted exchange rate combined with generous pay and extravagant spending by US troops (British and Canadian troops did not receive their full pay in the field) did much to accelerate inflation. Prices of those goods that were available in the shops quadrupled. Attempts by the Allied military government to impose price controls were ineffective.[52]

At the same time, the amount of Italian lire issued by the Bank of Italy in the north under the control of Italian fascists and German troops between August 1943 and April 1945 doubled. And yet, this did not produce the sort of behaviour that would normally be expected in such circumstances. Bank of Italy notes were saved in bank deposit accounts and hoarded at home. Consequently, money did not circulate as it should have done and so the commercial banks did what the private sector will often do when the public supply of money is perceived to be inadequate: they improvised a private sector solution. They issued Bearer cheques with pre-printed denominations, which were accepted at face value. This level of confidence in paper issued by the fascist side does not point towards a perception among the population of the north of Italy that the fascists were already losing. Quite the contrary. Hoarding and saving the currency issued by the fascist state indicated a level of confidence in the future of that currency and by extension in the state that issued it, reinforced by the determination of the German authorities to keep inflation under control.[53]

The stern occupation policy of the Allied forces, who to begin with saw Italy not as a new ally, but more as an erstwhile enemy, went so far as to limit food supplies to an absolute minimum. As the Allied military authorities did not see themselves bound to feed the Italian population, basic foodstuffs were available in the marketplace only in limited quantities. Unsurprisingly, the population became dependent on the black market, competing for scarce produce at increasingly high prices, with the inevitable consequence of surging inflation.[54] Substantial counterfeiting of the poorly printed Allied military lire containing elementary security weaknesses made matters worse. In stark contrast to the situation in the German-controlled north of Italy, the population in the south under Allied control had little confidence in the AM lire: people spent, rather than saved, them and were prepared to pay premium prices to get rid of them. If confidence in currency reflected confidence in a government, the weakness of the AM lire points towards a view among the population that an Allied victory was far from certain. As confidence waned and inflation rose, Allied military authorities fanned the flames by ensuring that their troops were well supplied with cash.[55] The act of excessive issue created a depreciating currency more in keeping with the economy of a failing government.

Italy's ambiguous position – a one-time enemy turned ally – left the authority of King Victor Emanuel's government compromised in American eyes, not least on the subject of currency control. Terms of the armistice had required the Italian government to redeem with Bank of Italy lire any Allied military lire and hand back free of charge the redeemed Allied military lire to the Allies. So, printed in America at a fraction of their face value, denominated in Italian lire, purchasable by US troops at a rate highly favourable to US dollars and spent by them freely in the local economy, AM lire became a liability on Italy's own balance sheet. Italy eventually had to produce vast quantities of Italian lire to support the spending of Allied forces. The more they spent, the more inflation rose, the more Bank of Italy notes had to be produced.

In the eyes of the Italians, however, these were conditions that one might expect to be imposed on a conquered country, not on a sovereign ally. In these new conditions, many felt it was only fair that the Allies should now pick up the bills for their own operations and associated expenditure in Italy.[56]

The mood shifted in October 1944 when Roosevelt announced plans to send more food to Italy and to supply the country with dollars to cover pay to US troops as well as payment for exports. These economic measures were wrapped up with other measures regulating diplomatic relations with Italy and recognising that it was no longer a hostile state. Although Italy did not receive as many US dollars to cover payment of US troops as it might have expected, it nevertheless signalled a change in the relationship with the Allies. America was now prepared to cover the direct costs to Italy of maintaining a foreign army by paying in dollars rather than Allied military lire. All the same, by November 1945, there were 366 billion lire in circulation (of which 81 billion lire were Allied military lire) compared to the value in circulation in 1939 of 24 billion.[57] In fact, Allied aid to Italy exceeded reparations paid by Italy almost ten-fold.[58]

The next major change in the monetary basis for the occupation – or liberation – of Italy occurred in January 1946 when the Allies ceased to issue AM lire altogether and undertook to cover the costs to Italy of troop maintenance. A new, commercial, exchange rate of 225 lire to the dollar was introduced and, although this helped to stimulate Italy's exports, it also stimulated inflation. From April to October 1946, the lire to dollar market exchange rate slumped from 281:1 to 1,000:1. By 1947 the Italian government had become so fearful of a general collapse of the Italian currency with dire consequences for social stability in the country that a series of new measures were put in place to stabilise the currency including devaluation of the official exchange rate to 350 lire to the dollar.

The contention then that an exchange rate of 100 lire to the dollar was too punitive for the local population at the height of the war, seen from one perspective, may be valid. Seen from the perspective of Italy's immediate post-war economic distress, however, it is not difficult to view it as having been too constraining. The country was simply not able to sustain an exchange rate of 100 lire to the dollar, much less the exchange rate of 60:1 that some commentators believed would have been 'fairer'.[59] Now even Harry Dexter White's exchange rate would seem unreasonably generous towards the failing lire.

The threat to social stability posed by monetary instability was of concern not only to the Italian government, but also to the Americans who were becoming increasingly agitated by the growing influence of the Communist Party in Italy. Although the measures introduced in 1947 succeeded in stabilising the lire, they were deflationary, and Italy's industrial production and exports suffered accordingly. This might well have given Italian communists a stick with which to beat the pro-American government, but as far as the Italian government was concerned, allowing the lire to spiral out of control was simply not an option.

Currency and Sovereignty in Liberated France

French colonies in Central Africa had already been liberated from Vichy French control by 1941 and in consequence Charles de Gaulle, leader of the Free French, ordered the creation of the Caisse Centrale de la France Libre to issue currency for these territories.[60] This wartime exigency marked the first step in the nationalisation of banknote issue for the colonies, reversing an earlier colonial policy of devolving banknote issue to private banks. Since the process of nationalising the Banque de France itself had begun in 1936, this change of policy of nationalisation of issue in the colonies was consistent with the metropolitan policy.[61]

The invasion and liberation of Italy had brought with it the liberation of France's island of Corsica from German occupation in September and October 1943. Allied authorities therefore began the process of replacing the circulating notes of occupied France there in October 1943, partly to exercise some control over the profits made by some businesses and individuals during the period of collaboration, but also to block off the possibility of notes flooding into Corsica from occupied mainland France. Existing Banque de France notes were replaced with notes from the Caisse Centrale and access to 75 per cent of any bank balance in excess of 20,000 francs was blocked. Some 1.8 billion of the old notes were withdrawn, but the overall money supply was not reduced for long: the large influx of troops to the island led to an overall increase in the currency in circulation and by autumn 1944, 2.2 billion of the new notes had been issued.[62]

Lessons had been learned in North Africa and Italy that de Gaulle's committee of National Liberation sought to apply prior to the invasion of France. It proposed constraints on the spending of US troops and a bar on the import of US dollars and their exchange into French currency. But the US War Department took the view that it was important for reasons of morale for its troops to enjoy strong purchasing power; moreover, it was a breach of federal law to withhold the pay of serving soldiers.[63]

There was also a question of the distinction between occupied and liberated countries and its relevance to the currency to be issued in mainland France. This time Roosevelt was not prepared to accept the compromise adopted for North Africa. In imposing a design very similar to that used for the Allied military lire in Italy he overruled or resisted the views of both the British and Free French, who emphasised the differences between France, which had been occupied, and Italy, which had started the war as an Axis power. Although the designs were printed in the US in preparation for the invasion of France, the initial plan to have them issued by Allied forces was revised in favour of responsibility for issue resting with the Committee of National Liberation. For the time being the issue remained unresolved, and when Allied troops landing in Normandy put the notes into circulation without prior agreement of the Free French authorities, de Gaulle described them in official communications as counterfeit. The Free French Provisional Government, which was based in Algiers and which had succeeded the Committee of National Liberation, objected in the strongest terms and refused to recognise the currency – known as supplementary francs – as legal tender.[64]

Among the Allies, attitudes towards the question of the supplementary francs became a touchstone for the bigger issue of sovereignty. Churchill was inclined to recognise French sovereignty over the issue as part of a wider recognition of the Provisional Government, while Roosevelt insisted on the right of the Allied command to issue the notes and in support pointed out that if the Provisional Government failed to recognise the supplementary currency, it would have a damaging effect on the French economy. Should the Provisional Government refuse to accept supplementary francs, the Allies would be forced to resort to American yellow seal silver certificates and British Military Authority occupation currency as they had in North Africa, with all the associated negative consequences.[65]

In reality, supplementary francs evoked quite a different set of behaviours in metropolitan France than did the military scrip among local populations in North Africa. It was not hoarded. Quite to the contrary, those who had accepted payment in the new currency concluded that it would be as well to get shot of it quickly by using supplementary francs to pay their taxes in advance. That is, until de Gaulle's Civil Affairs Commissioner in Bayeux, Normandy, instructed tax collectors to refuse supplementary francs in payment of taxes, exercising the ultimate embargo on recognition of a currency.[66]

This display of practical power and Churchill's resolute position on French sovereignty eventually persuaded Roosevelt to modify his own truculent position, and in August 1944 military representatives of the US and French forces signed an agreement that included confirmation that only the French government could issue currency, including supplementary francs in France. Francs issued by the French government to US forces for payments in France would be purchased with US dollars. This agreement was, however, one of military practicality, as it was not until a further two months had passed that Roosevelt's government formally recognised de Gaulle's own government.

The real monetary reform in France began nearly a year after D-Day and was announced by de Gaulle's finance minister on 2 June 1945. As elsewhere, the process of exchange was in part designed to identify those who had amassed wealth during the period of the occupation, but also to cancel currency that might have been obtained fraudulently through the black market. It was also a means of rendering void currency that might have been seized by the occupying German forces and were now leaking back into the French economy. Notes of 50 francs and above would be removed from circulation, but could be deposited at banks and replaced with lower denomination notes. This reduced the volume of notes in circulation, which had reached a high of 632 billion in 1944, to 473 billion in June 1945.

Elsewhere in Occupied Europe

During the period of German occupation, the exchange rate of the Belgian franc to the dollar had dropped by 33 per cent compared to the pre-war rate. The plan for monetary reform in liberated Belgium centred on the need to return the monetary supply to conditions consistent with stable prices, but also to constrain black-market transactions. In early October 1944 a census of cash was carried out and banknotes in circulation were estimated to be 350 per cent above the pre-war levels. During this initial census, notes of denominations above 100 francs were suspended and an exchange rate of 43.7 francs to the dollar established in contrast to the pre-war rate of 30 francs to the dollar. Limits were imposed on the amount of old currency that any family could exchange for the new notes that had been printed in England. Amounts of old francs above these limits were 'blocked': i.e. could not be exchanged but could be used for the payment of special new taxes. These measures successfully reduced the amount of money in circulation. The 300 billion francs circulating in September 1944 were reduced to 57.4 billion francs in October. As in the case of the currency exchange in Corsica, however, the contracted figure soon expanded as Allied armies spent money in the local economy.[67]

In Greece, the war had resulted in terrible depreciation and inflation: by 1944, bread cost 2 million times its pre-war price. A new currency was introduced with British support in November 1944 to replace the almost worthless old drachma at a rate of 1 new drachma for 50 billion old drachma. The speed and readiness with which the new currency was accepted, it has been suggested, may have been down to the knowledge that the new currency was backed by sterling reserves or, alternatively , that it was down to a new spirit of hope and optimism.[68] More simply, it might be concluded that the population was quick to embrace the new and alternative currency as a replacement for the old currency that had so manifestly failed. So demoralised was the population by the collapse of paper money that a gold sovereign could command four times the value in Greek drachma than its paper sterling counterpart. Paper sterling was good, but gold sterling was even better. In Greece, the stability of the currency and the stability of prices were the only guarantors of that currency's acceptability, as they had been in Italy.[69]

Currency Liberation

As the tide of war turned, the Allied authorities moved from the defensive and on to the attack. As countries were liberated or Axis countries invaded, the local currencies were replaced in a series of operations that enabled the Allies to build up an unprecedented level of experience in such operations. Between October 1944 and December 1945, currency replacement operations were conducted in Austria, Belgium, Czechoslovakia, Denmark, France, the Netherlands, Norway and Yugoslavia. As elsewhere, these operations had economic as well as policing purposes: to reduce currency in circulation and in accounts to something more akin to pre-war levels and to flush out profits accumulated by collaborators.[70]

At least one of the officials involved in implementing these currency exchange operations, Frank Southard, a financial adviser at the Allied headquarters in the Mediterranean, observed that the finer points of the social contract between issuing authorities and the public were not relevant in the event of wartime currency replacement operations. Public acceptance of a new replacement currency was not contingent on considerations such the legal status of the issuing authority or the state of the foreign reserves backing that currency, an issue that had become more cloudy since the dismantling of the gold standard. A general perception that the currency was issued by an institution that somehow must have had the authority to do so was good enough to afford it the status of an acceptable medium of exchange. Clearly, in wartime conditions when the established sources of authority have been swept away, the populace will readily accept new and competitive issues of currency from previously unknown authorities. In such circumstances, only stability of the currency and the stability of prices — or at least their relative instability — are valid evidence of a currency's legitimacy.[71]

This is certainly one view of the reaction by local populations to the introduction of new currencies by the victorious Allies, put forward by someone who had been closely involved in the operations themselves. An alternative view contradicts Southard's observation. The alternative view holds that the American military lire in Italy, for example, were not instantly accepted by the population of southern Italy, but were spent as quickly as possible rather than hoarded, implying a degree of mistrust. The performance of currency under wartime conditions and in the eyes of the local population is, above all, a reflection of public perceptions as to which side is winning in that particular theatre of war.

Monetary Preparations for the Occupation of Germany

Allied attitudes towards Germany's post-war future differed, unsurprisingly, from country to country. But perhaps it was not to be expected that the US, which had suffered less than the other Allies from the war with Germany, entertained the harshest of outlooks. The most extreme of economic proposals from the Roosevelt administration – the Morgenthau Plan, named after Roosevelt's Treasury Secretary – urged the reduction of Germany to an agricultural backwater without a developed industry of any sort. Although this most extreme plan was eventually shelved – partly due to pressure from the British side – Morgenthau and his adviser, Harry Dexter White, were determined to enfeeble the economy of the prime culprit and chose economic subversion as the means to achieve their objective. A Joint Chiefs of Staff directive forbade any measures to stabilise the Germany economy by wage or price controls. The occupying powers would take no steps to 'maintain, strengthen or operate' a sound German economy. The imposition of a currency of occupation, the supply of which would be entirely in the hands of the Allies, was to be one of their weapons in this campaign.[72]

The planning and implementation of a military scrip project for occupied Germany began well in advance of the invasion of Germany – in contrast to the lack of monetary preparation that preceded Operation Torch. Indeed, the Allies were discussing the options for a German occupation currency more than six months before the D-Day invasion of France and among the most powerful factors that they took into account was the relationship with the Soviet Union, its future in Europe and in the world. In setting America's policy towards the Soviet Union, Roosevelt began from a position of trust and confidence. He had concluded that the Soviet Union had arrived as a great power but that its aspirations and interests need not lead to conflict with the other Allies. He ensured that US representatives having direct contact with Soviet authorities were selected for their fundamentally positive attitude towards Stalin and the Soviet regime. He went out of his way to meet Stalin in person and make compromises to keep the Soviet Union within a concert of nations. This approach was supported most energetically by the US Treasury under Secretary Morgenthau, while doubters included officials of the State Department and Department of War. And the more pro-Soviet the department, the more active a policy it pursued in punishing Germany.[73]

On a political level, it was desirable for the sake of securing an inter-Allied understanding of the immediate post-war settlement that the main Allies including the Soviet Union should have a common approach, among other things, to the question of an occupation currency for Germany. Soviet authorities were therefore briefed on American and British plans in this respect in Moscow in November 1943 with the intention of obtaining Soviet agreement to a common currency. Agreement on volumes to be produced, common designs and the mark:ruble exchange rate also needed to be reached.[74]

On a practical level, this conciliatory approach towards the Soviet Union led to a significant departure from standard procedures in controlling the issue of a secure currency. While the policy of introducing a military scrip – the Allied military lire – in Italy had led to inflation and black-market trafficking in currency, at least the Allies were aware of how much AM lire had been issued since production was entirely in the hands of US authorities.[75] A general principle had been applied by America and Britain when it came to production of currencies for liberated and occupied countries: Britain would take care of the former, while the US would manage the production of the latter. Consistent with this principle, the preparation of designs and plates for a German currency to be issued by the occupying Allies had been completed by the US Treasury's Bureau of Engraving and Printing by January 1944 and a contract for the mass production of the notes had been agreed with the Forbes Company of Boston.[76]

In February 1944, the Soviet side finally responded to the plans that had been put to them in November of the previous year, agreeing to the adoption of a common military currency, but putting forward a proposal that part of the currency should be printed in Moscow, ostensibly to ensure adequate supplies would reach the Red Army. In order to achieve supplies of scrip identical to the notes due to be printed in the US, Molotov, who was Stalin's commissar for Foreign Affairs, requested printing plates, samples of paper and ink as well as lists of serial numbers.[77]

Military and Treasury experts in Washington debated this highly irregular request. It was unthinkable for a state-operated banknote printing operation to surrender printing plates for use by other powers. Washington's concerns might, moreover, have been heightened by the recollection of a Soviet intelligence operation counterfeiting US dollars in the 1930s. There was little reason to trust Soviet authorities when it came to such matters. But, if Stalin's covert counterfeiting operation had cropped up in these discussions, American reservations were gradually overcome by the persuasive lobbying of Harry Dexter White, who played the part of a Soviet agent of influence in effect, even if his true intentions and commitment to the Soviet ideology remain disputed.

White set out the possible negative effects on the Soviet–American alliance of a refusal. First, he explained that such a refusal to supply materials would be taken by the Soviets to reflect a lack of confidence in the alliance. Then he pointed out that because the product of these plates and other materials would be German occupation currency, not US dollars, there would be no impact on the US economy as the notes would not be valid in the US. He urged Treasury officials to continue talking to the Soviets on the matter rather than dismissing it out of hand and pushed the idea that the response should be discussed with Treasury Secretary Morgenthau, who was very much under White's influence. Subsequent analysis points towards a fundamental contradiction in White's promotion of a single occupation currency for Germany when set against the Allied plan to split up Germany.

Monetary unity implied a coherent economy and a single state jointly ruled by the Allies. On a political level it has been pointed out that White's energetic defence of the idea of sharing the printing plates ran counter to the agreed long-term policy for the division of Germany, of which he was a staunch supporter.[78] But to be consistent the analysis must accept also that the American and British authorities were equally supportive of dismemberment and yet promoted a joint occupation currency. White's inconsistency on this point might, then, have not looked so odd to the Allies. Similarly, in terms of practicalities, a joint occupation currency required only a single producer even if multiple issuing authorities were to be permitted. Why did the Soviets need to print notes when they could receive as many as they needed from the Americans? There were good grounds to smell a rat.[79]

Treasury Secretary Morgenthau, responding to the Soviet request for duplicate plates, attempted to explain that the Forbes Company that had been hired to produce the allied military marks would refuse to produce the notes if duplicate plates were surrendered. He reassured the Soviet side that they would have as many notes from the American side as they required.[80]

But Soviet Foreign Minister Molotov insisted that if the Americans would not provide duplicate plates, the Soviets would be forced to introduce their own occupation currency. This would have constituted the first threat to post-war Allied unity and as such would have been very unsettling for the US side. At the same time, White was making a forceful case for supply of the printing plates. If the Americans were prepared to supply unlimited amounts of occupation currency, what difference would it make if the Soviets were producing high volumes themselves with the same plates? Alternatively, if the Soviets were to introduce their own currency, the Western Allies would have little choice but to recognise it. By mid April of 1944 no final decision had been taken, and so White took advantage of a letter by Chairman of the Joint Chiefs of Staff General George Marshall that seemed to abdicate the decision-making in this matter. White seized the initiative and, instructing the Head of the Treasury Department's Bureau of Engraving and Printing, disingenuously reported that the Joint Chiefs of Staff had ordered the transfer to the Soviets of the glass film positives necessary to create plates.[81]

Treasury Secretary Morgenthau confirmed the decision to supply plates to the Soviet ambassador under conditions of secrecy so that the Forbes Corporation Printing company should be unaware of the deal. The argument in favour of a single unified currency for all Allied zones as a symbol of unity carried the day, despite the express view of the Allied leaders at the Tehran conference that Germany should be partitioned.

The State Department's Morgenthau Plan aimed to reduce Germany from being an industrial state capable of waging large-scale war to a largely agricultural one.

In keeping with this US Treasury department policy, money was 'an important offensive and defensive weapon of war', a strategic view that found concrete expression in a policy of fostering inflation in Germany. As in North Africa and Italy, a deliberate policy of overvaluation of the US dollar to the mark was adopted for Germany. Disagreements between Britain and the United States on the exchange rate to be adopted were eventually settled 'at the very highest echelons' of government.[82] A rate of 10 marks to the US dollar, in contrast to the British proposal of 5 marks to the dollar and a probable pre-war rate of 4 marks to the dollar, was pushed through at the insistence, again and to us in hindsight unsurprisingly, of Harry Dexter White. As, also, in those earlier cases of Italy and North Africa, this overvaluation was attractive to US troops as it guaranteed strong purchasing power for them. Experts such as Kindleberger who had been involved in the planning moreover contended that the rate of 10 marks to the dollar was not unreasonable given the wartime inflation.[83]

Unknown volumes of marks issued by the Soviet side, an overvalued dollar:mark exchange rate and heavy spending by occupying troops could only drive up inflation. Producing mark-denominated currency in this way placed the burden for supporting the occupation forces on the economies of the occupied lands as Germany was obliged to redeem allied military marks with notes of their own when the former eventually were to be withdrawn from circulation.[84] The notes issued became a liability on the German state, not on that of the US and Britain. It was, however, possible to convert allied military marks into dollar credits and to send those dollar credits (rather than dollars themselves) back to the United States in a perfectly legal transaction.[85]

At the same time, black-market activity facilitated the conversion of occupation marks into US dollars and their repatriation in unexpected numbers to the US. To neutralise this money-making opportunity, the United States introduced a military scrip – military payment certificates (MPCs) – in 1946. The MPCs were denominated in dollars that could be converted at a rate of 1 to 10 marks. However, the marks could only be spent in the local economy. Military payment certificates could be remitted back to the US, but not US dollars themselves.[86] The new arrangement was not, though, without its own problems. MPCs were poorly printed with poor security features and large-scale counterfeiting took place. A black-market trade in converting marks into US dollars – either the yellow seal version first used in North Africa as occupation currency or the original silver certificates on which the yellow seal dollars were based – flourished. A trade in illicitly imported US dollars consequently thrived.

A change of political direction in Washington emerged during the presidency of Harry Truman, following Roosevelt's death. The idea of dismembering Germany and denying it a degree of self-determination associated with the Roosevelt administration was replaced by a policy that regarded German unification and a degree of sovereignty over its own affairs as possible and even desirable. In 1945–46 the Allied Control Council based in Berlin discussed the possible introduction of a monetary reform to replace reichsmarks and the allied military marks in response to concerns that without monetary reform the economy of the new Germany could collapse, bringing with it civil disorder. Consistent with the Soviet position on allied military marks and their wish to have independent issue of them, they now insisted that in the event of the introduction of a new currency, duplicate plates should be held and used at printing factories in Berlin, which was under joint Allied control, and at Leipzig, which was under Soviet control. General Lucius Clay, US Military Governor of occupied Germany, flatly vetoed this demand, citing the inflationary problems caused by the Soviet Union's independent ability to issue allied military marks.[87]

The idea of a new currency for Germany became a bone of contention between the Soviet Union on the one hand and the US–British Allies on the other. American authorities proposed to produce the new currency at the German state print works in the American sector of Berlin, but suggested the operation be under joint four-power control. The Soviet side initially demanded their own set of plates, no doubt with the intention of producing unlimited volumes of the new currency just as they had with the allied military marks. This position, however, they surrendered, proposing instead that the issue of the notes be handed to German authorities which, at that time, were in no state to undertake such an operation. This idea was interpreted by some on the US side as nothing more than time-wasting.[88]

By late 1947, the Western line had hardened and the Soviet Union was advised that currency reform would proceed with or without Soviet participation. Clay's support for the proposed currency reform was reinforced by the belief that the Soviet side was already preparing its own new issue of currency. Should the Soviets introduce their own notes and declare the allied military marks no longer legal tender, vast volumes of the latter would have found their way to the Western zones and precipitated inflation. A currency race was already under way.[89]

Soviet Occupation – Currency as a Tool of Subjugation

From an early point in the war the Soviet Union had been alert to the monetary benefits of conquest. Prior to the German invasion of the Soviet Union, the Reich and Stalin's government had agreed to the division of spoils in Eastern Europe. When Soviet troops invaded the Baltic states in June 1940, Moscow ordered those states to arrange the transfer of their gold reserves held at the Bank for International Settlements to the State Bank of the Soviet Union. BIS senior managers, however, refused to comply with the request. As we have seen, the senior BIS administrators had become much more wary about transferring gold reserves out of the accounts of states that had been invaded after the embarrassment of its initial transfer of Czechoslovak gold to the Reichsbank. The second request for a transfer of Czechoslovak gold had therefore been refused as a result of personal intervention by Thomas McKittrick, the American President of BIS. The embarrassment attached to BIS compliance with the first of these requests was a factor in the decision not to hand over the Baltic states' gold to the Soviet Union.[90] But, it is also reasonable to assume that, while BIS appears to have found a modus vivendi in dealing with both Axis and Allied powers during the war, collaboration with Communist authorities in Moscow would have been an ideological step too far.

The Soviet Union had attempted, not unsuccessfully, to destabilise the economies of Italy and Germany by promoting through US Assistant Treasury Secretary Harry White monetary measures designed to stimulate inflation. In the case of Italy, these measures were applied indirectly via the introduction of the AM lire with skewed exchange rates and excessive spending in Italy by US troops. In the case of Germany, the Soviet authorities in possession of the printing plates for the allied military marks were able to introduce inflationary volumes of currency directly and at a pace to suit themselves. Having no doubt observed the destabilising effect of inflation on Germany in the 1920s, Stalin and his advisers resorted to this tool as a means of extending Soviet power to central Europe. An outbreak of Weimar-standard inflation would generally lower living standards and erode the savings and pensions of the middle classes. Whether Stalin and his advisers believed in Lenin's dictum regarding the debasement of currency as a means of bringing down a country's political system or not, they seemed to be pursuing precisely that method to undermine parts of Western Europe.

During a brief period of occupation of Poland and the Baltic states following the Molotov–Ribbentrop pact of August 1938, the existing currencies of those countries were allowed to circulate, but the money in circulation was vastly increased by the parallel use of the Soviet ruble, heavy spending by the occupying Soviet forces and massive labour wage increases.[91] During this brief period of peace, Soviet troops were able to buy quantities of items that had become scarce at home, thanks to an overvalued ruble. Vladimir Petrov suggests that the ruble was overvalued by as much as 2,000–3,000 per cent.[92]

When Soviet forces occupied Eastern European countries towards the end of the war, they resorted again to the crude measure of vastly overvaluing the ruble. Moreover, the governments of these countries – Poland, Romania, Bulgaria, Hungary and Czechoslovakia – were required to supply the occupying forces with local currency on demand. But evidently this approach was inadequate and before long the Soviet authorities took control of the national banknote production plants, either directly or through compliant local officials. The ability to issue notes at will supported a deliberate policy of fanning inflation, directly attacking the established wealth of the middle classes. Poland's experience in this respect is worth recording: in the years immediately following the Soviet occupation, zloty in circulation rose from 13.6 billion in January 1945 to 36.7 billion in 1946 and a staggering 130 billion in 1948 – a nearly ten-fold increase in three years.

Hungary, which had experienced inflation worse than Germany in the years following the First World War, fell prey to it again under Soviet occupation. The pengo unit of value was issued in denominations as ludicrously high as 100 quadrillion.[93]

The exchange rate of the Hungarian pengo to the US dollar plummeted:

1939	5
April 1945	250
November 1945	30,000
December 1945	265,000
May 1946	52 billion
August 1946	4,600 quintillion

Source: Petrov p.186-190, Bank for International Settlements 14th annual report, p.9.

Stabilisation was only achieved in the summer of 1946 when Hungary's gold reserves, seized by the Nazis during the war, were returned to Budapest to be used as backing for a new currency. During this period of hyperinflation in Hungary currency prices were doubling, astonishingly, every fifteen hours. The average monthly rate of price rise has been recorded at 19,800 per cent, according Hungary at this time the dubious distinction of having the worst recorded inflation in any country over the past 100 years, surpassing even that of Zimbabwe in recent years.[94]

While Soviet authorities made free with the issue of money – both local and rubles – in their occupied states, they took measures to ensure that rubles would be surrendered to the occupying authorities, avoiding the return of large volumes of rubles to the Soviet Union through currency trafficking or black-market operations.

The Soviet Zone of Occupied Germany

In 1946, East Germany and its communist-led government were burdened with the gargantuan task of supporting a Soviet army of occupation that numbered 700,000 as well as a German population swelled by several million refugees from eastern lands that they had settled during the war. In these circumstances food was scarce and commanded a premium, stimulating a black market and inflation. Moreover, Germany's economy was, as a result of the war, in a worse condition than that of any of the other occupied states.

Despite these highly unfavourable conditions, the highest denomination available in eastern Germany was the 1,000 allied military mark note. In contrast to the overwhelming monetary inflation of other states such as Hungary, there was a degree of inflation, but it did not get out of control. This was not, however, because of exceptional monetary restraint by the German or Soviet administrators. Rather, the fact that all Allied occupied zones used a single unified currency – the allied military mark – meant that money could flow from the Russian zone to the other Allied zones, thereby easing off the monetary excess in eastern Germany. Western goods flowed in the opposite direction. The Soviet Union's ability to issue as many of these allied military marks as they wished thanks to the US surrender of glass negatives to produce printing plates along with other printing materials provided unlimited scope to buy up available goods, especially as Soviet troops were paid up to six years of payment in arrears in these marks. Soviet-produced allied military marks were also carried into the Western-occupied zones in large numbers by refugees and black marketers. Significant volumes of these Soviet-produced allied military marks were converted into US dollars, alerting the US military authorities to the exceptional scale of the problem.[95]

Operation Bird Dog and the Division of Post-War Germany

The British and American zones of western Germany were officially merged on 1 January 1947, primarily for economic purposes, into a single unified entity known by those two Allies as Bizonia. The first volumes of a new currency – the deutschmark – were produced by the Bureau of Engraving and Printing in the United States under conditions of extreme secrecy and flown to Frankfurt am Main.[96] A very limited number of Allied and twenty-five German experts were aware of the planned currency reform – code-named, amusingly, Operation Bird Dog – and were cloistered during the six-week planning period at the US Air Force base at Rothwesten to ensure that the plans did not leak. The final decision to launch the currency reform planned at the so-called Rothwesten Conclave was taken by General Clay in response to the Soviet withdrawal from the Allied Control Council responsible for the administration of Berlin, a step that seemed to signal a final rupture in the relationship between Western and Eastern Allies. The planned currency reform was finally announced on 18 June 1948.

Three days later, authorities in the Soviet zone announced an emergency response – a currency reform for eastern Germany that was executed in the following four days by the simple expedient of attaching special stickers to the existing notes. Petrov concludes that the speed of the implementation reveals studied preparation for the reform.[97] We might, however, wonder whether a long-term preparation would have resulted in the launch of a new family of banknotes with designs specifically prepared for the occasion, rather than a cobbled together solution requiring the attachment of stickers.

Attempts by the Soviet side to impose their new currency as the sole legal tender for the whole of Berlin were interpreted by the Western Allies as an attempt by the Soviets to extend their control over the city and ultimately to absorb it fully into the Soviet zone. Both the Western Allies and, bravely, the Berlin mayor rejected the attempt. The introduction of the new Western currency, on the other hand, was cited by the Soviet side as the main reason for the Berlin Blockade, imposed on 24 June, out of an alleged concern that large volumes of the old currency would exit the Western zone and would be dumped on Berlin – much the same fear as had prevailed on the Western side with regard to the possible introduction of a new Soviet-produced currency. In practical terms, the dissolution of a single unified currency for Eastern and Western zones and the return of monetary sovereignty to the West German state deprived the Soviets of their free access to German goods but also relieved the United States of its responsibility for Germany's money supply.[98]

The monetary reform and the introduction of the deutschmark – along with the scrapping of price controls and other economic measures – were credited at the time with the turnaround in Germany's economic fortunes. In 1946, Germany's exports were valued at $160 million; in 1948, they reached $850 million.[99] Beyond these economic outcomes, one of the lead economists involved in the planning for Operation Bird Dog observed that in political terms the monetary reform was extraordinary in that it 'was in fact dictated by a Military Government that professed to be trying to introduce democracy'. Post-war reviews of this last, political, aspect of Operation Bird Dog have debated whether a benevolently despotic power (i.e. the military government) was indispensable to execute the operation and whether the same would be true in essence for any number of monetary reforms. Here we might recall the widespread view in Chile in 1925 that a military junta was indispensable to launch a monetary reform (but that it should be brought to a conclusion by an elected government).[100] Repeated instances of major monetary reform in entirely democratic and peaceful environments surely undermine this argument. The specific situation of Germany in 1948 – economic destruction and military defeat for the second time in twenty-five years, occupation and division by the wartime Allies, a growing Soviet menace and a loss of national political cohesion and leadership – present a set of circumstances where only extraordinary powers would work. Experiences in Japan where, critically, the Soviet Union presented no challenge to the American authorities as an occupying power, presented quite different circumstances where there was no need to force through, in conditions of secrecy, a currency reform of this type. Politico–military factors determined the monetary modus operandi.

Power and Money in the Post-War Settlement

By the end of July 1944, the tide of the war had definitively turned. Soviet forces had liberated Belorussia up to the pre-war border with Poland and Japanese forces finally began to withdraw from Imphal, the furthest point of their advance against British India. Rome had been liberated. On 1 July, economists and diplomats from Allied countries began to gather in New Hampshire, in the US, to plan the monetary framework of the post-war world. The Bretton Woods conference of 1944 had as its objective the establishment of institutions to regulate monetary systems and reconstruction of a post-war world. Participants included delegations from the US, United Kingdom and, as separate delegations, representatives from Britain's dominions Canada, India, Australia, New Zealand and the Union of South Africa. China and the Soviet Union were also represented, as were Greece and Mexico. In all, a total of forty-four countries had representatives present, but the driving forces of the conference were first and foremost the US and to a lesser extent the British delegations, led respectively by Assistant Treasury Secretary Harry Dexter White and the economist John Maynard Keynes.[101]

Of the two institutions that the conference designed, one – the International Monetary Fund – had as its primary purpose the establishment of an international monetary system to avoid a repeat of the economic conditions of the 1930s that had contributed to the rise of fascism.[102] The founding principle was to ensure the stability of the international monetary system.

Britain and the US, as the protagonists, came to the conference with differing perspectives on what a post-war world might look like and this coloured their attitudes towards the conference objectives and the means to those ends. Having been financially ruined a second time in thirty years and yet anxious not to be shorn of its status as a leading world power, imperial and financial, Britain started the conference already at a disadvantage. America was now indisputably the new world power. The output of its industry had already surpassed that of Britain towards the end of the previous century. Having been, at the beginning of the First World War, a debtor to British and other European banking houses, America's role as supplier of vital food produce and military materiel to France and Britain in 1914–18 and subsequently, as their reserves ran out, their financier during the First World War had reversed its position from that of debtor to that of the leading creditor. By the end of the First World War, America had accumulated a bigger gold reserve than any other country in the world and its industrial and military might during the Second World War had made it the undisputed senior partner in the wartime alliance against the Axis powers. The relative strengths of the two parties were reflected in the eventual outcome of the conference.

But, at least to begin, with both sides had common aims: the design of a system that would help to align currencies fairly on the basis of their purchasing power, reducing the possibilities for the sort of competitive devaluations driven by domestic political motives in the 1930s ,and achieving stable and 'realistic' exchange rates. With these thoughts in mind, Keynes and White had already exchanged ideas well before the Bretton Woods conference took place. To achieve this objective of stability in the system, the opening American proposal was to employ gold as an intermediating mechanism to fix exchange rates of currencies to each other.[103] Gold and certain other currencies convertible to gold would still be used as the primary medium of exchange to settle international transactions, but, in the event that a country lacked enough of a foreign currency to carry out that trade, the role of the American version of the International Monetary Fund would be to step in to help resolve the problem by means of loans until the country in trouble was able to correct its own problems. White's proposal unsurprisingly reserved a special position of power for the United States, which ultimately would have the power to veto a decision by the Fund's board of directors. There would also be limits on the ability of other countries to withdraw amounts of US dollars.

Keynes' original proposal, on the other hand, involved a permanent clearing union based to some extent on the system proposed by Hitler's Finance Minister Walter Funk, handling international transactions as and when they occurred. Unlike the American proposal, its operation was to be constant, not purely a means of exercising an ad hoc emergency set of measures.[104] Both concepts relied on fixed exchange rates, although Keynes' system removed the requirement for gold as a mediating mechanism.

As the national delegations convened in New Hampshire at the beginning of July 1944, White presented to the British side a refined design for his earlier version of the International Monetary Fund. He explained that the overall objective was to prevent a rerun of the conditions leading to the Depression, where some countries had been at a great disadvantage owing to their dependence on imports. Countries struggling to escape a current account deficit and which were therefore unable to borrow on the capital markets would be able to borrow from the Fund. Moreover, there would be in White's developed plan an ability for countries to devalue with the endorsement of the Fund, which would act as a referee in such cases, precluding uncontrolled competitive devaluations, but permitting them under agreed circumstances. This arrangement, ceding as it did a degree of national sovereignty over currency, did not go down at all well with the British delegation. Unsurprisingly, the creditor state wanted exchange rate stability, while the debtor was keen on the freedom to devalue, both parties following the time-honoured path of self-interest that had, after all, been universally adopted by Roosevelt in the 1930s. White was determined not to give ground in this area. But, in the joint statement of the Bretton Woods conference, it was accepted that the Fund could not impede a change of exchange rate by a member state on the basis of 'domestic, social and political policies'. So, on this point there was a compromise, but there were also other points of disagreement.[105]

America's place at the centre of this new financial architecture was due in large part to the fact that the dollar remained the only truly gold-convertible currency. As a result, there was a global demand for dollars, echoing the scramble for gold in the last quarter of the nineteenth century. As representatives of the pre-eminent industrial and military power, the possessor of by far the largest reserve of gold and now the leading creditor in the world, American negotiators saw gold as the surest means of preventing debtor nations from inflating away their debts. There were other advantages attached to securing for the dollar a pre-eminent position as the world's preferred foreign reserve currency. The Federal Reserve issuing the dollar would not have to hold vast quantities of another country's currency as a reserve, and would indeed earn huge amounts of seigniorage on the notes issued. As the dollar would become the primary trading currency, US companies would suffer less as a result of exchange rate risk.[106] It was Harry Dexter White's objective to secure this commanding position for the dollar, toppling sterling from the position it had held as the ultimate gold standard currency for more than a century and a half. To achieve his objective he manoeuvred with consummate finesse, packing the various committees with his own team who would prepare the minutes to reflect the US objectives, exploiting the British consciousness of its own financial fragility and dependence on US loans while trading improved quotas for some countries in return for their support for the US position. The British team, starting from a weak and vulnerable position, was comprehensively out-manoeuvred.

But there were responsibilities attached to America's pre-eminence and its insistence on retaining gold as the bedrock of the new system: the American delegation agreed to penalties that would be imposed on the United States should it fail to issue sufficient dollars to match world demand. Given that the US then held something like two-thirds of the world's gold reserves [107] and was the leading exporting power-house, it seemed at the time perfectly possible that the US would be able to comply with that obligation for the foreseeable future. Thus, the US dollar emerged as the only currency that was recognised as having a status equivalent to gold because of its full convertibility. One ounce of gold was fixed at $35, the rate that Roosevelt himself had settled on prior to the war, and other currencies were then fixed to the dollar at individual rates.[108] White explained the purpose of gold as that of a sta-biliser: a means of fixing currencies to each other, but claimed that its purpose was not to act as a brake on the money supply of any one coun-try's currency. In this he probably had one eye on the widely held view that gold reserves inhibited the appropriate level of money issue and helped to make the Depression of the late 1920s worse.[109]

Britain, notwithstanding its long-held position as the ideal and origi-nal gold standard economy, knew from the more recent experience of the 1920s that gold imposed too great a constraint on any but the most robust and wealthy economies. But America had Britain over a barrel. To secure a $4.4 billion US government loan, Britain had little option but to toe the line when it came to the American position on gold and in particular its demands for sterling gold convertibility that had proven so unsustainable in 1931.

When it came to jockeying for position, however, American–British tensions over the role of gold were relatively straightforward compared to the multiple rivalries prompted by the question of quotas. As the quota – or financial investment a country would make in the Fund's capital and its corresponding voting power – would determine its influence on key decisions, many countries were keen to invest as much as possible from the start. Quotas were also seen as a reflection of a country's economic prestige and its position in the post-war pecking order. While most countries seemed to have accepted that the US would hold the highest investment and therefore the greatest number of votes on IMF matters, below that there was a scramble for position. Britain's second place seemed assured, but Russia wanted equal status with Britain and China, and India wanted parity with Russia. A country's quota at the Fund reflected, obviously, its status in a world emerging from war. Following White's determination to capture this national pecking order, members of the US delegation were charged with coming up with the economic rationalisation that, improbably, would show the size of the Russian and Chinese economies to be greater than that of France, a pecking order that understandably infuriated France's representatives. But White's plan appeared to reward countries that were perceived to have put up the strongest resistance to the Axis powers and, more fundamentally, to establish a post-war economic entente that reflected the wartime alliance. And White got his way.[110]

As far as the Russians were concerned, there was little likelihood that their country would engage economically with the West in a post-war world. But they could not ignore the participants' intention of creating this new economic world. Thus they elected (after much reference to Moscow) to participate in the negotiations and in the institutions that would be created, but without any strong conviction that participation was going to make any difference to the Soviet Union's closed economy and land-locked monetary system. In the end, Russia succeeded in securing with White's assistance their desired place in the International Monetary Fund hierarchy – third place in terms of quotas, only a little behind Britain, but with a special dispensation that permitted the Soviet Union to lodge rather less gold – 25 per cent less – than might otherwise have been expected. As Russia was a major producer of gold, it would plainly prefer to sell gold on the market in a world where the metal was still a significant element in currency reserves, especially in the US. Russia was moreover indulged to the extent that it would be permitted greater freedom to manipulate its exchange rate to other countries in a way that White had objected to when it was a British objective.[111]

For Britain there were additional difficulties to manage during the conference. During the war it had taken substantial loans from its dominions, which were now determined that Britain would not default on that debt. For the dominions – notably Canada, Australia, India, South Africa and New Zealand – wartime exigencies had altered the nature of their relationship with Britain. On the open international stage of the Bretton Woods conference they demonstrated their increasing degree of independence from and equality with the mother country. Australia, for instance, had notably stood its ground against Churchill's attempts to divert Australian troops towards theatres of war that were clearly less immediately pressing than the defence of Australia against a possible Japanese invasion. It was also Australia that was described by White at Bretton Woods as likely to be the most 'troublesome' of delegations, active to an extent beyond its 'size and importance'.

Other countries under British control – India, which had been moving towards home rule during the 1930s, and Egypt, the status of which had been that of protectorate and not a colony – came to the conference aiming to resolve issues surrounding the debts owed to them by Britain as a result of exceptional wartime borrowing. As Britain fell heavily into debt with these and other countries of the Empire, their accounts at the Bank of England were credited with sterling represented by British government securities. For the period of the war, those credits would be frozen, denying the creditor states the option to convert sterling into other currencies – notably the dollar – and repatriate the proceeds. As some compensation and to reflect the growth created by exports to Britain, the British government authorised large increases in the issue, for instance, of rupees in India backed by the securities in London. For India and Egypt, the Bretton Woods conference presented an open international forum at which they could appeal to a wider group of states on the matter, increasing the pressure on Britain for a resolution. India, in particular, sought to convert its blocked sterling balances into US dollars. From Britain's point of view, an open debate rather than a bilateral, or rather unilateral, settlement was to be avoided.[112] The shaping of a new world financial order in which Britain and sterling would formally cede its leadership to the US and the dollar was intersected at Bretton Woods by the loosening of its command of Empire and an increasing assertiveness on the part of its colonies.[113]

Although Britain's ability to marshal the voting power of its dominions was thus on the wane, White and the American delegation were still concerned that US proposals could be outvoted by a combination of the British imperial delegations. To counterbalance the numbers, White sought to win over the Latin American states to the US position, even if it meant accommodating some of the particular interests of those states, including their interest in promoting silver as an integral part of the reserve system of the Bretton Woods agreement. Moreover, White ensured that the quota and thus the voting power of the United States alone would exceed the quotas and voting power of all the constituent members of the British Commonwealth combined.[114]

Britain's commitment to the convertibility of sterling, forced on it by White's plan, predictably enough, ended badly. Countries with major sterling balances found that Britain was not producing the goods on which they might want to spend that sterling. Instead, it made sense to convert sterling into US dollars that could then be converted to gold or used to buy some of the many goods being manufactured in America. In the four weeks following the resumption of convertibility in July 1947, British reserves were drained of dollars: $106 million in the first week, then $126 million, $127 million, and in the fourth week $183 million.[115] Countries still forming the sterling area took advantage to switch monetary allegiance by converting their sterling into dollars. Convertibility was unsustainable and was rapidly suspended on 20 August.[116] Two years later, Britain went further and devalued against the dollar. In an echo of the competitive devaluations of the 1920s and '30s that the International Monetary Fund had expressly set out to prevent, a further thirty countries devalued in the following weeks. Devaluations of sterling and of the French franc as well as Italy's use of multiple exchange rates drove a coach and horses through the principle of stable but realistic exchange rates. In the longer term, the British experience in which that country had rapidly lost much of the value of a huge US government loan precisely because it agreed to the US conditions served as a salutary lesson to other European states. There was thereafter little enthusiasm in those countries for American proposals to relax exchange controls.[117]

And the new arrangement was not without problems for America in the long run. The status of the dollar as ersatz gold made it attractive to other countries, which sought to increase their dollar reserves to the point where the US would be unable to convert them all on demand to gold. Despite this danger, America continued to issue large volumes of dollars to settle its international debts. The dollar's privileged status as the only currency considered equivalent to gold encouraged the US authorities to continue issuing vast sums in dollars in order to promote trade since other countries needed dollars to buy American goods. But the more dollars were issued, the more likely it was that the dollar would depreciate. Rather than hold depreciating dollars, other countries would seek to convert their dollar holdings to gold as a more reliable store of value. In turn, the reduction in America's gold stocks would make it increasingly difficult to support the fixed gold:dollar exchange rate of $35 to the ounce, placing yet more pressure on the dollar. Known as the Triffin Dilemma, named after the Belgian-born economist who had first explained the problem, the dollar's position as the principal global reserve currency convertible to gold contained within it a paradox: issue too many dollars, and they depreciate to a point where international preferences switch from dollars to gold; issue too few, and American exports would decline as the dollar would strengthen and American goods would become too expensive to buy in in the export markets.[118]

Despite the problems this raised for America, some leading Europeans continued to resent the advantage that it enjoyed by reason of the dollar's status as the desirable global reserve currency – the 'exorbitant privilege' as it was described by Valerie Giscard D'Estaing, de Gaulle's Finance Minister and subsequently President of France. Opinion in Germany differed to some extent as the political leadership there recognised the debt owed by Germany to America's security guarantees. Although, in 1966 Germany's minister of economics wanted to fall in with France's policies on the dollar, the consensus among decision-makers was that Germany should continue to support the dollar wherever possible, partly because of national security considerations, but also because the French policy of dumping dollars would simply have undermined the value of Germany's large dollar-denominated foreign reserves.[119] Triffin's dilemma had exposed the problem confronting US policy-makers when it came to issuing insufficient or excessive volumes of dollars. At the same time there was a dilemma confronting other governments that had become dependent on the dollar as the principal reserve currency: on the one hand they recognised that they were dependent on responsible US policy to provide the world with an adequate supply of US dollars without exploiting that position, but on the other they feared any attempt to walk away from the dollar would diminish the value of their reserves, which were so dependent on the dollar and its continuing value in the marketplace. This was in effect the corollary of Triffin's dilemma, which continues to challenge emerging powers such as China.

And America's commitment to gold as the foundation of the dollar's pre-eminence would come to haunt it during the Vietnam War.

8

CURRENCY AND CONFLICT SINCE 1945

It is a matter of relief that there have been no instances since 1945 of monetary upheaval as a direct result of war between states on anywhere near the same scale as the widespread turmoil experienced during the Second World War. The unification of North and South Vietnam at the end of the Vietnam War in 1975 was sure enough followed by the unifi-cation of the currencies in 1978, but that was an isolated event and any link – ideological or otherwise – to the introduction of new currencies in Cambodia and Laos following the civil wars there at roughly the same period is tenuous. There was no domino reaction in collapsing curren-cies, just as the feared domino sequence of countries across Asia falling to communist revolution had failed to materialise.

Vietnam and the End of the Gold Standard

If the Vietnam War had any special significance in monetary politics, it was in the role it played in driving America off the gold standard. In 1967–72, money supply in the US increased by 50 per cent as the government sought to subsidise the war through the printing press. During the 1960s US exports declined and imports increased; increasing volumes of dollars left the country. By 1968, foreign-held dollar assets – both money and government debt – far exceeded America's gold reserves.[1] From a point at the end of the First World War when America held more gold than any other country, it now found itself threatened by an outflow on demand of the nation's creditors. The dollar's purchasing power fell and those who held dollars elected to convert them to gold. In 1971, northern European countries – Belgium, Austria and the Netherlands – followed Germany out of the fixed rate of exchange to the dollar.

In classical gold standard terms, America's predicament was no dilemma at all: any country which could not support full convertibility would simply be forced to reduce the rate at which it issued paper money or stop altogether. The Bretton Woods agreement, however, in raising the dollar's status to that of the international reserve, placed American policy-makers in a difficult position. National pride obliged them to sustain convertibility; the social policies of President Johnson, foreign aid commitment and prosecution of the Vietnam War demanded the issue of more money; only rapidly increasing gold reserves could have supported both requirements. But new sources of gold were not available in adequate amounts as they had been in the nineteenth century. Devaluation seemed the most likely course – just as it had been for Roosevelt in 1933-and foreign exchange markets, sensing that that was the most likely outcome, intermittently sold off large volumes of dollars.[2]

Inflation during the early 1960s, before America had truly engaged in the war, was in the region of 0.7–1.6 per cent, establishing a low base for comparison with inflation in the war years of 1965–71. At its peak, annual consumer price index levels increased by no more than 6.1 per cent in any one year (1969), inflationary levels that would be positively modest in comparison with so many other cases of war-induced inflation. As the war ramped up, the number of troops deployed in Vietnam increased, from 80,000 in 1965 to 538,000 in 1968, and spending on defence procurement over the same period increased by about 50 per cent. In addition to the mounting costs of the war, the then President, Lyndon Johnson, was determined to maintain spending on his social programme, the Great Society. Only the size of the American economy enabled the country to absorb these costs without the economic burden becoming untenable. In fact, spending on the war in 1968, the peak year of that war in terms of expenditure, amounted to only 9.5 per cent of GDP. This is put in perspective by Britain's defence spending during the Second

World War, which exceeded 40 per cent of GDP in each of four years and peaked at 52 per cent of GDP in 1945. Nevertheless, the difficulty of pursuing the war to a successful conclusion was the principal reason for the refusal of Johnson to run for a second term of office.[3]

The pragmatic government of Richard Nixon, agitated by news that European states including France and Britain were planning to convert more dollars to gold, took the decision to abandon the convertibility of the US dollar to gold. The founding principle of White's International Monetary Fund – a dollar convertible to and therefore as good as gold – was dead within one generation of the Bretton Woods conference. An attempt to prolong the fundamental concept of Bretton Woods based on a devaluation of the US dollar to gold – the Smithsonian Agreement – collapsed in 1973 after only two years in effect.[4] Nixon cited the end of the war in Vietnam as the right juncture for the launch of a new economic strategy, of which the abandonment of gold was a key part. The collapse of America's adherence to the gold standard was not purely attributable to the Vietnam War, but it certainly contributed to it in a major way.

What conclusions can we reach from the US abandonment of the dollar:gold fixed exchange rate at the end of the Vietnam War? It is not realistic to conclude that all major conflicts will end in the reconfiguration of the international monetary order.

The fact is that the overwhelming majority of new currencies introduced since the end of the Second World War have emerged as a result of a decolonisation or secession, most of which was peaceful.

That is not, however, to say that war has not led to the replacement of one currency by another. There have been at least two cases in the past twenty years where the armed overthrow of regimes by hostile alliances have resulted in the introduction of new currencies. In Afghanistan in 2002, a year after the overthrow of the Taleban regime in Afghanistan by NATO forces, the Bank of Afghanistan, with the assistance of the International Monetary Fund, introduced a new currency to replace that circulating before the overthrow of the Taleban regime in Kabul. And in Iraq, following the Second Gulf War of 2003, a new currency was introduced to replace the discredited and depreciated currency bearing the portrait image of the ousted President Saddam Hussein. But these were relatively isolated incidents, unlike the wave of new currencies introduced by the end of imperialism.

Nevertheless, the instances of Iraq and Afghanistan are worth recording, together with what may be the only case of war seemingly linked to currency competition between states in modern history – that of the Eritrean–Ethiopian War.

Eritrea–Ethiopia 1998

There have been few instances of armed conflict breaking out as a result of monetary rivalry between states. The East India Company's attempts in the eighteenth century to usurp the local rulers' rights of *sikka* (currency issue) in India in the eighteenth century brought about punitive action on that commercial organisation, but it was local and not a case of states going to war. Benjamin Franklin believed (as well he might, as a banknote printer) that Britain's obstinacy in denying the colonies their own currency was the key factor in provoking the War of Independence. But it is difficult to identify with certainty any cases where one country's monetary policy alone has led to war with another. Eritrea's introduction of its own currency in 1997 is often cited as one of the key causes of the conflict between it and Ethiopia in 1998, but no serious assessment suggests that it was the only cause.

Eritrea had been Italy's first overseas colony, acquired from an Italian steamship company in 1882 and then integrated with Italy's other East African colonies during the inter-war fascist era to form Italian East Africa. At the end of the Second World War, and following lobbying by the then Emperor of Ethiopia, Haile Selassie, the United States and the United Kingdom supported the idea of a federation of Eritrea with Ethiopia. As a result, UN Security Council Resolution 390A of December 1950 ensured that a British post-war transitional administration was succeeded by the federation of Eritrea with Ethiopia, much against the wishes of Eritrean activists, who pressed for a referendum on the future of the country. In 1961 the emperor dissolved the Federation, annexing Eritrea formally and sweeping aside any pretence of autonomy. At that point, Eritrean separatists took up arms against the government, first of the emperor and then against the regime of the communist Derg ('military coordinating council') that had overthrown the emperor in 1974.

Eritrea's thirty-year armed struggle for independence drew to a close in 1991, when the repressive regime of the Derg's leader, Colonel Mengistu Haile Mariam, was overthrown by the combined efforts of the Eritrean People's Liberation Front (EPLF) and the Tigrean People's Liberation Front (TPLF), whose leader, Meles Zenawi, became the President of the Transitional Government of Ethiopia from 1991–95.[5] During this transitional period, the central government led by Zenawi agreed to the Eritrean leadership's proposal for a referendum on the question of independence. From 1991 to 1993 a transitional government formed by the EPLF ran Eritrea, until at the end of that period a referendum, endorsed by the UN, resulted in a vote for independence. In May 1993, the United Nations recognised Eritrea's independence by admitting it as a full member.[6]

Despite the collaboration between the TPLF and the EPLF in the fight against Mengistu and a direct professional relationship between the two leaders, Meles Zenawi and Isaias Afewerki, who had – to some extent – been brothers-in-arms in that struggle, tensions arose between the two countries.

Minor border incursions had already taken place when, in 1997, Ethiopian troops crossed into Eritrean territory in pursuit of rebels from the Afar region with the approval of the authorities in Asmara, but had then occupied land in Eritrea.[7]

It was against this backdrop of tension that the two states took divergent economic paths. By mutual agreement with Ethiopia, Eritrea had used the birr as its currency since independence, even though, during the transitional period after Mengistu had been overthrown, Eritrean officials negotiating with their Ethiopian counterparts complained that Eritrea had been given little influence over matters such as currency.[8]

In early 1997 Eritrea put forward to Ethiopia proposals for its own currency, the nakfa, which, it suggested, should be exchanged at par with the birr. Apparently, it took some eight months for Ethiopia to respond to these proposals, presumably while the TPLF leadership in Addis Ababa evaluated the proposal and weighed up the pros and cons.[9]

For Eritrea, the immediate advantages would include seigniorage as well as full control over the issue of notes. These objectives were not in themselves unreasonable. But the proposed one-to-one rate of exchange to the birr was a problem. The Eritrean side might produce excessive quantities of nakfa to be exchanged for birr that could then be used to buy goods and produce in Ethiopia. There was no suggestion that the nakfa would be issued under the disciplined conditions of, for instance, a currency board, and indeed it was widely believed that Eritrea did not have foreign currency reserves or gold to back the issue of notes. Under those circumstances, it was reasonable to assume that the nakfa would soon depreciate, making a one-to-one exchange rate unrealistic. At least one Ethiopian report suggests that Eritrea also proposed that the nakfa be fully accepted as a medium of exchange in Ethiopia. If true, this would mean that there would be no need to exchange nakfa for birr: an uncontrolled issue of nakfa and one-to-one exchange rate with birr, together with full circulating currency status in Ethiopia, would have provided every opportunity for Eritreans to buy up Ethiopian produce and goods at advantageous prices and export them to Eritrea. We are reminded of the Soviet exploitation of unrestrained access to allied military marks during the occupation of Germany immediately after the Second World War. Like so many other aspects of the build-up to war, however, the claim that Eritrea requested 1:1 parity has been contested.

The choice of 'nakfa' – the name of a town in Western Eritrea that had been the site of Eritrean resistance to military assaults by Derg forces from 1978 onwards – was also likely to be seen as a slap in the face for Ethiopia. In October 1997, Ethiopia rejected the proposals and upped the stakes by proposing that future transactions should be settled in hard currency based on letters of credit.[10]

In November 1997, Eritrea began to issue the nakfa. Unable to comply with Ethiopia's demand for cross-border transactional settlements in hard currency, Eritrea in its turn raised the stakes by embargoing trade with Ethiopia. Given that the latter's main export and import route was through the Eritrean port of Assab, this in the longer term has had the effect of forcing Ethiopia to seek alternative routes to the sea, notably through Djibouti, but also through Berbera in Somaliland. It has also had the effect of decreasing commercial activity at Assab port. Tensions tipped over into outright hostilities.

In May 1998, Eritrea invaded the border regions of Ethiopia, precipitating a war lasting two years, which at the time was held to be the worst conflict anywhere on the globe. Estimates suggest that when Ethiopian troops drove deep into Eritrea in a massive counter-attack in 2000, one in three of all Eritreans were displaced from their homes. In December 2000, a peace deal was signed by the two countries providing for UN peacekeeping forces to patrol a buffer zone between the two opposing forces and creating a commission to settle the border dispute.

The exchange rate value of the nakfa to the dollar halved between 1997 and 2002. At the start of the conflict, the nakfa:dollar exchange rate was 8:1. At the peak of Ethiopia's military success and Eritrea's military failure in June 2000, it fell to 18:1, before recovering to 13:1 in early 2001, shortly after the peace agreement had been signed and UN peacekeepers deployed. At the peak of the war in 2000, inflation reached 26 per cent before dropping back in 2001 to 7.7 per cent, although in 2002 it climbed back up to 23.8 per cent. The poor quality of Eritrea's land, drought and the weakness of the nakfa among other things following the war combined to produce dreadful conditions for the supply of food. By 2004 some 70 per cent of food requirements had to be imported, a particular concern given Eritrea's poor foreign reserves.[11]

The situation in Ethiopia during and after the war was quite different. The birr:dollar exchange rate declined modestly from 7.5:1 to 8.3:1 over the period 1999–2003. Between 1998 and 2000 the inflation rate moved from 3.9 to 6.2 per cent. Surprisingly, between 2000 and 2002 there was a period of deflation while Eritrea was experiencing double digit inflation, although in 2002–03 inflation in Ethiopia did reach 15 per cent. Throughout the period of the war and just after, Ethiopia's foreign reserves amounted to two to three times those of Eritrea.[12]

Expert commentators investigating the causes of this war find it difficult to understand the true reasons for its outbreak, but some ascribe its origins to a permutation of factors ranging from internal Eritrean politics through conflicting models of state and governance, to rival economic models and eventually to mutual rivalry between the leaderships of the two countries. The consensus, however, seems to be that while the introduction of the nakfa was not the sole cause – or perhaps even the main cause – of the hostilities it added significantly to the tensions between the leadership of the two countries, making it yet more difficult for them to defuse the tensions building over border disputes and economic rivalry.[13] As the charge brought against the introduction of the new nakfa currency as a cause of war must at worst be described as 'not proven', there seem to be no known historical incidents of countries going to war on currency matters alone.

Afghanistan 2002

When on 11 September 2001 terrorists attacked the World Trade Center in New York by flying hijacked aircraft into the Center's Twin Towers, the worst single act of modern terrorism was played out in front of a global audience via international television networks. This direct challenge to the world's superpower could invoke only one response. When it very quickly became clear that the individuals who had inspired the attack were being sheltered by the Islamic regime governing Afghanistan – the Taleban – and when the Taleban refused to surrender those individuals to the US government, the administration of President George Bush launched Operation Enduring Freedom, the military campaign to overthrow that regime.

By the time of the US invasion of Afghanistan in October 2001, the country's currency was already in disarray. This was partly because, since seizing power, the Taleban had not ordered any new banknotes; but also because, as the crisis developed, United Nations sanctions prevented the regime from ordering new notes from foreign printers to pay its soldiers. The Taleban had in any case already lost control of banknote issue even before the UN sanctions had been imposed. Matters were made worse by the fact that since the Taleban had seized control in 1996, opposition groups located in the north of the country amongst the Uzbek and Tajik communities close to the borders with former Soviet states were importing notes from Russia. These new afghani notes were identical in appearance to the existing notes in circulation and were therefore

accepted beyond the areas controlled by the opposition. As the Taleban
had not issued any notes of their own since 1996, they attempted to
block this monetary intrusion by banning notes with serial numbers
indicating production after 1996. The opposition groups and their
Russian suppliers simply navigated around this minor obstacle by producing notes with pre-1996 serial numbers.[14]

In addition to these new, covert supplies of currency entering the
country, there were legacy notes bearing the portrait of King Zaher
Shah issued before he was ousted in a coup in 1973. Of all the notes
available in Afghanistan, these held their value best and were accepted at
a premium in comparison with other notes in circulation. Other notes
issued prior to the Taleban seizure of power in 1996 were also preferred
(although not quite so much as the notes of the ex-king) when compared to notes produced after 1996 by the Russians or by the Uzbek
warlord Rashid Dostum. Thus, the older the note and the less it was
associated with the current warring factions, the more valued it was.
Moreover, major transactions conducted by merchants or traders wishing to import goods were usually settled by payments in US dollars
or Pakistani rupees. In total, then, there were six different sets of notes
being used in Afghanistan and the lack of confidence in the currency
was reflected in the international exchange rate. By March 2001 the
afghani had fallen to 78,400 to the dollar.[15]

As the prospect of American military action approached, some serious change in the exchange rate downward might have been expected.
Yet only slight variations – and those favourable – were observed, for
instance when there seemed to be a failure by the US side to push forward with an invasion or when the Taleban fended off any attempt at
internal revolt. But curiously, as America's military might bore down
on the country in October 2001, the afghani to dollar exchange rate
rose to 73,000:1. This increase in value, which seems to run counter to
normal expectations (of a collapse in value when a government appears
to be losing ground), is ascribed by some to a cautious sense of optimism
among those in Afghanistan who were banking on an early American
victory. This interpretation seems to be supported by the fact that when
the Taleban fled Kabul in November 2001, the exchange rate rose briefly
but dramatically to 23,000:1.

There was a further temporary downturn in the value of the afghani when an IMF representative visiting Kabul in January 2002 following the invasion suggested that the country might adopt the US dollar, prompting many people to part with their afghanis. In the previous two years, the dollar had been adopted by Timor-Leste, Ecuador and El Salvador as the local legal tender and seemed to be on the rise as a truly international currency. However (and in opposition to the ideas of some at the IMF), members of the US Treasury were less enthusiastic about the idea, observing privately that the dollar at the time was 'systemically overvalued by some 15 per cent'. US officials noted that, were the dollar to be introduced as Afghanistan's currency, it would attract huge quantities of imports from neighbouring countries and at the same time would have a very negative impact on Afghanistan's own efforts to export. These arguments no doubt carried weight with the Afghan authorities, but questions of sovereignty and unity also played a significant part in their decision not to go for dollarisation. When the prospect of a dollarised economy quickly receded, the afghani climbed again to 27,000:1.[16]

Members of the new transitional government installed in Kabul, having been involved with the procurement of afghani notes from Russia when they were in opposition, were all too well aware that further stocks were available in the north of the country. Those stocks, if introduced covertly, had the potential to destabilise further an already fragile economy. A major currency reform was therefore in the view of both the new transitional government and IMF advisers a matter of urgency.[17] Accordingly, 27 billion afghanis worth of new notes were produced in Europe to replace approximately 15 trillion worth of the old Afghanis of various types. Some 2,500 officials manned forty-seven exchange offices around the country, where surrendered notes of the old type were also to be incinerated.

When the new notes were introduced in October 2002 to replace the existing afghanis that, according to some reports, had reached the rate of 42,000 to the dollar (although official US figures suggest it was closer to 39,000 at that time), the rate of the new notes was set at 49 to the dollar. Holders of notes issued by the Northern Alliance, which were not bona fide, were permitted to exchange them at a 50 per cent discount. Pragmatically, the possibility of converting old for new afghanis would flush out unauthorised issues once and for all, concentrating the issue of national currency in the Afghan National Bank. However, the success of the currency exchange was not quite as instantaneous as had been anticipated. During the early stages of the exchange period of October–December 2002 (subsequently extended to January 2003) the new afghani lost value and monthly inflation was in double digits – 16 per cent in September, 12.4 per cent in October and over 20 per cent in November.

Attempts to carry out currency replacement programmes while conflict is still under way usually fail, or at least falter, and the poor performance of the new afghani immediately after launch, when it briefly fell to 70:1 US dollar, might have given cause for concern. But 2002 had been a militarily successful year for the coalition forces and at that stage decision-makers might have been forgiven for thinking that the hot phase of the war was over, permitting reconstruction to proceed.[18] From December 2002 onwards the rate of inflation was slowing, reflecting the growing success of the currency replacement. By March 2003, the afghani had appreciated some 20 per cent against its original launch rate of 49:1 dollar.

Over the next three years after its introduction, the afghani, set originally at close to 50 to the dollar, moved within a narrow band between 49 and 51 to the dollar. Official inflation figures during that period were reported as having fallen from 29 per cent to 9 per cent, although unofficial sources in 2006 suggested the true figure might be in the region of 20 per cent.[19]

US Treasury currency statistics[20] give a dollar:afghani exchange rate as follows:

Pre-2002 afghani		'New' afghani	
March 2001	78,400	Mar 2003	40.3
June 2001	73,000	June 2003	49.1
30 September 2001	71,500	September 2003	49.25
31 December 2001	38,200	December 2003	48.17
March 2002	35,000	March 2004	49.87
June 2002	36,807	June 2004	57.69
September 2002	38,600	September 2004	45.67
December 2002	39,000	December 2004	45.21

With the exception of the quarter October–December 2010, when the new afghani hit a high of 44.5 to the dollar, it had remained within the range of 45–50. The Bank of Afghanistan had launched the new currency on the basis that it would not be fixed to any reserve currency as in a currency board, nor would the bank seek to defend a rate of exchange by interventions using its reserves to purchase afghanis in the marketplace. If the stability of the currency could not be ascribed to major interventions by the bank, market perceptions of the political and military stability of the regime, backed by US and other foreign forces, did play a significant role. As the US government proceeded to wind down the number of its troops in Afghanistan in 2014–15, the new afghani started to weaken and breached 60 to the dollar in the quarter ending June 2015. From April to September 2015, a long-running battle for control of the city of Kunduz pitched Taleban fighters against Afghan government troops in an early test of the Afghan National Army's ability to hold ground. When the Taleban seized the city in October, it dealt a blow to popular confidence in both the Afghan Army and the national currency. The new afghani reached a new quarterly low of 67.9:1 US dollar in the quarter ending December 2015. By April 2017 it had only slightly strengthened to 67.3:1.

Iraq 2003

The legal justification for the invasion of Iraq in 2003 by a limited alliance of the United States, United Kingdom, Australia and Poland to overthrow the regime of Saddam Hussein has been debated elsewhere and is not for discussion here. While the military campaign with its limited objectives was over relatively quickly, the post-invasion settlement of the country has been seen as a failure, with critics particularly observing that there was no plan for an effective reform of the civil administration of Iraq. The process of de-Ba'athisation – of removing from the civil service, the military and other public services anyone with a background in the Ba'ath party – left the country short of experienced administrators and personnel to enforce public order and security. Thirteen years later, the internal security of Iraq remains threatened by sectarian and ethnic rivalry and conflict.

In this fairly dismal context, one civil operation that has been generally acclaimed as an organisational success was the replacement of the banknotes issued by Saddam Hussein with new notes produced in Europe. Backed into a corner by effective international sanctions, the Saddam regime had produced poor-quality notes bearing the portrait of Saddam in ever larger volumes to finance the government. The replacement of these notes, which had low levels of security, low purchasing power, poor durability and quality as well as the unwanted portrait of Saddam, was a high priority for the coalition government led by the US.

The decision to introduce new notes was announced by the American chief administrator of Iraq, Paul Bremer, in July 2003 after discussions with senior Iraqi officials at the Ministry of Finance and central bank and with representatives of the Kurdish region in the north of the country. The involvement of Iraqi officials in the decision-making process thus resembled more closely the collaboration between American authorities and German experts during Operation Bird Dog for the introduction of an independent German currency in 1948, than the imposition of allied military marks at the invasion and occupation of Germany: this was not the enforcement of a project favourable to the conquering forces and punitive towards the defeated country, but rather a genuine attempt to offer the entire Iraqi population a new currency that would best serve its economic interests and reflect the change of regime.[21]

Under Saddam's leadership in the twenty-three years prior to the invasion, the regime had fought a war against Iran, invaded and been thrown out of Kuwait, and used chemical weapons in parts of the country where the local population was held to be opposed to the regime. The results had been the declaration of an autonomous region in the Kurdish area in the north protected by a no-fly zone defended by foreign (US, UK and French) air assets and the imposition of punishing sanctions by the United Nations. Under the UN sanctions, Iraq's primary foreign currency earner, oil, could only be sold in return for food, medicine and other humanitarian necessities. What additional foreign currency was earned was diverted into the acquisition of arms and to pay for vanity architectural projects. Internal public sector payments were covered by excessive recourse to the printing press – at least one of which was not under control of the Central Bank of Iraq – with the product being passed directly to the government, undermining the credibility of the dinar. As noted by Mervyn King, governor of the Bank of England at the time of the invasion, the face value of cash in circulation had increased from 22 billion dinars to a massive 584 billion dinars in the period between the end of 1991 and the end of 1995. Over the same period inflation was averaging 250 per cent a year.[22] At its worst, inflation peaked at 500 per cent per year, but tough budget cuts were then imposed and inflation dropped to 20–30 per cent per year. Despite the monetary expansion, prices were to a considerable degree controlled and in the case of energy and water at least subsidised until the 2003 invasion. In 2001, cash expanded in the country at an estimated 21 per cent with inflation in prices running at 29 per cent. Cash in circulation in 2002 was estimated to have increased by 44 per cent over the previous year while, thanks to the pricing controls, inflation fell to 15 per cent.[23]

These political, military and economic conditions were reflected in the country's circulating currency. In the autonomous north a separate currency known as the Swiss dinar (named after its putative country of production) circulated. It was badly worn but otherwise of a high quality in terms of security. In the rest of Iraq, poor-quality dinars with a portrait of Saddam and poorer security features were in circulation. The inept management of the Saddam dinar issuance was also reflected in the fact that in the later years prior to the fall of the regime, those dinars were available in only two denominations: the 250 dinar and the 10,000 dinar, worth about 14 US cents and US $5.50 respectively, which in an economy relying on cash for transactions made for a very inconvenient denominational structure. As the Kurds, unlike the authorities in Baghdad, had no means of increasing the numbers of notes in circulation, the notes in that region held their value well. By 2003 one of the dinars from the Kurdish north was worth 300 times more than the Saddam dinars when measured against the US dollar.[24]

Unsurprisingly, conditions became much worse on the outbreak of the war: the central bank was looted and $1 billion worth of foreign currency removed, although much ($800 million) of this was later recovered. The destruction of commercial bank branches made access to cash more difficult and one of the central bank's printing presses was stolen, leading to mistrust of the 10,000-dinar note, which as a result traded at a discount of 20 or 30 per cent. To address the collapse in confidence in the 10,000-dinar note, the newly reconstituted central bank began a programme a month after the end of the war to produce large volumes of the 250-dinar note, for which 10,000-dinar notes could be exchanged. Individuals were also permitted to exchange 10,000-dinar notes for US dollars up to a maximum of $2,000 per person. News of the planned currency exchange rendered these emergency measures unnecessary.[25]

The decision to undertake a currency exchange – which in the long context of money and war should hardly in itself have come as a surprise – was based on five requirements:

- The desirability of unifying the currency of the country, introducing a single currency to replace both the Swiss dinar in the north and the Saddam dinar in the rest of the country.
- The need to introduce a currency not bearing the portrait of Saddam Hussein – i.e. a symbolic break with the previous regime.
- An urgent economic requirement to bring inflation under control and to break with the previous regime's monetary financing by over-issue of currency.
- A practical decision to create a new family of banknotes with a spread of denominations more convenient than the two denominations of the Saddam notes.
- And finally a recognition that the security of the new family needed to be greater than those of the old notes to reduce the opportunity for criminal or political counterfeiting.

In contrast with Soviet monetary policies at the end of the Second World War, there was no attempt to stoke inflation as a means of punishing former enemies. Nor was there any policy of carrying out a currency exchange to flush out profiteers or to block the possible return of large volumes of old notes that might have been seized by hostile forces. This was a currency for Iraqis, not for occupying forces. Acknowledging the sovereignty of the Iraqi people and its institutions over their own currency, Bremer's announcement in July 2003 stated that: 'We have not designed *a new currency for Iraq*. Only a sovereign Iraqi government could take that decision. So we have taken the designs from the former national dinar (the "Swiss" dinar).' In design, the new notes were variations on the Swiss dinar, thereby presenting images familiar to the population prior to the introduction of notes with Saddam's portrait.[26]

In common with currency exchanges at the end of the Second World War, however, setting the appropriate exchange rate between existing and new currencies became of central importance to secure immediate acceptability and price stability in the short and longer terms. The idea of a redenomination, replacing the 10,000-dinar note with a 100-dinar note, was ruled out when Iraqi officials recommended that the currency exchange should involve the least possible change. A redenomination that would strike three zeros from each note could be misinterpreted by the population as a loss of value. Thus, to make the operation as simple as possible, the rate of exchange was fixed at one new dinar for one Saddam dinar.[27]

However, choosing the right rate of exchange for the so-called Swiss dinar was more complicated. The established exchange rate of the Swiss to the Saddam dinar at 1:250 had reflected the weakness of the latter and a recent appreciation of the former. This appreciation was attributed to growing conviction in the Kurdish area in an imminent American invasion of Iraq and a belief that it would lead to greater independence for the Kurdish region. An alternative explanation, which would appear to contradict the first perception, was that a new institution governing banknote issue for all of Iraq would be created and that this would support the value of the Swiss dinar.[28] Plainly the idea of a single issuing authority for the entire country would have been at odds with the possibility of independence for the north. That is not to say, though, that both ideas did not gain ground in the run-up to the invasion, pushing up the value of the Swiss dinar. Different expectations may contribute simultaneously to the same end result. Just as possible an explanation might have been a drive by people holding Saddam dinars, which might have been seen as a poor long-term bet, to exchange them for Swiss dinars, the currency most likely to benefit from an American invasion. Such an explanation is entirely consistent with the behaviour of populations in civil war, where the currency of the losing side becomes increasingly worthless, while that of the winners appreciates. This behaviour may have started even before the first US troops entered Iraq.

To fix the exchange rate at the prevailing rate of 1 Swiss dinar to 250 Saddam dinars would have had the effect of sealing in an exceptionally high rate in the Kurdish north, attractive for purchasing goods from elsewhere in Iraq, but unhelpful in selling produce and goods from the north to the rest of Iraq. The currency planning team looked closely at the examples of the euro exchange and the exchange of East German marks for deutschmarks at the time of German reunification. In the latter case, it was generally believed that too high a rate favouring the East mark had been responsible for higher labour costs in the east and consequently a high level of unemployment. A comparison of the purchasing power (purchasing power parity) of the Swiss and Saddam dinars to an identical basket of basic foods in both areas pointed towards a more realistic rate of 1 Swiss dinar to 100 Saddam dinars. Drawing on these various lessons, a decision was taken to exchange Swiss dinars for new dinars at the compromise rate of 1:150.

Although there was a belief within the International Monetary Fund that eighteen months to three years would normally be required to design, produce and deliver a new banknote series, the Iraq currency exchange took three months from date of signature of the contract for production to the first date of the exchange, partly because the designs used were based very closely on the designs of the original Swiss dinars. Between the beginning of production in summer 2003 and June 2004 a total of 3.25 billion notes were delivered worth 12.4 trillion dinars, of which 1 billion notes were a reserve. The exchange operation was conducted at 244 commercial bank branches across Iraq, an extraordinary feat of organisation given that the country was still not peacefully settled, especially as the time allowed from Bremer's announcement to the first day of the exchange was no more than thirteen weeks. A more convenient value structure of six different denominations was introduced.[29]

The determination of the central bank and its international advisers to break with the past was given constitutional form with a law that formalised the independence of the central bank from the Finance Ministry, establishing for as long as that law held a barrier to monetary financing of future public-sector debts. Despite strong support from eminent (mainly American) economic specialists, the idea of fixing the exchange rate to the dollar or the euro was ruled out by the Iraq currency advisers, largely on the grounds that wild fluctuations in the value of the dinar and a lack of adequate data from the Saddam regime's central bank would make it difficult to identify the appropriate exchange rate. Too strong a dinar would inhibit exports; too weak and inflation could be triggered. The reserves necessary to defend a fixed exchange rate were also in short supply in the immediate post-war period, making it virtually impossible to fix an exchange rate and stick to it. Given the state of the damaged economy in a country emerging from war, there was little confidence that the central bank would be able to defend a fixed rate, so a decision was taken to allow the dinar exchange rate to float. This arrangement seems to have served the country well: after the pre-invasion depreciation and an initial surge in value following the war and the currency conversion operation, the dinar was stable at 1,400 dinars to the dollar from 2004 to 2006 and then from 2008 to 2014 at about 1,170 dinars to the dollar.[30]

As the currency exchange programme came to an end some nine months after the start of the invasion of Iraq in March 2003, the Central Bank of Iraq took over the running of monetary operations. The objectives set out for the currency conversion operation – the unification of the currencies on issue under a single issuing authority, the removal of the Saddam portrait from the currency as a symbol of the change in regimes, the stabilisation of the currency and of prices, and the introduction of a more secure set of convenient denominations – had been achieved.

9

MONETARY SANCTIONS

States have a number of options by which they can apply pressure to the national monetary systems of other states for politico-economic reasons. There is counterfeiting, as described in Chapter 6. There is also the deliberate debasement of the currency of a conquered territory, described in Chapter 7. And then there is the application of national laws or the application of multilateral sanctions to interdict the supplies of national currency to another country or to disrupt access to foreign currency reserves or systems. All of these measures have been or are being applied now. But as monetary systems develop on new digital 'platforms' that are rapidly replacing coins, cheques and notes, there may be other means of undermining another country's monetary system that have yet to be experienced on a large scale.

General economic sanctions, blockade and the economic hardship and the eventual breakdown that comes with war will wear down a nation's currency, for the losers, obviously, but sometimes even for the winners, albeit less obviously. But there are few instances where an attack on a monetary system alone can force a country to reverse military, diplomatic or other political strategies. Interventions by one country to interdict supplies of currency to another can certainly be an irritation or worse. But, as a means of applying pressure on the policies of a foreign country short of war, currency attacks have yet to be proven to be reliably effective.

On one level, supplies of national currency are particularly susceptible to intervention if they are being produced in another country. In such a case, the supply can be disrupted by legal action in the country in which currency is being prepared. Perhaps the leading example was that of a case brought by the Emperor of Austria against the Hungarian national- ist Lajos Kossuth and the British printing company W. Day & Sons in the London law courts in 1861. The Austrian government in this case sought an injunction to prevent W. Day & Sons printing banknotes for Kossuth, who intended to use them as currency for an independent Hungary once the country had broken away from Austria's control.

The case was prosecuted on the grounds that an attempt to introduce new currency into Hungary in support of revolution was a breach of the sovereign's prerogatives in the issue of currency. The case was also based on the contention that the introduction of an unauthorised cur- rency would cause economic damage to the emperor's subjects. Initially, an injunction was granted on the basis of the emperor and the Austrian government's sovereign prerogative and that British courts had an obli- gation to support that prerogative. However, in an appeal held in the House of Lords – the highest court of appeal – the judges hearing the case concluded that an English court could not pass judgement on mat- ters relating to the political prerogatives of a foreign sovereign. They did, however, agree that a case relating to prospective financial damage to the subjects of a foreign power could be heard in an English court. On those grounds, and not on the political grounds, both judges found for the government of Austria and upheld the injunction preventing W. Day & Sons printing notes for Kossuth. All the notes that had been printed, together with the plates used by the printers, were surrendered and destroyed.

The case of the Emperor of Austria versus Kossuth and Day remains an important precedent in law and was cited in the US courts in a comparable case during the Mexican revolution. The case involved production of notes in the US for the armed uprising against Mexico's military dictator Victoriano Huerta led by the head of the Constitutionalist party, Venustiano Carranza. The banknotes were seized by US authorities in Texas near the border with Mexico in August 1913, in conformity with a US Presidential decree of 1912 forbidding the export of arms or munitions of war. The seizure was made on the grounds that the notes would be used to buy arms or munitions and that they were therefore as good as arms or munitions themselves.

The Constitutionalist party applied for the release of the seized notes and the case was heard in a US federal court. The US State Department held the view that the constitutionalists' attempts to issue notes were in breach of the federal Mexican government's prerogatives in the issue of notes, a breach of the prerogative of sovereignty; one of the arguments considered but ruled out in the London courts hearing the case of the Emperor of Austria versus Kossuth and Day. The US Department of Justice, on the other hand, based its argument in court on the financial damage that the issue of those notes could cause, consistent with the finding of the appeal court in the London case. As the US court ruled in favour of releasing the notes to the constitutionalists, however, the outcome was quite the opposite to that of the Austro-Hungarian case in London.[1]

The Agadir Incident 1911

One early example of monetary operations successfully reversing military and political confrontation occurred in 1911 when France and Germany squared up against each other during the so-called Agadir Crisis. Very much in the spirit of the times, the great powers of Europe had recognised France's special position of influence in Morocco following an earlier Moroccan Crisis of 1905–06. When, however, France intervened in support of the sultan against a local rebellion in 1911, Germany launched countermeasures, sending a gunboat and then a cruiser to the port of Agadir, partly to test the strength of Britain's support for France. Within a week of the outbreak of these near-hostilities, however, Germany recognised France's protectorate of Morocco, in return for recognition of German territorial interests elsewhere in Africa.

The Agadir incident was very much a product of its time and of the jostling of European powers for territory and influence in Africa. But rather than erupting into full-blown conflict, the tension was effectively defused by a major monetary operation believed to have been orchestrated by the French finance minister. French commercial banks and those of its ally Russia began to withdraw their deposits from Germany, prompting the German public to begin converting its own notes to gold. Within a month the Reichsbank lost a fifth of its gold reserve and was in danger of having insufficient gold to back the notes on issue, with a potential outcome of Germany being forced off the gold standard. Emperor Wilhelm II consequently backed down. The lesson for Germany and for the emperor was clear: in the event of a future conflict, Germany had to be able to defend its monetary front as well as its military positions.[2] While the gold standard provided a solid barrier against domestic inflation, it could be an Achilles heel in times of war.

Monetary influence exercised between the wars

The inter-war years in Western Europe seem to have been the heyday of France's use of the currency attack as a tool of foreign policy. The success of its operation at the time of the Agadir incident and the fragility of the monetary system of Germany immediately after the Weimar hyperinflation provided evidence of the efficacy of such an attack and perfect circumstances for a repeat of the means. But first France suspected Germany of such methods. Between January and March 1924, the French franc lost more than 20 per cent of its value. Raymond Poincaré, a strongly anti-German Prime Minister of France who had the previous year ordered the reoccupation of the Ruhr, announced in the National Assembly that a German plan to conduct a currency attack on the franc had been uncovered. Poincaré alleged that German Foreign Minister Gustav Stresemann had prepared an attack to be launched from the Netherlands exploiting a reserve fund of 13 billion francs that had been accumulated there by German businesses. The claim has been disputed, with those rejecting the allegation pointing out that there is no record of the German government's involvement in any German archive, a specious argument in the eyes of those who suspected a secret plot. An alternative interpretation of the causes of the fall in the franc place the blame firmly on the economic mismanagement of the French economy by Poincaré's own government; the German 'plot' simply provided convenient cover and reflected Prime Minister Poincaré's anti-German disposition. Yet another explanation, one that might seem all too plausible in our own time, is that the sale of francs for dollars in New York and

Amsterdam was a purely commercial operation by currency speculators. At least as possible as these individual theories is the idea that German authorities were prepared to accelerate any market decline in the franc's value: political forces jumping on a market bandwagon. We might also conjecture that, as France itself was well aware of the power of monetary influence, it could all-too-easily conceive of the same techniques being exploited by other countries.[3]

In the eyes of some senior French public figures, Germany was not its only rival in matters of monetary influence. The governor of the Banque de France, Emile Moreau, was deeply exercised by what he saw as Britain's monetary imperialism as the Bank of England, with the assistance of the financial committee of the League of Nations in Geneva, established itself as the dominant partner of central banks in Norway, Austria, Hungary and Italy. When Yugoslavia required substantial loans in 1927, the Banque de France sought to exclude British participation primarily because France wanted to be Yugoslavia's main creditor for political – that is, for foreign policy – reasons. Moreau confided to his diary an intention to buy gold in London if the Bank of England were to take the Yugoslavian business away from his own bank.[4] The scale of his threat is understood by the massive increase at this time in France's sterling holdings. Between November 1926 and May 1927, France increased its sterling holdings from £5 million to an astonishing £160 million. In May 1927, Moreau exercised his threat when the League of Nations stepped in to stabilise Poland's currency, removing the opportunity for France to intervene. As Moreau considered the League of Nations to be under British control, he responded by converting sterling into gold in London and withdrawing it to France, repeating the ploy that France had first used at the time of the Agadir incident. Moreau had not, however, thought his gambit through. Britain held £600 million pounds' worth of French Treasury bills as war debt and threatened to dump them on the market, causing a crash in the value of French sovereign debt. Moreau promptly brought the sterling to gold conversion operation to a halt.[5] Where the application of direct monetary pressure had failed, Moreau tried diplomacy. With the blessing of his Prime Minister Poincaré, he sought to agree spheres of monetary influence in Europe with the Bank of England. But his counterpart at the Bank of England, Montagu Norman, was having none of it.

Germany remained the primary concern, however. France's gold reserves made it, of all European states, the one best placed to exert economic power and Germany's fragile economy made it particularly vulnerable. Over the period 1929–30 the economy was showing worrying signs of rapid decline. Some $500 million, much of it gold, left the country, leaving only about $250 million in gold reserves. To put this in perspective, Germany had begun the First World War with approximately $1 billion worth of gold and finished the war with about $150 million worth in its reserves. At the end of the war America held approximately $4.5 billion worth of gold reserves. Britain had, in 1913, gold reserves worth in the region of $800 million.

During the Young conference of 1929, convened in Paris to settle the thorny ten-year-old problem of Germany's First World War reparations, the Paris press, banking sector and government colluded to conduct public attacks on the policies of the Reichsbank and the value of the German mark. Perhaps again drawing on the experience of the Agadir incident, French banks scaled back their credit arrangements to German banks and the Reichsbank's gold cover for banknote issue fell almost to its legal minimum of 40 per cent. Hjalmar Schacht, governor of the Reichsbank at the time and the man who had halted Germany's runaway post-war inflation in 1923, exposed the weak foundations of the French policy: if the German economy was so weak that its monetary stability could be undermined by a relatively low-level intervention in this way, the country was clearly not sufficiently robust enough to pay reparations on the scale that France demanded. Schacht threatened to default on further payments unless the attack on the mark ceased.

Schacht's daring gamble might appear to have been excessively risky for a country that, as hyperinflation and the occupation of the Ruhr had shown, was still vulnerable to military and political action on the part of the Allies. However, Schacht was nothing if not wily. He understood that a suspension of reparations payments would have led to a series of financial responses as damaging to the Allies as to Germany. The first reaction to a suspension of reparations would have been the withdrawal of foreign money invested in a risky German financial system. That in turn would have forced many German institutions – public and private – to default on their debt-servicing commitments to foreign lenders.

Schacht's calculation had been canny. The central bankers of America, Britain and even of France grasped the implications for their own countries and pulled back.[6]

Emergency measures may have enabled Germany to stave off France's political demands, but they did not rescue the country's economy from disaster. By summer 1931 the German banking system was collapsing and German industry was operating at 60 per cent of its 1928 output. By 1932, 6 million men were out of work.[7]

The plan for a customs union of Austria and Germany announced in March 1931 also prompted action against Austria. It was an unwelcome development for France, all too well aware of the creation of Germany's customs union in the nineteenth century as a precursor to full political union. The proposed customs union was referred to the International Court of Justice by France, which contended that the union would be in contravention of the Treaty of Saint-Germain by which Austria was forbidden political union with Germany.

With its economy already in a bad way and dependent on foreign loans, Austria was vulnerable to economic pressure. French banks were encouraged by the government in Paris to withdraw deposits from Austria, aggravating the situation and, taking with one hand and giving with the other, France stepped forward to offer the necessary loan subject to Austria dropping the planned customs union. Rather than accept these conditions, the Austrian government resigned and on this occasion the effectiveness of monetary pressure for political purposes was undermined by Britain's willingness, expressed a day after the Austrian government's resignation, to offer a loan without punitive conditions.[8] Before long, France encouraged in revenge a series of withdrawals in gold from British banks, deploying against its apparent ally the same monetary tactics as it had used against Germany as early as 1911. Having adopted the gold exchange standard, but on the basis of a much-reduced gold backing for sterling, Britain was more susceptible than ever to this attack on the venerable yet vulnerable foundation of its monetary system. At other times the standard response would have been for the Bank of England to raise its interest rate to attract foreign money into the country. At the height of the inter-war Depression, however, any attempt to raise interest rates, choking off loans for the little domestic economic development that was under way, would have been extremely unpopular. The Bank, moreover, recognised that an inflow of foreign money would only have reversed at the first sign of a relaxation of interest rates. The idea was, then, not only a short-term solution but likely to aggravate an already terrible position in the economy.[9]

The year 1931 also marked a turning point for Britain and its historical adherence to the gold standard. Coming to terms with the inevitable and recognising that strict loyalty to the gold standard that had made Britain the country to be emulated in monetary terms was no longer viable, Britain came off the gold standard. From this point onwards, Britain was no longer vulnerable to France's exploitation of the convertibility and export of British gold, but, economically weak, would be susceptible to other forms of pressure. This would be all too obvious in the period following the Second World War.

Suez 1956

When, in 1956, Egypt's President Gamal Abdul Nasser nationalised the joint British–French company that ran the Suez Canal, Britain and France conspired with Israel to regain management control of that vital waterway. For Britain's fragile post-war economy, the closure of the Suez Canal, interrupting as it would the flow of oil from the Middle East and other raw materials from the Far East, threatened severely negative effects. Military operations launched by Israel acted as a pretext for a pre-arranged invasion by French and British troops seeking to 'protect' the canal. While Britain's Prime Minister, Anthony Eden, viewed Nasser's action in seizing the canal-operating company as a breach of international agreements, the joint Franco–British invasion was seen in quite a different light by US President Dwight Eisenhower. In his eye, the expropriation of the management company was not a justifiable *casus belli*.[10] Indeed, Eisenhower saw the invasion as an expression of colonial power, the sort of adventure that America did not expect to see in the new international settlement reached at the end of the Second World War. The United Nations charter, which had been issued at the end of the first UN gathering in San Francisco in 1945, set out agreed constraints on the use of force that would only be used 'in the common interest'. The Suez operation, coming only eleven years after the San Francisco conference, would be viewed as a contravention of Article 1.2 of the charter, which called for respect for the principle of self-determination. On a domestic level, the president, who was running for re-election as a peacemaker, had good reason to use hard-edged persuasion to defuse military conflict. The president decided to intervene by exploiting the weakness of sterling.

Sterling's once admired strength as a currency had dwindled since the First World War. Following the suspension of gold convertibility in 1914, an attempt to return to the gold standard between 1925 and 1931 had ended in failure, largely because the government had gone back to too high a sterling:gold fixed rate that was no longer sustainable. Having barely recovered from the Great Depression, a dollar:sterling exchange rate was similarly held at an artificially high level of $4.03:£1 from 1941 to the end of the Second World War. Sterling's fragility was further highlighted in 1948 when, under the terms of a US government loan, Britain was obliged to resume gold convertibility. Creditor countries swiftly converted their sterling to gold and then bought dollars, as a result of which, much of a $4.4 billion loan from the US ended up returning promptly to the US. From this point onwards sterling rapidly slipped back from its wartime rate of $4.03 to $2.80 or thereabouts and stayed there for the next ten years.

As pressure on sterling increased, some delaying tactics were mounted by the Conservative government to prevent the drain of Britain's remaining reserves. Capital controls were, however, only partially successful and purchasers of British goods, believing the pound would soon be devalued, delayed purchases and payment. British reserves declined by 15 per cent over the period September–November 1956.[11]

Against this background and the scale of Britain's wartime debts, sterling presented a convenient pressure point, which Eisenhower duly exploited. The Secretary to the Treasury instructed the Federal Reserve Bank of New York to sell pounds, which it did, commencing on 5 November 1956. Deploying America's powerful voting majority at the IMF, the White House was also able to block Britain's access to its own IMF reserves. Having applied the stick, the US side also offered a carrot. Should the British government agree to withdraw troops from Egypt,

America would unblock access to Britain's IMF reserves and extend trade credits to soften the pressure on UK's reserves. The carrot and stick gambit was reminiscent of the ploy used by France to persuade Austria to abandon its prospective customs union with Germany.

Recognising that the value of UK reserves was declining rapidly and faced with the unavoidable responsibility for publicly declaring the value of those reserves, Eden's government buckled and conceded to the US government's demand that it withdraw troops from Suez. Eisenhower's Secretary of State agreed to unblock the UK's access to its IMF credit line. This effectively brought the financial crisis to an end, although sterling continued to plummet and indeed lost 20 per cent in value in December 1956.[12]

America's pressure on sterling as the UK's weak point during the Suez crisis is quoted by some as the clearest case of monetary systems being successfully exploited to achieve non-economic foreign policy objectives. But one aspect of this case calls into question its value as a model for the exertion of monetary influence. Unlike most other cases, the pressure was being applied by one country on another that had been the closest of allies in the recent world war and remained a staunch ally during the ensuing cold war. It was, moreover, being applied to a country that had already demonstrated at Bretton Woods its inability to stand up to America's industrial and financial dominance. Other countries on the receiving end of American foreign policy sanctions in the sixty years following Suez have been less willing and much slower to comply with US demands. In a world that remains stubbornly multipolar, where other states such as Russia and China refuse to accept America's hegemony, countries placed under sanctions will find alternative means of mitigating the vulnerability of their monetary systems. This alternative was simply not available to Britain in 1956.

Iraq

When Iraq under the leadership of Saddam Hussein invaded Kuwait on 2 August 1990, the United Nations reacted rapidly and decisively, passing on the same day UN Security Council Resolution 661 (1990), condemning the invasion and demanding that Iraq withdraw. Article 4 of the resolution required member states of the UN to deny to Iraq funds, financial and economic resources for anything other than medical or humanitarian purposes. Iraq, an oil-dependent economy relying on the supply of banknotes from other countries, was thus hit twice: access to dollars was denied and ability to source national currency from overseas suppliers was severely constrained. Restrictions on any form of financial transaction between US citizens and entities were imposed by presidential decree 12724 of 9 August 1990 signed by President George Bush, reinforcing the UN decision.

The Iraqi government made efforts to manage the impact of the second of these two sanctions by seeking to acquire its own banknote production line. Under the terms of an 'Oil for Food Programme' overseen by the United Nations, Iraq was permitted to sell oil in order to earn money to buy pharmaceuticals and food for humanitarian purposes, but all proposed disbursements had to be cleared in advance by the UN. Correspondence between Benon Sevan, Executive Director of the Office for the Iraq Programme of the United Nations, and Mohammed al-Douri, the Permanent Representative of Iraq to the United Nations, in February 2001 referred to the proposed purchase of a banknote production line with the proceeds of oil sales. Sevan informed al-Douri that such a request would be considered by the sanctions committee of the Security Council.[13] The request was rejected and the Iraqi government and population continued to accept the circulation of extremely poor-quality banknotes in the absence of anything better. The case of Iraq demonstrates that even a country with few international allies can limp on without access to supplies of a securely printed national currency for twenty years without collapsing.

Syria

Quite a different perspective is supplied by the case of Syria, a country riven by multi-polar civil war since 2011. In Western capitals there had been a growing belief in the efficacy of sanctions on banknote supplies to countries that did not have their own indigenous banknote supply.

In the case of Syria, it was widely believed that until the outbreak of the civil war, contracts for the supply of banknotes were held by Austrian and German companies. The European Union consequently moved to ban the supply of notes and coins to Syria by European Council decision 2011/782/CFSP of December 2011. During the period March 2011–November 2012, the Syrian pound lost nearly 50 per cent of its value against the dollar and although this was not solely a consequence of the currency embargo, it plainly raised the demand for reliable supplies of currency.[14]

Perhaps naively, the European Union had not taken into consideration the possibility that Russia might step in to fill the vacuum. Investigative journalists revealed that the cargo manifests of a Syrian Air Force cargo plane showed that Russia had supplied at least eight plane-loads of banknotes through the summer of 2012 – less than six months after the imposition of the EU sanctions. The Russian state banknote printing operation Goznak confirmed that it had printed the notes. What remained unclear from this episode, however, was whether Syria had been obliged to pay for the notes with hard currency (in much the same way that Stalin had exacted a fee in gold for the supply of arms to Republican Spain) or whether it was a form of military aid. Whichever of those two scenarios is true, the Syrian case demonstrates that, as with all other types of sanctions, monetary sanctions will only have a chance of having a major impact so long as the target country has no alternative 'work-round' in the form of supplies from another country.[15]

Iran

A nuclear programme with the potential to be upgraded to military purposes threatening Israel has been the motive for American sanctions on the Islamic Republic of Iran in recent decades. When Iran seemed determined to ignore the demands of the International Atomic Energy Authority to suspend its nuclear programme, the United Nations passed Resolution 1696 in 2006, indicating willingness to impose sanctions until Iran was ready to comply. Five months later, in December 2006, the UN set out clearly in Resolution 1737 the sanctions it was imposing, specifying goods and technology that might assist Iran's nuclear programme and freezing funds, financial assets and economic resources of specified organisations and individuals linked to the nuclear programme.

UN Security Council Resolution 1747, passed in March 2007, further tightened the restrictions and forbade the supply or export of arms to or from Iran and sanctioned all financial transactions with the exception of those destined for humanitarian or development purposes. By 2010, UN Resolution 1929 had ramped up its list of sanctioned activities to cover banking services in general and oil shipments.

But, rather than the UN sanctions, it was US sanctions that really bit. From 2007 the US Treasury had barred a number of Iranian banks from carrying out transactions with US banks. Even attempts to evade this embargo by means of the personal hawala system that arranged money transfers by informal methods also attracted legal action by the US government, which sought to close loopholes in the financial sanctions system.

The key sanction was the 10 November 2008 US Treasury embargo on so-called 'U-turn transfers' – an operation in which a bank in a third country would act as an intermediary for illicit transfers between American and Iranian banks. In this operation, a transfer from the intermediary bank in one currency to a US bank is converted into dollars and then transferred back to the intermediary. According to the new sanction, US depositary banks were 'no longer authorised to process such transfers, thereby precluding transfers designed to dollarise transactions through the US financial system for the direct or indirect benefit of Iranian banks or other persons in Iran or the Government of Iran'. The US continued thereby to close off all of Iran's possible sources of the world's leading reserve currency in which most commodities were denominated and traded.[16]

Banking sanctions were further tightened considerably in late 2011. As oil shipments were always denominated and paid in dollars, the embargo on trade between US and Iranian banks disrupted the medium of exchange for the international settlement of oil transactions with Iran. The majority of the American commercial banks conducting these transactions hold accounts with the US Federal Reserve banks and so were subject to pressure from the Federal Reserve. As pressure mounted on Western banks, prohibiting any transactions with Iran, the effect reached far and wide to deter those banks from handling any transactions for businesses dealing with Iran, even if the products or services concerned were not specifically sanctioned. In effect, Iran's sources of access to US dollars were drying up. The only alternative for Iran was to take payments for its oil and other exports in currencies other than dollars – notably in Chinese renminbi and Indian rupees paid via Russian banks that did not have branches or accounts in the US and which were therefore beyond the reach of the US authorities.[17] The disadvantage was that renminbi and rupees were not nearly so desirable in the wider world as a medium of exchange or a store of value.

The tightening UN resolutions were in turn supported by the European Union, which passed EU regulation 267/2012, forbidding the trade with Iran in gold and the supply of 'newly printed banknotes and coinage to or for the benefit of the Central Bank of Iran'.

It is difficult to imagine that the sanctions on the supply of newly printed banknotes would have made that much of a difference. Unlike other countries whose banknote supplies had been sanctioned in recent years but were dependent on external supplies, Iran had its own banknote-printing capability and the ability to produce its own banknote paper. It was to all intents and purposes self-sufficient in production of its own currency. So, what was the point? It may be that EU legislators were simply unaware of Iran's self-sufficiency in these areas. On the other hand, it may have been more a case of a gesture of solidarity. In reality, what hurt Iran was the banking services sanctions that prevented US banks from supplying dollars.

As Iran's oil exports shrank and access to dollars declined rapidly, the value of the riyal suffered: between December 2011 and October 2012, the riyal's value against the dollar declined by 80 per cent, causing a steep rise in food prices.[18] Popular discontent at the deteriorating economic situation in Iran did not go unnoticed by the most senior political authorities in the land.

When an agreement – the Joint Comprehensive Plan of Action (JCPoA) – was reached in 2015 between Iran on the one hand and France, Germany, UK, US, Russian Federation and China on the other, resolving the stand-off concerning the Iranian nuclear programme, the UK and EU countries lifted sanctions on 16 January 2016. The EU announcements specifically announced the lifting of sanctions on the supply of gold and 'newly printed banknotes'. US primary sanctions remain in place, however, blocking any trade in dollars that ultimately has to pass through New York.

Banking and currency controls were only one aspect of the wider sanctions on Iran, among which the oil embargo was far reaching. However, sanctions applied to the international banking system had the effect of attacking the central nervous system of the Iranian economy, freezing payments for Iran's primary export, oil, depriving the country of the world's premier medium of exchange for imports and store of value. Furthermore, US and foreign banks were deterred from conducting transactions in many other business sectors that otherwise were not embargoed, simply from fear of incurring penalties levied by the US.

Iran's expectations of a significant improvement in the state of its economy following the signature of the JCPoA were unfulfilled. Some sectors of the political leadership in the country had reasonable grounds to feel they had been duped into giving up a nuclear programme, but had been denied the reward. Matters, however, became far worse when US President Donald Trump, elected in late 2016 and taking office in 2017, withdrew the United States from the nuclear agreement in May 2018. Major European companies that had entered into contracts in Iran following the implementation of the nuclear accord started to withdraw from them during the spring and summer of 2018. Some banks in Europe and elsewhere which had been willing to handle transactions with Iran in 2016 and 2017 now turned away business with the country. Public confidence in the riyal was already declining sharply before Trump's withdrawal. Between 10 April 2018 and 8 May 2018, the riyal:dollar exchange rate had declined from 37,500:1 to about 43,000:1. By 3 September 2018 it had reached a new low of 128,000 to the dollar.[19] With such a depreciated value, the purchase of hard currency to pay for imported essentials such as food and pharmaceuticals, which are not in themselves subject to sanctions, has become increasingly difficult. Even though these items were in themselves not subject to sanctions, the secondary effect on them was to make it more difficult to buy them.

The responses in Iran to this further pressure on its currency have been predictable. The government announced that the dollar would no longer appear on its official exchange rate reporting portal, where it has been replaced by the Chinese yuan. Such a move is perfectly consistent with the likely ascendancy of the yuan, especially as China remains Iran's primary trading partner. But European states are also working on the development of a 'special purpose vehicle' – an alternative to a bank – that will facilitate transactions, particularly in pharmaceuticals and food, without recourse to the American dollar system. Furthermore, Turkey, Russia and Iran have reached an agreement to conduct trade in their own currencies rather than in US dollars.[20] And, on the local market, some entrepreneurs in the real estate sector are demanding gold in settlement of major transactions. None of these developments is surprising, but there must be some doubt as to whether they will help the riyal to regain a measure of its value, even when traded against the Turkish lire and the Russian ruble.

Cuba

More than half a century of sanctions on Cuba by the US, incorporating the same monetary measures as those that have been applied to Iran, were eased back as part of the general effort to resolve long-standing foreign policy issues during the second term of President Barack Obama. As the administration prepared the ground for Obama's visit to Cuba in March 2016, two key sanctions were lifted. The US Treasury made the following announcements:

- U-turn payments through the US financial system. US banking institutions will be authorised to process U-turn transactions in which Cuba or a Cuban national has an interest. This provision will authorise funds transfers from a bank outside the United States that pass through one or more US financial institutions before being transferred to a bank outside the United States, where neither the originator nor the beneficiary is a person subject to US jurisdiction.

- Processing of US dollar monetary instruments. US banking institutions will be authorised to process US dollar monetary instruments, including cash and travellers' checks, presented indirectly by Cuban financial institutions. Correspondent accounts at third-country financial institutions used for such transactions may be denominated in US dollars.[21]

The removal of monetary sanctions can be as potent a tool of foreign policy as their imposition – perhaps, given the unproven reliability of monetary sanctions, more so.

China's Dollar

It would be naïve to think that emerging powers will be content to live indefinitely with the political power America enjoys through its leverage of the dollar and the US clearing system. In China, this issue will exercise the minds of the leadership of the Communist Party for some time to come.

In recent years, China has emerged as the second largest economy in the world: at $10.3 trillion of GDP in 2014 compared to the US' $17.4 trillion, still some way behind, but more than double the GDP of Japan, the next largest economy at $4.6 trillion.[22] China is, however, the world's leading trading state, exceeding the US in exports and the second largest importer after the US.[23] Moreover, it is now also the largest single foreign holder of US Treasury debt, with $1.25 trillion worth, compared to Japan's holding of $1.12 trillion.[24] China's holding of dollar-denominated debt was, at 2011, approximately eight times that of Russia.[25]

At the same time, China is recognised increasingly as a great power, moving, perhaps, to re-establish a bipolar great power balance as had existed during the cold war between the US and the Soviet Union. Commentators point towards China's establishment of military facilities on islands in the South China Sea, the sovereignty of which is disputed by other states in the region, as an indicator of growing Chinese ambition. As other countries in the region are long-term American allies, it is not difficult to see tensions ramping up. However, given China holds so much US Treasury dollar-denominated debt and trades so heavily in dollars, can it afford to confront America just now without damaging the value of the dollar and its dollar-denominated debt holdings or prompting financial sanctions that could severely constrain its export-led economy, with possible implications for internal stability? In these circumstances the observer could be forgiven for recalling John Paul Getty's bon mot: if you owe the bank $100, it's your problem. If you owe the bank $100 million, that's the bank's. In storing up so much of the United States' dollar debt, China may have stored up a problem for itself.

It would seem that the only option available to China to mitigate this risk is a long-term programme to reduce its dependence on the dollar. But it has to be careful in doing so: to drop the dollar too quickly, to exchange dollars on such a huge scale for other currencies, would be to cause the dollar to depreciate heavily and the value of China's remaining dollar reserves to decline. And yet to wean itself off the dollar, China must diversify its holdings of foreign debt, reduce the amount of trade it transacts in dollars and position the renminbi as an independent trading currency in its own right. On this last point, the country is already making progress. From 2009, when very little of China's trade was invoiced in renminbi, by 2013 17 per cent of its trade was invoiced in the national currency. But a measure of the distance to go is demonstrated by the fact that one-third of China's imports are dollar-denominated commodities, vital to supply the Chinese miracle economy. While those commodities remain denominated in dollars, the dollar remains pre-eminent. If eventually they are denominated in another currency, the compulsion to earn and hold dollars will decline.

A further measure adopted to reduce the role of the dollar in China's trade is a series of currency swap arrangements with other countries, enabling Chinese companies to swap renminbi for the currencies of its partner companies in other countries without going through foreign exchange markets.[26]

While China's calculations will be based on economic, domestic grounds as much as on geo-political considerations, it is unrealistic to imagine that independence of action in military and diplomatic spheres free of the threat of monetary intervention will not be a factor in its plans.

It is also not lost on the Chinese leadership that great power prestige – certainly in the case of Britain and the US – brought with it leading global reserve currency status, even if there is a time lag between achieving economic dominance and reserve currency leadership. It is, of course, also possible that China has calculated that there is no better alternative to the US dollar in the foreseeable future and that, until an alternative global currency emerges, the country has no choice but to hold fast to it.

Instances of over-dependence on a single monetary regime such as gold or the US dollar have demonstrably created for some economies a disproportionately greater vulnerability to currency attack or sanctions. In the event that the United States were to increase its use of monetary sanctions as a policy tool around the world, it is easy to imagine countries choosing to spread the risk by increasingly trading in currencies other than the dollar. There are indications, as we have already seen, that this is happening in Iran, by necessity. The euro is one such option, although the EU's tendency to ally itself with the US on most major foreign policy issues would cast doubt on the reliability of the euro in the long term for any country that sees itself as potentially at odds with the US. Current efforts of the EU to develop alternative trading mechanisms for trade with Iran may put this point to the test. In this particular respect – the protection of trade and of an economy from US intervention – the renminbi seems likely to emerge as an alternative trading currency of choice, not only because of the growing strength of the Chinese economy, but also because of China's role as an independent rival to the United States on foreign policy matters.

10

THE MONETARY MACHIAVELLI

The question 'who controls money', which was once contested by sovereigns and parliaments, has not gone away. In Britain, Parliamentary committees still hanker after a greater role in the oversight of the Bank of England, particularly after the credit crunch of 2008. The sovereign debt crisis in the Eurozone that followed the banking crisis highlighted differences between Germany and southern European states as to the degree of freedom from political interference the European Central Bank should enjoy. Entirely new technologies – cryptocurrencies such as bitcoin – have been developed by shadowy individuals who promote the merits of a system that is beyond government control. New stakeholders and aspiring power-brokers in the world's monetary systems always emerge to challenge the existing sources of monetary authority.

Governments and central banks are as willing to absorb new ideas from the private sector and turn them to advantage today as they have been in previous centuries. Central banks are now studying the 'distributed ledger system' known as blockchain, by means of which any monetary transaction in a crypto currency system is authorised and executed not by a single central authority or bank, but rather by multiple actors with the digital capability to participate. With some irony, some professionals believe that such a distributed system may remove the vulnerability that comes with a single processing authority, which in itself presents a single point of weakness. But the bitcoin exchanges themselves have been successfully attacked, in Tokyo in 2013 and in

Hong Kong in 2016. No monetary technology is immune to attack. At present, central banks seem unlikely to adopt the distributed ledger system, but do acknowledge a growing trend towards a reduction in the use of cash by the private sector and populations. Policy-makers are therefore now considering the implications of this increasingly digital world for the long-standing monetary architecture that relies on a partnership between the central bank and commercial banks to generate a nation's monetary supply.

In the mainstream, currency systems have adapted quickly to new technologies designed to make life easier for commercial operations and even, perhaps, for the public. Automatic teller machines dispense banknotes without any requirement for the customer to meet a member of the bank's staff. Bank transfers can be made by telephone or via computer without the necessity of leaving home, all via the ultimately convenient medium of the internet. But we should beware. The easier monetary transactions become, the more vulnerable. The internet connections that permit currency transactions to take place in the modern world are also accessible to cybercriminals intent on digital theft. And if the system is accessible to criminals in this way, how much more vulnerable would it be to well-organised hostile powers with significantly greater resources? Where currency attacks by hostile powers in the past have taken the form of counterfeiting, in the future they will come as large-scale cyber attacks where a nationwide and coordinated 'denial-of-service' inflicted on the national and commercial banking system could bring transactions to a halt and cause runs on banks across the entire banking system. It will not be necessary to divert the entire national wealth from one country to another to cause bedlam (although, of course, some large-scale theft of money at times of hostility would represent a substantial success even if, as Germany found in the course of the Second World War, the gain might only be short-term). The ability merely to deny access to money by sabotaging digital systems would be enough to paralyse an economy.

Lest anyone should consider this scenario implausible, we have only to look at the evidence of cyber attacks in a range of sectors. Cyber attacks on accounts held by Russian commercial banks at the Central Bank of Russia in 2016 resulted in the theft of $31 million.[1] Some $81 million was stolen from the account of the Central Bank of Bangladesh held at the Federal Reserve Bank of New York in February of the same year. (Other reports total the losses at $101 million.)[2] Between 2011 and 2015, more than fifty separate cyber attacks on the United States Federal Reserve Bank System were detected.[3] Other attacks have been recorded on the Reserve Bank of Australia (2013), Bank of Indonesia and Bank of Korea (2016).[4]

The Bank of England takes this sort of scenario sufficiently seriously to carry out a series of cyber attack exercises under the generic title 'Waking Shark' involving the leading wholesale banks with bases in London. 'Waking Shark 2' was tested in 2013. The exercise set out a scenario where a hostile power carries out a coordinated 'distributed denial of service' (DDOS) attack on a number of banks, affecting their ability to carry out transactions in the financial sector. The exercise was focused on testing the systems and methods of service suppliers and financial organisations operating in the wholesale financial markets and in identifying areas for improvement. A number of participating organisations, however, felt that the exercise was not sufficiently challenging. It did not, for instance, test the potential impact of a truly major 'denial of service' attack on the retail system and on the public at large, and it did not explore outcomes that might include a run on a number of banks.

Experiences of the Northern Rock Bank in England in September 2007, Greek banks during the financial crisis of 2015 and of India following that country's demonetisation of two top value denominations in 2016 demonstrate that banking and monetary systems and their ability to serve the public can be put under extreme pressure, even in the absence of major hostile cyber attacks. The ability of hackers to carry out coordinated attacks on private and public institutions is increasing steadily, as proven by the May 2017 attacks on the British National Health Service, the Russian Interior Ministry and the US carrier FedEx by means of the WannaCry malware. Such an attack on the banking system of one country by well-resourced and nationally supported defence services of another with the intention of denying the public access to its money would cause extreme civil disruption. The central bank of the attacked country would be forced to revert to the distribution of large volumes of cash around the country. The effect of such an attack could be more far-reaching than the shortage of coins and notes in Britain and elsewhere on the eve of the First World War.[5]

There is evidence that central bank authorities are starting to understand the magnitude of the threat. Stefan Ingves, the highly respected governor of Sweden's Riksbank, the oldest central bank in the world, has urged his government to consider the dangers of an attack on the national payments network in time of a 'serious crisis or war'. A fellow Swede and former head of Interpol, Bjorn Erikson, echoing the specific threats currently feared by many of his compatriots, points towards the ability of Russia to 'switch off the payments network' at the point of an outbreak of hostilities in which Russia might seize Swedish territory.[6] This is no doubt a very valid concern, but global interconnectivity means that a serious cyber attack could immobilise a national monetary system without a single shot being fired. The nature of hostility has changed from a simple binary war–peace option to that of a spectrum of activities that might precede war, or indeed might replace wars with other forms of hostility between states.

In this new world, what should wise leaders do? The first thought must be for defence: how can a country protect itself from a possible catastrophic cyber attack on the monetary system? As things stand, it may be that governments can do something to shield against such an attack, but complete security is unattainable. It is perfectly possible that 'sleeper' malware exists undetected in some systems, waiting to be activated by a hostile regime. Even if such 'sleepers' are detected and neutralised, new malware might be regularly distributed to payments networks so that governments and other key participants in payments systems such as the clearing banks and managers of clearing systems will need to be constantly vigilant, scouring their networks for potential threats and removing them. But then a so-called zero-day attack that takes place on the same day that a system vulnerability is identified leaves the initiative in the hands of the hostile aggressor attacking an unsuspecting victim.

One thing that governments cannot afford to do in planning defence against monetary cyber attack, however, is rely on commercial clearing banks to maintain the very highest standards of cyber security. There have been enough instances to prove that commercial banks are vulnerable to cyber attack and have taken insufficient steps to protect their systems.

Governments are ultimately responsible for the protection of these payment networks, or if they are unable to guarantee an attack-proof system, to have an alternative solution at their disposal. Prior to the outbreak of the First World War, the most calculating governments had taken steps to prepare their monetary systems for a major shock. Others had to react rapidly to come up with new solutions to the weaknesses that became apparent in the run-up to war. In the most extreme cases of attack, where an entire system is crashed beyond repair or is subjected to repeated attacks making it inoperable, it is difficult to imagine a more convenient and trusted response than a resort to cash. The logistic challenges to distributing such an emergency issue of currency can be addressed in advance as was demonstrated by US, German and French preparations prior to the First World War.

Wise governments have a duty not only to plan for the defence of their monetary systems, but also to plan attacks on the monetary systems of prospective enemies. It is perfectly reasonable for a country to aim to 'distress an enemy' in time of war by attacking his currency, as Lord Kenyon pronounced in the case of the French assignats counterfeited by Britain at the end of the eighteenth and beginning of the nineteenth centuries. This is no less true in the twenty-first century. Indeed, some countries with a more flexible and aggressive approach to their relations with other countries may seek to carry out such an attack before a state of war occurs or even as an alternative to outright hostilities. Such attacks might have no objective other than to weaken another country politically and economically and might well be delivered so as to be unattributable to the government of origin, or at least 'deniable'.

In the Middle Ages, some jurists considered that the counterfeiting of a state's currency was a *casus belli*. In fact, history records no instances where a country has gone to war over such a provocation. Indeed, the deployment of cyber attacks on one country by another has hitherto not led to an outbreak of war primarily because of the deniable nature of such attacks, but also because of the prevailing modern view that the response to a hostile act should be appropriate and proportionate. Where it is difficult to prove that one country has carried out a major cyber attack on another, it has become even less likely that a digital monetary attack as a tool of foreign or security policy would lead to a case of war – at least among states of approximately equal power. That is not, however, to rule out an unequal resort to military force by a first-rate power convinced that a minor player has incapacitated its monetary system by cyber attack. It would thus be unwise for a weak state to provoke a much stronger one by carrying out this sort of attack while hoping to rely on deniability as an adequate insurance against a disproportionate military response. Generally, only powerful states will take such a risk, although weaker states that, for whatever reason, do not fear military intervention by apparently much more powerful adversaries, may be tempted to take the risk.

And if any lessons have been learned from the Second World War and again from conflicts in the past twenty years, it is that planning for a post-war monetary world is as important to secure the recovery of the victors as it is to secure the stability of economic conditions for the vanquished. Leaving a vanquished country in monetary chaos (as was the case in Germany at the end of the First World War) threatens to breed conditions for further conflict.

What of monetary subversion as a tool of domestic power plays? In those cases of civil war and revolution we have reviewed, monetary systems under such circumstances have tended to collapse as a result of the military failure of the losing side. There are no historical cases that prove that one of the sides in any such conflict has defeated another due to the failure of the latter's monetary system. Indeed, populations tend to cope with debased money even in its most extreme forms. Only in the case of Portugal in 1925–26 has the compromise of the national monetary system been used as the pretext for a military coup. However, it requires no great effort of the imagination to see that an ambitious and malign military or security service could subvert its own government by covertly attacking the national currency, perhaps blaming the attack on an external actor. And yet, in the event of a government being toppled in this way, the coup plotters would be confronted by the challenge of repairing chaotic monetary conditions of their own making.

In these and other cases, it is to be hoped that the actors would think carefully before taking extreme measures.

NOTES

Introduction

1   Niall Ferguson, *The Ascent of Money: A Financial History of the World*, Penguin, 2008.
2   *Ibid.*, but Richard Von Glahn (*Fountain of Fortune: Money and Monetary Policy in China 1000–1700*, University of California Press, 1996, p. 25) dates the introduction of knife and spade money to the fifth century BC.
3   Walter Scheidel, 'The Divergent Evolution of Coinage in Eastern and Western Eurasia' in *The Monetary Systems of the Greeks and Romans*, ed. W.V. Harris, Oxford University Press, 2010, p. 274.
4   Richard Von Glahn, *Fountain of Fortune*, p. 19.
5   *Ibid.*, p. 55.
6   *Ibid.*, p. 67.
7   Thomas J. Sargent and François R. Velde, *The Big Problem of Small Change*, Princeton University Press, 2002, pp. 271, 302.
8   Richard Von Glahn, *Fountain of Fortune*, p. 56.
9   J.M. Keynes, *The Economic Consequences of the Peace*, Penguin, 1995, p. 235.

Chapter 1

1   Glyn Davies, *History of Money*, University of Wales Press, 2010, p. 89. Although Professor Davies does not specify the period covering this calculation – which, given the inflating cost of a soldier's pay throughout the history of the late republic and empire, is not entirely helpful – it seems that it relates to a legion of 5,000 men paid at 300 denarius each at the time of the Emperor Domitian.
2   Tacitus, *The Annals of Imperial Rome*, Penguin Classics, 1996, p. 198.
3   David B. Hollander, 'The Demand for Money in the Late Roman Republic', in *The Monetary Systems of the Greeks and Romans*, ed. Harris, p. 129.
4   Wolfram Eberhard, *A History of China*, H. Schuman, 1977, pp. 212–3.
5   Richard Von Glahn, *Fountain of Fortune*, p. 151. See also Debin Ma, 'Money and monetary systems in China in the 19th and 20th centuries: an overview', Economic

History Working Papers, London School of Economics and Political Science, 2012, p. 4, recording observations that the situation regarding variations in money standards was virtually unchanged in the late nineteenth century.

6   Şevket Pamuk, *A Monetary History of the Ottoman Empire*, Cambridge University Press, 2000, p. 132.

7   *Ibid.*, p. 41.

8   R.B. Wernham, *The New Cambridge Modern History: Volume 3, Counter-Reformation and Price Revolution, 1559–1560*, Cambridge University Press, 1968, pp. 371–2; Şevket Pamuk, *A Monetary History of the Ottoman Empire*.

9   Şevket Pamuk, *A Monetary History of the Ottoman Empire*, p. 95.

10 *Ibid.*, pp. 103–4.

11 *Ibid.*, pp. 155–6.

12 *Ibid.*, pp. 198–200.

13 Paul W. Drake, *The Money Doctor in the Andes: The Kemmerer Missions 1923–1933*, Duke University Press, 1989, p. 14.

14 *Ibid.*, pp. 17, 23.

15 *Ibid.*, pp. 81–2.

16 *Ibid.*, pp. 85–7.

17 *Ibid.*, pp. 86–8, 90, 97–8.

18 *Ibid.*, pp. 121–2.

19 *Ibid.*, p. 131.

20 *Ibid.*, p. 136.

21 *Ibid.*, p. 150.

22 This section based on the author's paper on Ecuador to the Monetary History Group, 'Ecuador – Country in Search of a Monetary Regime', 25 September 2015, and George Lauderbaugh, *The History of Ecuador*, ABC-CLIO, 2012; Carlos Mendoza, 'Monetary Authority: Similar Beginning but Different Trajectories: Bolivia, Ecuador and Guatemala in comparative perspective', 2004; Paul W. Drake, *The Money Doctor in the Andes*, p. 15.

23 Henry Wigan, 'The effects of the 1925 Portuguese bank note crisis', London School of Economics Working Papers, 2004, pp. 10–11; Ana Bela Nunes, Carlos Bastien, Nuno Valerio, Rita Martins de Souza, Sandra Domingos Costa, 'Banking in the Portuguese Colonial Empire 1864–1975', University of Lisbon Working Papers, 2010, p. 17.

24 Henry Wigan, 'The effects of the 1925 Portuguese bank note crisis', pp. 14–15, 23, 27, 41.

25 *Ibid.*, pp. 30, 32–3, 37.

26 Benn Steil, *The Battle of Bretton Woods: John Maynard Keynes, Harry Dexter White, and the Making of a New World Order*, Princeton University Press, 2013, p. 84; Charles P. Kindleberger, *A Financial History of Western Europe*, George Allen and Unwin, 1984, pp. 379–80.

27 Staff Reporter, 'Zimbabwe Army demands special dispensation on salaries', *Bulawayo 24 News*, 1 July 2016; Chris McGreal, 'Zimbabwe starts paying soldiers and other government workers in US dollars', *The Guardian*, 19 February 2009.

28 *Reuters*, 12 May 2016; World bank WITS database for Zimbabwe; Peter Oborne, 'Zimbabwe will sink into horror and depravity unless Mugabe quits now', *The Spectator*, 10 September 2016, notes that the Finance Minister Tendai Biti had increased the government's revenues from $280 million in 2008 to $4.3 billion in 2013.

29   Ed Cropley, 'As Zimbabwe's money runs out, so does Mugabe's power', *Business Report*, 28 November 2016; 'Zimbabwe Army demands special dispensation on salaries', *Bulawayo 24 News*; Abdur Rahman Alfa Shaban, 'Zimbabwe to pay most December salaries in January 2017', *AfricaNews*, 15 December 2016; Godfrey Marawanyika and Brian Latham, 'Dollar shortage forces Zimbabwe to delay military pay', *Bloomberg*, 19 June 2016.

Chapter 2

1   Rebecca L. Spang, *Stuff and Money in the Time of the French Revolution*, Harvard University Press, 2015, p. 100.

2   Glyn Davies, *History of Money*, p. 459; David Sinclair, *The Pound: A Biography*, Vintage, 2000, p. 166.

3   David Sinclair, *The Pound*, p. 194, notes the Massachusetts Bay credit notes were issued from as early as 1681.

4   Benjamin Franklin, *A Modest Enquiry Into the Nature and Necessity of a Paper-Currency*, University of Virginia Library, 1729.

5   Alexander Hamilton and United States Department of the Treasury, 'Report on a National Bank, December 13, 1790,' in Hamilton, Alexander and United States Department of the Treasury, *Official Reports on Publick Credit, a National Bank, Manufactures, and a Mint*, William McKean, 1821, pp. 67–118.

6   Glyn Davies, *History of Money*, p. 465.

7   *Ibid.*, p. 462.

8   Walter Isaacson, *Benjamin Franklin: An American Life*, Simon and Schuster, 2002, pp. 222–3.

9   *Ibid.*

10   Forrest Capie, 'Conditions in which very rapid inflation has appeared', *Carnegie–Rochester Conference Series on Public Policy*, 24, issue 1, 1986, pp. 115–68.

11   David McCullough, *John Adams*, Simon and Schuster, 2002, p. 141.

12   Glyn Davies, *History of Money*, p. 467.

13   Michael D. Bordo and L. Jonung, 'The future of EMU: What does the history of monetary unions tell us', *National Bureau of Economic Research*, 1999. Bordo and Jonung note that the rate of exchange between Continentals and specie in payment of taxes was 40:1 in 1780, 'a value much lower than the exchange rate of 1780'. This is at variance with Chown, who reports a much lower exchange rate than 40:1 in 1780.

14   John Chown, *A History of Money from AD 800*, Routledge, 1994, p. 220.

15   Eugene White, 'France and the Failure to Modernize Macroeconomic Institutions', 12th International Economic History Congress, Madrid, 25 August 1998, p. 22.

16   Rebecca Spang, *Stuff and Money in the Time of the French Revolution*, pp. 9, 49, 100; Eugene White, 'France and the Failure to Modernize Macroeconomic Institutions', p. 22.

17   Charles P. Kindleberger, *A Financial History of Western Europe*, p. 99; Rebecca Spang, *Stuff and Money in the Time of the French Revolution*, pp. 62, 73.

18   John Chown, *A History of Money from AD 800*, p. 224; Forrest Capie, 'Conditions in which very rapid inflation has appeared', notes 3 per cent interest.

19   Rebecca Spang, *Stuff and Money in the Time of the French Revolution*, p. 77.

20   Georges Lefebvre, *The French Revolution*, Routledge & Kegan, 1962, p. 154; Glyn
      Davies; *History of Money*, p. 557.
21   Stephen D. Dillaye, *Assignats and Mandats: A True History*, Ulan Press, 1877, p. 16,
      puts the second issue of assignats at June 1790.
22   Georges Lefebvre, *The French Revolution*, p. 155; Pierre Vilar, *A History of Gold and
      Money*, 3rd ed., Verso, 1984, p. 303.
23   Stephen D. Dillaye, *Assignats and Mandats*, p. 19; Forrest Capie, 'Conditions in which
      very rapid inflation has appeared'.
24   Glyn Davies, *History of Money*, p. 557; Georges Lefebvre, *The French Revolution*, pp. 155,
      255; Rebecca Spang, *Stuff and Money in the Time of the French Revolution*, p. 112.
25   Pierre Vilar, *A History of Gold and Money*, pp. 304–5.
26   *Ibid.*, p. 305.
27   Stephen D. Dillaye, *Assignats and Mandats*, pp. 32, 35.
28   Rebecca Spang, *Stuff and Money in the Time of the French Revolution*, p. 229.
29   John Chown, *A History of Money from AD 800*, pp. 228–9.
30   Eugene N. White, 'Measuring the French Revolution's inflation: the tableaux de
      dépréciation', *Histoire & Mesure*, 1991, p. 246.
31   John Chown, *A History of Money from AD 800*, p. 229.
32   Noel Maurer, *The Power and the Money: The Mexican Financial System, 1876–1932*,
      Stanford University Press, 2002, p. 14.
33   *Ibid.*, p. 50; Edwin Walter Kemmerer, *Inflation and Revolution: Mexico's Experience of
      1912–1917*, No. 04, HG229, K6, 1940, p. 5.
34   Noel Maurer, *The Power and the Money*, pp. 23, 27.
35   *Ibid.*, pp. 49, 54.
36   *Ibid.*, p. 64.
37   Eric Helleiner, *The Making of National Money*, Cornell University Press, 2003, p. 78.
38   Noel Maurer, *The Power and the Money*, pp. 136–7; Edwin Kemmerer, *Inflation and
      Revolution*, pp. 7–8.
39   Simon Prendergast, 'Constitutionalist Cartones', *The Paper Money of Sonora*, published
      online; Noel Maurer, *The Power and the Money*, pp. 149–50; Aurora Gomez-
      Galvariatto, 'The transformation of the Mexican banking system from the Porfiriato
      to 1925', published online by the World Business History Conference, p. 9; Frank
      McLynn, *Villa and Zapata: A Biography of the Mexican Revolution*, Random House,
      2001, pp. 117, 217; Edwin Kemmerer, *Inflation and Revolution*, pp. 9, 16–18, 21, 27, 30,
      32 (Kemmerer states (p. 36) that the depreciation of the peso against the US dollar
      between May 1913 and August 1914 represented a 'fall of over 40 per cent'); 41, 47,
      49, quoting the *New York Times* of 24 August 1915, (Kemmerer, p. 61).
40   Noel Maurer, *The Power and the Money*, p. 146.
41   Frank McLynn, *Villa and Zapata*, pp. 305, 314; Edwin Kemmerer, *Inflation and
      Revolution*, pp. 43, 46; Kemmerer (*Inflation and Revolution*, p. 67) states that the peso
      issued by Villa was already worth as little as 3 US cents in the marketplace in July
      1915, while Villa's finance minister demanded they be accepted at a value of 30 cents.
42   Edwin Kemmerer, *Inflation and Revolution*, pp. 73, 99.
43   *Ibid.*, p. 101.
44   Noel Maurer, *The Power and the Money*, pp. 151–2; Aurora Gomez-Galvariatto, 'The
      transformation of the Mexican banking system from the Porfiriato to 1925', p. 9, n.
      25; Banco de Mexico website.
45   Edwin Kemmerer, *Inflation and Revolution*, p. 107.

46   *Ibid.*, pp. 114–17.

47   *Ibid.*, pp. 119–21.

48   Noel Maurer, *The Power and the Money*, pp. 153, 156; Aurora Gomez-Galvariatto, 'The transformation of the Mexican banking system from the Porfiriato to 1925', p. 9 n. 25; Frank McLynn, *Villa and Zapata*, p. 340; Clause 10, Article 123, Mexican Constitution, constituteproject.org; Edwin Kemmerer, *Inflation and Revolution*, p. 135.

49   Noel Maurer, *The Power and the Money*, pp. 138–44, 153, 166–7, 169; Banco de Mexico website.

50   Jacques Gernet, *A History of Chinese Civilization*, 1996, pp. 324–5, 415.

51   *Ibid.*, p. 540.

52   *Ibid.*, p. 609.

53   Wolfram Eberhard, *A History of China*, pp. 312–13.

54   Debin Ma, 'The rise of a financial revolution in Republican China in 1900–1937: an institutional narrative', Economic History Working Papers, London School of Economics and Political Science, 2016, p. 5.

55   Debin Ma, 'Money and monetary systems in China in the 19th and 20th centuries,' pp. 11–12.

56   Niv Horesh, *Chinese Money in Global Context: Historical Journies Between 600 BCE and 2012*, Stanford University Press, 2013, pp. 156–8, 161.

57   *New Zealand Herald*, 16 October 1911; Debin Ma, 'The rise of a financial revolution in Republican China in 1900–1937', p. 14; Debin Ma, 'Money and monetary systems in China in the 19th and 20th centuries', p. 11.

58   Debin Ma, 'Money and monetary systems in China in the 19th and 20th centuries', p. 14; Niv Horesh, *Chinese Money in Global Context*, p. 195.

59   Forrest Capie, 'Conditions in which very rapid inflation has appeared'.

60   Bokarev et al., *Monetary Circulation of Russia*, Bank of Russia, 2010, pp. 235–6; Steve H. Hanke, Lars Jonung and Kurt Schuler, *Russian Currency and Finance: A Currency Board Approach to Reform*. Routledge, 2005. p. 43.

61   Bokarev et al., *Monetary Circulation of Russia*, pp. 239, 241, 247.

62   *Ibid.*, p. 252.

63   *Ibid.*, pp. 265–6.

64   *Ibid.*, pp. 262–7.

65   *Ibid.*, p. 273; Hanke, Jonung and Schuler, *Russian Currency and Finance*, p. 150.

66   Bokarev et al., *Monetary Circulation of Russia*, p. 277.

67   *Ibid.*, p. 278; Hanke, Jonung and Schuler, *Russian Currency and Finance*, p. 150.

68   Bokarev et al., *Monetary Circulation of Russia*, pp. 286–91.

69   Hanke, Jonung and Schuler, *Russian Currency and Finance*, pp. 44, 151–3.

70   *Ibid.*, pp. 154.

Chapter 3

1   Lucan, *Pharsalia*, trans. Robert Graves, Penguin Classics, 1956, p. 37.

2   *Ibid.*, p. 71.

3   Forrest Capie, 'Conditions in which very rapid inflation has appeared'.

4   Ben Tarnoff, *A Counterfeiter's Paradise: The Wicked Lives and Surprising Adventures of Three Early American Moneymakers*, Penguin, 2012., p. 195; Karl Rhodes, 'The

counterfeiting weapon: attacks against American currency began in 1776', Federal Reserve Bank of Richmond, *Econ Focus*, issue 1Q, pp. 34-37, 2012.

5   John Chown, *A History of Money from AD 800*, p. 247.

6   *Ibid.*, p. 249; gold convertible currency known as 'yellowbacks' continued to circulate on the west coast, where gold-rich California had declared for the Union at the beginning of the war; Hugh Rockoff, 'How long did it take the United States to become an optimal currency area?', *National Bureau of Economic Research*, 124, April 2000.

7   Forrest Capie, 'Conditions in which very rapid inflation has appeared'.

8   Kwasi Kwarteng, *War and Gold: A Five-Hundred-Year History of Empires, Adventures, and Debt*, Public Affairs, 2014, p. 72.

9   Ben Tarnoff, *A Counterfeiter's Paradise*, pp. 177-9; Karl Rhodes, 'The counterfeiting weapon'.

10   Ben Tarnoff, *A Counterfeiter's Paradise*, p. 206.

11   *Ibid.*, p. 207.

12   *Ibid.*, pp. 215–16.

13   *Ibid.*, pp. 215–16.

14   *Ibid.*, p. 217.

15   *Ibid.*, pp. 225–6; Forrest Capie, 'Conditions in which very rapid inflation has appeared'.

16   Ben Tarnoff, *A Counterfeiter's Paradise*, pp. 230, 232, 249.

17   Inflationdata.com, Confederate inflation; Forrest Capie, 'Conditions in which very rapid inflation has appeared'.

18   Hanke, Jonung and Shuler, *Russian Currency and Finance*, p. 146.

19   Bokarev et al., *Monetary Circulation of Russia*, pp. 252, 254.

20   *Ibid.*, p. 262.

21   *Ibid.*, p. 258.

22   Hanke, Jonung and Schuler, *Russian Currency and Finance*, p. 149.

23   *Ibid.*, p. 148; Bokarev et al., *Monetary Circulation of Russia*, p. 255.

24   John Chown, *A History of Money from AD 800*, pp. 268–9; Hanke, Jonung and Schuler, *Russian Currency and Finance*, p. 149.

25   Adam LeBor, *Tower of Basel: The Shadowy History of the Secret Bank that Runs the World*, Public Affairs, 2013. p. 55, states that Spain had the fifth largest gold reserves after the US, France, Britain and the Soviet Union.

26   Daniel Kowalsky, *Stalin and the Spanish Civil War*, Columbia University Press, 2004.

27   *Ibid.*

28   Antony Beevor, *The Battle for Spain: The Spanish Civil War*, Penguin Books, 2006, pp. 154, 174–5; Martín-Aceña et al. (see n. 30 below) p. 12 suggest that 174 tons rather than 124 tons of gold were sent to France. It should be noted that there is a distinct lack of material in English on monetary trends in the Spanish Civil War. The author is almost entirely dependent on the excellent work of Martín-Aceña and team.

29   Antony Beevor, *The Battle for Spain*, pp. 365, 382; Adam LeBor, *Tower of Basel*, p. 55.

30   Pablo Martín-Aceña, Elena Martínez Ruiz and María A. Pons, 'War and economics: Spanish Civil War finances revisited', *European Review of Economic History*, Vol. 16, No. 2, 2012, p. 3.

31   *Ibid.*, pp. 8–9.

32   *Ibid.*, p. 9.

33   *Ibid.*, p. 9.

34   *Ibid.*, p. 14.

35   *Ibid.*, pp. 10, 15–16.

36   *Ibid.*, p. 17.

37   *Ibid.*, pp. 22–4; Adam LeBor, *Tower of Basel*, p. 56.

38   Stathis N. Kalyvas and Nicholas Sambanis, 'Bosnia's Civil War', *Understanding Civil War*, Yale University, 2005, pp. 192–3; Vladimir Gligorov, 'Stabilisation of a War Economy', Institute for Advanced Studies, Vienna, 1995.

39   World Heritage Encyclopedia, self.gutenberg.org/articles/eng/Hyperinflation; Steve H. Hanke, '1997: A field report from Sarajevo and Pale', *Central Banking* 12, No. 3, 1996, pp. 36–40.; Misha Glenny, *The Fall of Yugoslavia: The Third Balkan War*, Penguin Books, 1974, p. 219; Steve Hanke and Nicholas Krus, 'World Hyperinflations', Cato Working Paper, Cato Institute, pp. 4–6 set out the difficulties in tracking down the data on Bosnia's hyperinflation; Warren Coats, *One Currency for Bosnia*, Jameson Book Inc., 2007, pp. 24, 44.

40   United States Department of the Treasury, 'Reporting Rates of Exchange', Bureau of the Fiscal Service, 1992–95.

41   Merima Zupcevic and Fikret Čaušević, 'Case study: Bosnia and Herzegovina', McGill University and the World Bank, 2009, p. 15 (quoting the Bosnian Statistics Agency and others).

42   Warren Coats, *One Currency for Bosnia*, pp. 10–11, 25. The range of Coats' experience in helping to resolve some of the thorniest currency problems in recent decades is extraordinary. One can only hope that the IMF has bottled his knowledge and experience to be uncorked on the occasion of future crises.

43   *Ibid.*, p. 44.

44   *Ibid.*, pp. 52–5. See also Coats for a detailed explanation of the debates surrounding the non-cash payment systems and their reform.

45   *Ibid.*, pp. 85–6; 221 UN press release SC /6755; Central Bank law article 42.2 and 42.4 quoted by Coats, pp. 218–19, 221.

46   *Ibid.*, p. 225.

47   *Ibid.*, pp. 222, 241.

48   Kurt Schuler, 'Introduction to currency boards' in 'Monetary Politics in Post-Conflict Countries: Restoring Credibility' (archived webpage), Working Paper, American University, 2004, pp. 8–10. UN Dayton Agreement, Annex 4, Article VII; Warren Coats, *One Currency for Bosnia*, pp. 33–4, 226.

Chapter 4

1   Richard Roberts, *Saving the City: The Great Financial Crisis of 1914*, Oxford University Press, 2013, p. 67.

2   *Ibid.*, p. 73.

3   Liaquat Ahamed, *Lords of Finance: 1929, the Great Depression and the Bankers who Broke the World*, Windmill Books, 2010, pp. 31, 43, 44; Richard Roberts, *Saving the City*, p. 80.

4   Richard Roberts, *Saving the City*, p. 116.

5   *Ibid.*, pp. 123, 125.

6   *Ibid.*, p. 233.

7   *Ibid.*, p. 172.

8   *Ibid.*, p. 172; John Powell, *A History of the Gold Standard*, Bank of Canada, 2005, p. 37; M. Bordo, A. Reddish and R. Shearer, 'Canada's monetary system in historical perspective: two faces of the exchange rate regime', University of British Columbia working paper, 1999, p. 19.

9   Charles P. Kindleberger, *A Financial History of Western Europe*, p. 294; Adam Fergusson, *When Money Dies: The Nightmare of the Weimar Hyper-inflation*, Old Street Publishing, 2010, p. 9.

10   Although, Gerd Hardach, *The First World War, 1914–1918*, Vol. 2, Uni of California Press, 1981 (p. 140) says convertibility was suspended on 4 August in Germany. Richard Roberts, *Saving the City* (pp. 202–3), also cites 31 July as the date of suspension of convertibility; Adam Fergusson, *When Money Dies*, p. 9.

11   J.M. Keynes, *Indian Currency and Finance*, Cambridge University Press for the Royal Economic Society, 1911, p. 15 n. 1.

12   Richard Roberts, *Saving the City*, p. 199.

13   Liaquat Ahamed, *Lords of Finance*, pp. 69–71; Richard Roberts, *Saving the City*, p. 201, and on p. 199 states that specie payment – i.e. convertibility – was suspended on 6 August.

14   Richard Roberts, *Saving the City*, p. 199.

15   Jonathan Kirshner, *Currency and Coercion: The Political Economy of International Monetary Power*, Princeton University Press, 1995, p. 87.

16   *Ibid.*, p. 89.

17   *Ibid.*

18   J.M. Keynes, *The Economic Consequences of the Peace*, pp. 271, 278; Liaquat Ahamed, *Lords of Finance*, p. 87, and p. 100 states that money supply doubled in Britain, tripled in France but increased four-fold in Germany. Ahamed also notes that the franc had dropped from 5 to the dollar at the start of the war to 15 in the early 1920s and 27 to the dollar in March 1924 (pp. 203–4).

19   J.M. Keynes, *The Economic Consequences of the Peace*, pp. 244–5.

20   *Ibid.*; Adam Fergusson, *When Money Dies*, pp. 1, 10.

21   J.M. Keynes, *The Economic Consequences of the Peace*, pp. 241–2.

22   Liaquat Ahamed, *Lords of Finance*, p. 158; according to Kwasi Kwarteng, *War and Gold* (p. 101) there were 2 billion marks in circulation in 1914 and 27.5 billion marks in circulation in November 1918. Adam Fergusson, *When Money Dies* (p. 33), records 2.7 billion marks in circulation at the beginning of the war and 27 billion at its end. The post-war volumes issued continued to soar.

23   Adam Fergusson, *When Money Dies*, pp. 19, 23.

24   Richard Roberts, *Saving the City*, p. 205.

25   Şevket Pamuk, *A Monetary History of the Ottoman Empire*, pp. 222–3.

26   *Ibid.*, p. 224.

27   Bokarev et al., *Monetary Circulation of Russia*, pp. 219–20.

28   Hanke, Jonung and Schuler, *Russian Currency and Finance*, p. 43.

29   Jonathan Kirshner, *Currency and Coercion* (p. 88), suggests that gold cover for ruble notes had declined to 8 per cent by the time of the revolution.

30   *Ibid.*

31   Bokarev et al., *Monetary Circulation of Russia*, p. 223.

32   Richard Roberts, *Saving the City*, pp. 215–16.

33   *Ibid.*, p. 173; Hugh Rockoff, 'Until it's over, over there: the US economy in World War 1', Working Paper 10580, *National Bureau of Economic Research*, 2004, p. 4; Homer Joseph Dodge, JSTOR archive.

34   Richard Roberts, *Saving the City*, p. 174.

35   Liaquat Ahamed, *Lords of Finance*, pp. 91, 100; Ed Conway, *The Summit: Bretton Woords, 1944: J.M. Keynes and the Reshaping of the Global Economy*, Pegasus Book, 2016, p. 70; Hugh Rockoff, 'Until it's over, over there', pp. 5–6.

36   Barry Eichengreen, *Exorbitant Privilege: The Rise and Fall of the Dollar*, Ocford University Press, 2011, pp. 26–7, 32, 37.

37   Richard Roberts, *Saving the City*, p. 206.

38   Maartje M. Abbenhuis, *The Art of Staying Neutral: The Netherlands in the First World War, 1914–1918*, Amsterdam University Press, 2006, p. 69.

39   *Ibid.*, pp. 160, 168.

40   Although R. Matthee, W. Floor and P. Clawson, *The Monetary History of Iran*, I.B. Taurus, 2013 (p. 259), describes continuing commercial rivalries between British and Russian banks based in Iran.

41   J.M. Keynes, *The Economic Consequences of the Peace*, pp. 209 n. 1, 214, 227.

42   Text of the Financial Agreement of 27 August 1918 between Russia and Germany, Article 3; J.M. Keynes, *The Economic Consequences of the Peace*, p. 114 and footnote.

43   'A Brief History of Belgian Banknotes and Coins', National Bank of Belgium website.

Chapter 5

1   J.M. Keynes, *The Economic Consequences of the Peace*, pp. 170–2; Liaquat Ahamed, *Lords of Finance*, p. 119.

2   J.M. Keynes, *The Economic Consequences of the Peace*, p. 173.

3   Adam Fergusson, *When Money Dies*, pp. 80–3.

4   Eric Helleiner, *The Making of National Money*, p. 158.

5   Jonathan Kirshner, *Currency and Coercion*, p. 222; Adam Fergusson, *When Money Dies*, pp. 89, 112, 115, 120, 122, 167, 175.

6   Adam Fergusson, *When Money Dies*, pp. 195–202.

7   Liaquat Ahamed, *Lords of Finance*, pp. 120–1; Brian Johnson, *The Politics of Money*, John Murray, 1970, p. 64.

8   Steve Hanke and Nicholas Krus, 'The Hanke–Krus hyperinflation table', p, The Official Monetary and Financial Institutions Forum (OMFIF), October 2012.

9   Hjalmar Schacht, *The End of Reparations: The Economic Consequences of the War*, J. Cape, 1931, pp. 148–9; Brian Johnson, *The Politics of Money*, p. 66; Adam LeBor, *Tower of Basel*, p. 7; Charles P. Kindleberger, *A Financial History of Western Europe* (p. 326), states that the exchange rate of the rentenmark to the reichsmark was in fact 1:1 billion, not a trillion, as does Johnson (p. 66). See also Kindleberger (p. 326) for an interesting debate as to who exactly came up with the idea of the rentenmark.

10   Hjalmar Schacht, *The End of Reparations*, p. 159; Liaquat Ahamed, *Lords of Finance*, p. 186; Adam Fergusson, *When Money Dies*, p. 206.

11   Liaquat Ahamed, *Lords of Finance*, pp. 189–91. Charles P. Kindleberger, *A Financial History of Western Europe*, p. 326. Adam Fergusson, *When Money Dies*, pp. 206–9, 216–17, 210.

12   H. Clark Johnson, *Gold, France and the Great Depression 1919–1932*,Yale University Press, 1998; Germany's Bundesbank continues to place great emphasis on gold: as at 2015, two-thirds of the country's reserves were held in gold – the second largest gold reserve in the world after the US. Bundesbank website, 7 October 2015.
13   Liaquat Ahamed, *Lords of Finance*, p. 481.
14   Adam LeBor, *Tower of Basel*, p. 20.
15   Steve Hanke and Nicholas Krus, 'The Hanke–Krus hyperinflation table'.
16   Eric Helleiner, *The Making of National Money*, p. 145.
17   Luis W. Pauly, 'The League of Nations and the foreshadowing of the International Monetary Fund', *Essays in International Finance*, No. 201, Princeton University, December 1996, pp. 14-15; Steve Hanke and Nicholas Krus, 'The Hanke–Krus hyperinflation table'; Eric Helleiner, *The Making of National Money*, p. 157; Adam Fergusson, *When Money Dies*, pp. 93-5.
18   Liaquat Ahamed, *Lords of Finance*, p. 89.
19   www.voxeu.org/article/did-france-cause-great-depression; Liaquat Ahamed, *Lords of Finance*, p. 377.
20   Mark Metzler, *Lever of Empire:The International Gold Standard and the Crisis of Liberalism in Prewar Japan*, University of California Press, 2006, p. 133.
21   Forrest Capie, 'The development and institution of the International Financial Architecture', *Elsevier Encyclopedia*, 2010.
22   For unemployment rates see: Unemployment Statistics from 1881 to the Present Day, Office of National Statistics.The data shows that while unemployment from 1881 to 1920 was in single figures, from 1921 to 1939 it was in double figures, peaking at 22 per cent.
23   www.gold.org/sites/default/files/documents/1925apr28.pdf.
24   H. Clark Johnson, *Gold, France and the Great Depression*, pp. 3, 135.
25   *Ibid.*, p. 4.
26   *Ibid.*, pp. 46, 48.
27   Liaquat Ahamed, *Lords of Finance*, p. 374.
28   *Ibid.*, pp. 428–9.
29   H. Clark Johnson, *Gold, France and the Great Depression*, p. 145.
30   Mark Metzler, *Lever of Empire*, p. 237; Liaquat Ahamed, *Lords of Finance*, pp. 432–3.
31   Ed Conway, *The Summit*, p. 82.
32   Mark Metzler, *Lever of Empire*, pp. 102, 104.
33   *Ibid.*, pp. 104–5.
34   *Ibid.*, pp. 123–4.
35   *Ibid.*, p. 123.
36   *Ibid.*, pp. 19, 131.
37   *Ibid.*, p. 142.
38   *Ibid.*, pp. 230–1.
39   *Ibid.*, pp. 246–7.

Chapter 6

1   Peter Spufford, *Money and its Use in Medieval Europe*, Cambridge University Press, 1988, p. 11
2   Glyn Davies, *History of Money*, p. 125.

3   Peter Spufford, *Money and its Use in Medieval Europe*, pp. 173–4.

4   Bokarev et al., *Monetary Circulation of Russia*, pp. 46–7.

5   *Ibid.*, p. 47.

6   Şevket Pamuk, *A Monetary History of the Ottoman Empire*, p. 25.

7   Karl Rhodes, 'The counterfeiting weapon'; Forrest Capie, 'Conditions in which very rapid inflation has appeared'.

8   Eric P. Newman, 'The successful British counterfeiting of American paper money during the American Revolution', *British Numismatic Journal*, Vol. 29, 1958.

9   Karl Rhodes, 'The counterfeiting weapon'.

10   Eric P. Newman, 'The successful British counterfeiting of American paper money during the American Revolution'.

11   'An address of the Congress to the inhabitants of the United States of America', Minutes of 8 May 1778, *Journals of the Continental Congress*, cited in Eric P. Newman, 'The successful British counterfeiting of American paper money during the American Revolution'.

12   Stephen D. Dillaye, *Assignats and Mandats*, p. 33, and the story is also quoted in *The Moreton Bay Observer*, 30 June 1849, citing a report in *The Gateshead Observer*, although the latter report differs from the former in the location of the counterfeiting operation.

13   Stephen D. Dillaye, *Assignats and Mandats*, p. 33.

14   *Ibid.*, p. 34.

15   Rebecca Spang, *Stuff and Money in the Time of the French Revolution*, p. 191.

16   *Ibid.*, p. 180.

17   Johann Wolfgang von Goethe, *Campaign in France*, Ricardo Cunha Mattos Portella Publishing, 1849, p. 82, 91; Eugene N. White, 'Measuring the French revolution's inflation: the tableaux de dépréciation', *Histoire & Mesure*, pp. 249, 255.

18   Bokarev et al., *Monetary Circulation of Russia*, pp. 151–2; Philipe Comte de Segur, *A History of Napoleon's Expedition to Russia*, Project Gutenberg, 2006.

19   *Montreal Gazette*, 14 October 1935.

20   Andor Klay, 'Hungarian counterfeit francs: a case of post-World War I political sabotage', *Slavic Review* 33, No. 1, 1974, pp. 107–13.

21   *Montreal Gazette*, 14 October 1935; The Advocate (Tasmania), 26 August 1926.

22   Arnold Krammer, 'Russian Counterfeit Dollars – A case of early soviet espionage', Slavic Review 30, No. 4, 1971, pp. 762–73.

23   Vladimir Petrov, *Money and Conquest: Allied Occupation Currencies in World War II*, John Hopkins Press, 1967, pp. 36–7.

24   *Ibid.*, p. 44.

25   Craig Karmin, 'Biography of the Dollar', *New York: Crown Business*, 2008, p. 4, and www.federalreserve.gov/newsevents/press/other/20061025a.htm.

26   www.federalreserve.gov/paymentsystems/coin_currcircvalue.htm.

27   www.independent.ie/irish-news/workers-party-boss-linked-to-counterfeit-super-dollars-26243360.html.

28   'The Superdollar Plot', *Panorama*, BBC, 20 June 2004 [transcript at: news.bbc.co.uk/nol/shared/spl/hi/programmes/panorama/transcripts/superdollar.txt].

29   www.federalreserve.gov/boarddocs/RptCongress/counterfeit/default.htm#toc6.5.7.

30   Interpol website: Orange Notice 'To warn of an event, a person, an object or a process representing an imminent threat and danger to persons or property.'

Chapter 7

1   Jonathan Kirshner, *Currency and Coercion*, pp. 51–3.
2   Mark Metzler, *Lever of Empire*, p. 264; *Ibid.*, pp. 59–60
3   Jonathan Kirshner, *Currency and Coercion*, p. 60.
4   *Ibid.*, p. 57
5   *Ibid.*, p. 60.
6   *Ibid.*, pp. 54–7.
7   *Ibid.*, p. 91.
8   Peter Pugh, *The Highest Perfection: A History of De La Rue*, Aubrey Books, 2011, p. 115.
9   Mark Metzler, *Lever of Empire*, p. 264.
10   Gregg Huff and Shinobu Majima, 'Financing Japan's World War II occupation of South East Asia', *The Journal of Economic History*, 73, No. 4, 2013, p. 9.
11   Marilyn Longmuir, *The Money Trail: Burmese Currencies in Crisis, 1937–1947*, p. 33; Gregg Huff and Shinobu Majima, 'Financing Japan's World War II occupation of South East Asia', pp. 6, 22 and Table 5.
12   Mark Metzler, *Lever of Empire*, p. 264; Marilyn Longmuir, *The Money Trail*, pp. 31–4; Gregg Huff and Shinobu Majima, 'Financing Japan's World War II occupation of South East Asia', Table 5.
13   Kurt Schuler, 'Episodes from Asian Monetary History: A Brief History of Hong Kong Monetary Standards', *Asian Monetary Monitor*, Vol. 12, No. 5, September–October 1989.
14   Marilyn Longmuir, *The Money Trail*, pp. 8–13.
15   *Ibid.*, p. 43. Longmuir notes that in April 1945, ten times as many rupees were in circulation than were circulating in May 1942. By August 1945, 5.6 billion rupees were in circulation.
16   *Ibid.*, pp. 30, 41, 54–7, 85.
17   *Ibid.*, p. 46.
18   *Ibid.*, pp. 78, 89.
19   *Ibid.*, pp. 73, 78.
20   *Ibid.*, pp. 88, 96.
21   *Ibid.*, pp. 112–13.
22   *Ibid.*, pp. 80, 82.
23   Mark Metzler, *Lever of Empire*, p. 266; Bank for International Settlements, 15th Annual Report, 1945, p. 67.
24   Mark Metzler, *Lever of Empire*, p. 267; Kwasi Kwarteng, *War and Gold*, pp. 194–5.
25   Mark Metzler, *Lever of Empire*, pp. 258, 264.
26   Ed Conway, *The Summit*, p. 100.
27   Vladimir Petrov, *Money and Conquest*, pp. 23–5.
28   Adam LeBor, *Tower of Basel*, pp. 53, 60.
29   Ed Conway, *The Summit*, pp. 93–4; Adam LeBor, *Tower of Basel*, pp. 59–61.
30   Filippo Occhino, Kim Oosterlinck and Eugene White, 'How Occupied France financed its own exploitation in World War II', NBER Working Paper 12137, pp. 17–18.
31   Adam LeBor, *Tower of Basel*, p. 85.
32   Vladimir Petrov, *Money and Conquest*, p. 28 and n. 12; Adam LeBor, *Tower of Basel*, pp. 84, 114.

33   Bank for International Settlements, 15th Annual Report, 1945, p. 24.

34   Charles P. Kindleberger, *A Financial History of Western Europe*, p. 404, quoting Pierre Cathala, Finance Minister of the Vichy French Government, and p. 406; Filippo Occhino, Kim Oosterlinck and Eugene White, 'How Occupied France financed its own exploitation in World War II', p. 9.

35   Vladimir Petrov, *Money and Conquest*, p. 32.

36   Occhino, Oosterlinck and White, 'How Occupied France financed its own exploitation in World War II' (p. 8) points out that it was forbidden to spend Reichskreditkassenscheine in Germany. Nevertheless, other sources suggest they were repatriated to Germany, perhaps to be traded there for reichsmarks.

37   Vladimir Petrov, *Money and Conquest*, pp. 33–4.

38   Charles P. Kindleberger, *A Financial History of Western Europe*, p. 405.

39   Vladimir Petrov, *Money and Conquest*, pp. 35–6. Note: on p. 31 Petrov states that the net debt rose during the course of the war from 3 billion to 40 billion reichsmarks. It is not altogether clear whether Petrov means only the net debt recorded in the clearing accounts, or really does think this is the total of Germany's net debt. Other sources record the net debt as much greater: Charles P. Kindleberger, *A Financial History of Western Europe*, p. 405, records a net debt of 400 billion reichsmarks by the end of the war. The Bank for International Settlements 14th Annual Report (p. 78), issued following the defeat of the Axis powers, records an estimated net debt of 400 billion reichsmarks.

40   Bank for International Settlements, 15th Annual Report, 1945, pp. 67, 91.

41   Jonathan Kirshner, *Currency and Coercion*, p. 144.

42   Bank for International Settlements, 15th Annual Report, 1945, pp. 85–6, 103; Trade and Payments Agreement between His Majesty's Government and the Government of the Turkish Republic, 4 May 1945, Article 5.

43   P.J. Symes, 'Banknotes and banking in Ethiopia and Abyssinia', pjsymes.com.au, November 2013.

44   *Ibid.*

45   Vladimir Petrov, *Money and Conquest*, pp. 44–5.

46   *Ibid.*, p. 47.

47   *Ibid.*, pp. 47, 52.

48   Charles P. Kindleberger, *A Financial History of Western Europe*, p. 407.

49   Vladimir Petrov, *Money and Conquest*, p. 53; Frank Southard, *Some Currency and Exchange Experiences*, Department of Economics, Princeton University, 1946, p. 10.

50   Vladimir Petrov, *Money and Conquest*, p. 76.

51   *Ibid.*, p. 77; Frank Southard, *Some Currency and Exchange Experiences*, p. 7.

52   Vladimir Petrov, *Money and Conquest*, pp. 78, 83, 84; Charles P. Kindleberger, *A Financial History of Western Europe*, p. 407.

53   Vladimir Petrov, *Money and Conquest*, pp. 87–8.

54   *Ibid.*, pp. 90, 93.

55   *Ibid.*, pp. 94, 96.

56   *Ibid.*, p. 97.

57   *Ibid.*, pp. 99–100.

58   Eugene White, 'Making the French pay: the costs and consequences of the Napoleonic reparations', NBER Working Paper series, Working Paper 7438, p. 27.

59   Vladimir Petrov, *Money and Conquest*, p. 102; Jonathan Kirshner, *Currency and Coercion*, p. 239. See also Kirshner pp. 240–2 for opportunities missed by the US authorities to support the Italian government at this critical time.

60   Banque de France, The Franc Zone Fact Sheet, No. 127, July 2010.

61   *Ibid.*

62   Bank for International Settlements, 15th Annual Report, 1945, p. 59.

63   Vladimir Petrov, *Money and Conquest*, p. 63.

64   *Ibid.*, pp. 55–7.

65   *Ibid.*, pp. 58–9.

66   *Ibid.*, p. 60.

67   Charles P. Kindleberger, *A Financial History of Western Europe*, pp. 410–11; Bank for International Settlements, 15th Annual Report, 1945, p. 61.

68   Frank Southard, *Some Currency and Exchange Experiences*, p. 3.

69   Bank for International Settlements, 15th Annual Report, 1945, p. 89.

70   *Ibid.*, pp. 63–5.

71   Frank Southard, *Some European Currency and Exchange Experiences*.

72   Brian Johnson, *The Politics of Money*, p. 141.

73   Vladimir Petrov, *Money and Conquest*, pp. 108–10.

74   *Ibid.*, p. 113.

75   *Ibid.*, p. 111.

76   *Ibid.*, pp. 112–13.

77   *Ibid.*, p. 114.

78   *Ibid.*, p. 117.

79   *Ibid.*, pp. 116–17.

80   *Ibid.*, p. 118.

81   *Ibid.*, pp. 122, 126–7.

82   Senate Sub-Committee hearing on Government Operations Abroad, 20 and 21 October 1953, p. 26.

83   Vladimir Petrov, *Money and Conquest*, p. 194; Charles P. Kindleberger, *A Financial History of Western Europe*, p. 407.

84   Vladimir Petrov, *Money and Conquest*, p. 224 citing clause 20 of the Allied agreement on Certain Additional Requirements to be imposed on Germany of September 1945. Benn Steil, *The Battle of Bretton Woods*, p. 274 (quoting Petrov) suggests that the Soviet side issued nearly 80 billion occupation marks – nearly eight times the amount issued by the Western Allies.

85   Senate Sub-Committee hearing on Government Operations Abroad 20 and 21 October 1953, p. 18.

86   Vladimir Petrov, *Money and Conquest*, pp. 214–15.

87   *Ibid.*, pp. 239–40; Stephen Meardon, 'On Kindleberger and Hegemony, From Berlin to MIT and Back', Bowdoin College, 2013, p. 7.

88   Stephen Meardon, 'On Kindleberger and Hegemony', p. 9.

89   Vladimir Petrov, *Money and Conquest*, p. 241.

90   Adam LeBor, *Tower of Basel*, p. 25.

91   Vladimir Petrov, *Money and Conquest*, p. 173.

92   *Ibid.*, p. 252, later states that the ruble was overvalued by as much as 4,000 per cent. Petrov's personal view on the Soviet regime was hostile and some of his positions have to be taken with a pinch of salt.

93   Vladimir Petrov, *Money and Conquest*, pp. 173–8; Brian Johnson, *The Politics of Money*, plate facing p. 50 and p. 140–1 footnote ‡, where Johnson records the number as 100 quadrillion but describes the value as 100 quintillion.

94   Steve Hanke and Nicholas Krus, 'The Hanke–Krus hyperinflation table'; Forrest Capie, 'Conditions in which very rapid inflation has appeared'.

95   Vladimir Petrov, *Money and Conquest*, pp. 186–90.

96   Charles P. Kindleberger, *A Financial History of Western Europe*, p. 413, claims the notes were printed in England. Although Kindleberger was directly involved in the post-war currency arrangements for Germany and Austria, he may have got this wrong as other sources suggest the notes were indeed printed in the US. Petrov was in Western Europe during the planning for monetary reform but certainly had no first-hand involvement in the operation and yet it seems he got it right while Kindleberger was in error. The notes were printed in America, consistent with the agreement between Britain and the US, according to which new notes for liberated, friendly states would be produced in Britain, while those for conquered Axis states would be produced in America. The contract was indeed awarded to the American Banknote Company (ABN). It has been suggested to me that the confusion may have its origins in the fact that ABN at that time owned the British company Bradbury Wilkinson, which may have been involved in producing some part of the Operation Bird Dog currency for its American owners.

97   Vladimir Petrov, *Money and Conquest*, pp. 248–9; Kwasi Kwarteng, *War and Gold*, p. 185.

98   Vladimir Petrov, *Money and Conquest*, p.245.

99   Stephen Meardon, 'On Kindleberger and Hegemony', p. 13.

100   *Ibid.*

101   For a comprehensive list of the participants, see Kurt Schuler and Mark Bernkopf, 'Who was at Bretton Woods?', Center for Financial Stability, 1 July 2014.

102   The second institution – the World Bank – was tasked with the reconstruction of countries whose economies had been destroyed by the war. Monetary issues rested not with the World Bank, but with the International Monetary Fund.

102   Ed Conway, *The Summit*, p. 131; Forrest Capie, 'The Development and Evolution of International Financial Architecture'.

103   Ed Conway, *The Summit*, pp. 131–2.

104   *Ibid.*, pp. 169, 369; Brian Johnson, *The Politics of Money*, p. 118.

105   Benn Steil, *The Battle of Bretton Woods*, p. 195.

106   US dollar reserves peaked in 1949 at US $24 billion worth of the reserve metal. Kwasi Kwarteng, *War and Gold*, 2014, p. 167.

107   Ed Conway, *The Summit*, pp. 170–1.

108   Benn Steil, *The Battle of Bretton Woods*, p. 257.

109   Ed Conway, *The Summit*, pp. 172, 224, 232; Benn Steil, *The Battle of Bretton Woods*, p. 229.

110   Ed Conway, *The Summit*, pp. 253, 265; Benn Steil, *The Battle of Bretton Woods*, p. 234.

111   Ed Conway, *The Summit*, pp. 218–20; Ben Steil, *The Battle of Bretton Woods*, p. 218.

112   Ed Conway, *The Summit*, pp. 192–3, 207.

113   *Ibid.*, p. 223.

114   Barry Eichengreen, *Exorbitant Privilege*, p. 41, states that Britain lost $1 million of reserves in the first month, nearly double the amount quoted by Steil.

115   Benn Steil, *The Battle of Bretton Woods*, p. 310; Kwasi Kwarteng, *War and Gold*, p. 174; Brian Johnson, *The Politics of Money*, p. 133.

116   Benn Steil, *The Battle of Bretton Woods*, p. 331; Brian Johnson, *The Politics of Money*, p. 134; Forrest Capie, 'The development and evolution of the International Financial Architecture'.

117   Kwasi Kwarteng, *War and Gold*, p. 158.

118   Barry Eichengreen, *Exorbitant Privilege*, p. 53.

Chapter 8

1   One suggestion is that the value of dollars issued exceeded the gold cover by 300 per cent.

2   United States State Department, 'Nixon and the End of the Bretton Woods System 1971–1973', *Milestones in the History of US Foreign Relations*, Office of the Historian; Forrest Capie, 'The development and evolution of the International Financial Architecture'.

3   Tom Riddell, 'Inflationary impact of the Vietnam War', *Vietnam Generation*, Vol. 1, Article 4, 1989, table 3; Institute for Economics and Peace, 'Economic Consequences of War on the US Economy', p. 12; UK Public Spending, 'Past Spending', www.ukpublicspending.co.uk/past_spending.

4   Ed Conway, *The Summit*, p. 381; Benn Steil, The Battle for Bretton Woods, pp. 258, 333, 339.

5   Haggai Erlich in Paul Henze, *Eritrea's War: Confrontation, International Response, Outcome, Prospects*, Shama Books, 2001, preface.

6   Paul Henze, *Eritrea's War*, pp. 10–11.

7   Ross Herbert, 'The end of the Eritrean exception?', The South African Institute of International Affairs, 2002, p. 8.

8   Bereket Habte Selassie, 'Dreams that turned to nightmares: the Ethio–Eritrean War of 1998–2000 and its aftermath', in *The Search for Peace: The Conflict between Ethiopia and Eritrea*, ed. Leenco Lata, Proceedings of Scholarly Conference on the Ethiopia–Eritrea Conflict, Oslo, 6–7 July 2006, www.fafo.no/media/com_netsukii/20014.pdf, p. 26. The author had been party to the conversations with the Eritreans during which the latter complained about the currency issue.

9   Seyoum Yohannes Tesfay, 'Eritrea–Ethiopia Arbitration: a "cure" based on neither diagnosis nor prognosis', *Mizan Law Review*, Vol. 6, No. 2, 2012, pp. 164–99.

10   HaileSelassie Girmay, 'Ethiopia–Eritrea border conflict: the role nakfa played', issued by the Ethiopian Embassy to the United Kingdom. This article obviously puts across the Ethiopian point of view. Bereket Habte Selassie, 'Dreams that turned to nightmares', p. 27; Leenco Lata, 'The causes, mediation and settlement of the Ethio–Eritria Conflict' in *The Search for Peace: The Conflict between Ethiopia and Eritrea*.

11   Ross Herbert, 'The end of the Eritrean exception?', p. 17; IMF figures quoted by Temesgen Kifle in 'Can border demarcation help Eritrea to reverse the general slowdown in growth?', University of Bremen, 2004, pp. 11, 12; IMF Eritrea, selected issues report, ISCR, 2003, pp. 19, 20.

12   International Monetary Fund – Ethiopia, selected issues report, 2005, p. 45.

13   Ross Herbert, 'The end of the Eritrean exception?', pp. 9, 13, 16.

14   Manabu Fuijmara, 'Post conflict reconstruction of the Afghan economy', Asian Development Bank, 2004, p. 36, suggests that it was the Taleban who ordered banknotes with pre-1996 serial numbers and issued them in the north of the country.

Since the north was largely controlled by the opposition Northern Alliance, it would seem difficult for the Taleban to accomplish this with ease. Moreover, what exactly would have been the purpose of such an operation in the north? The Taleban would have been able to top up their finances by issuing such notes anywhere else in the country with greater ease. Journalistic reporting of the time takes the view that it was the Northern Alliance that was inserting these new covert stocks into the economy.

15   Michael Griffin, 'Money Matters in Afghanistan', *Los Angeles Times*, 6 January 2002.

16   Anon., 'The Politics of Trade', *The Economist*, 28 February 2002; Author's personal discussions in Kabul and Washington with IMF and US Treasury officials; Charles Recknagel, 'Pakistan: Afghan currency blown by political winds', *Radio Free Europe Online*, 29 October 2001; Tom Cleveland, 'Do you know the history of the Afghani currency?', *News Central Asia*, 30 November 2012; Asia Development Bank, report on the reconstruction of Afghanistan's economy, p. 77.

17   Marc Kaufman, 'Afghans advised to unify currency', *The Washington Post*, 30 January 2002.

18   Liz Sly, 'Afghans see money value turn to dust', *Chicago Tribune*, 29 October 2002; Anon., 'Afghanistan switching to new currency', *Voice of America Online*, 22 October 2002; Anon., 'Afghan currency replacement delayed', *Radio Free Europe Online*, 5 December 2002; Asia Development Bank, report on the reconstruction of Afghanistan's economy, pp. 37, 39, 197.

19   Eric Ellis, 'Afghanistan gets back to business', *Euromoney*, 4 September 2006; US Bureau of Fiscal Services, US Treasury exchange rate figures.

20   Bureau of the Fiscal Service, US Treasury, Treasury reporting rates of exchange online.

21   Simon Thorburn Gray and Jacob Nell, *A New Currency for Iraq*, Central Banking, 2005, p. 5.

22   Mervyn King, *The End of Alchemy: Money, Banking, and the Future of the Global Economy*, WW Norton & Company, 2016, p. 238.

23   Simon Thorburn Gray and Jacob Nell, *A New Currency for Iraq*, pp. 5, 20; IMF – Iraq macroeconomic assessment, 21 October 2003, www.imf.org/external/np/oth/102103.pdf; Mervyn King, *The End of Alchemy*, p. 238.

24   Mervyn King, *The End of Alchemy*, p. 239.

25   IMF – Iraq macroeconomic assessment, 21 October 2003, www.imf.org/external/np/oth/102103.pdf.

26   Simon Thorburn Gray and Jacob Nell, *A New Currency for Iraq*, p. 6.

27   *Ibid.*, pp. 31–2.

28   J.P. Koning, 'Disowned currency: the odd case of Iraqi Swiss dinars', *Moneyness: The Blog of J.P. Koning*, 27 May 2013, jpkoning.blogspot.co.uk/2013/05/disowned-currency-odd-case-of-iraqi.html; Simon Thorburn Gray and Jacob Nell, *A New Currency for Iraq*, p. 25; Mervyn King, *The End of Alchemy*, p. 240.

29   Simon Thorburn Gray and Jacob Nell, *A New Currency for Iraq*, pp. 6–8, 13.

30   *Ibid.*, p. 29; World Bank Databank data.worldbank.org/indicator/PA.NUS.FCRF?end=2015&locations=IQ&start=2001.

Chapter 9

1   Simon Prendergast, 'The legal status of the Monclova issue', *The Paper Money of Sonora*, www.papermoneyofsonora.com/history/monclova/legal-status.html.

2   Liaquat Ahamed, *Lords of Finance*, p. 43.
3   *Ibid.*, p. 204; Jonathan Kirshner, *Currency and Coercion*, p. 224, describes the theory
    that the sale was not a political operation by Germany but a shorting operation by
    speculators. Charles P. Kindleberger, *A Financial History of Western Europe*, p. 351,
    describes the speculation and its primary plotters in further detail and France's
    countermeasures.
4   Jonathan Kirshner, *Currency and Coercion*, pp. 182, 185.
5   *Ibid.*, p. 183; Charles P. Kindleberger, *A Financial History of Western Europe*, pp. 343, 359.
6   Hjalmar Schacht, *The End of Reparations* pp. 102–3, 334.
7   Liaquat Ahamed, *Lords of Finance*, pp. 412–15, 419–20.
8   *Ibid.*, p. 406; Brian Johnson, *The Politics of Money*, p. 87; Jonathan Kirshner, *Currency and
    Coercion*, p. 182; Charles P. Kindleberger, *A Financial History of Western Europe*, p. 372.
9   Brian Johnson, *The Politics of Money*, pp. 87–8.
10 Jonathan Kirshner, *Currency and Coercion*, p. 66.
11 *Ibid.*, p. 69.
12 *Ibid.*, p. 77.
13 United Nations, 'Letter from Benon Sevan to Mohammed al-Douri', Office of the
    Iraq Programme, 13 February 2001.
14 'The European Union has announced new sanctions against Syria',
    Exportcompliance.eu, 2 December 2011. Dafna Linzer, Michael Grabell, Jeff Larson,
    'Flight records say Russia sent Syria tons of cash', *Propublica*, 26 November 2012.
15 Shaun Walker, 'Plane loads of cash: flight records reveal Russia flew thirty tonnes of
    banknotes to Syrian regime', *The Independent*, 26 November 2012; Dafna Linzer et
    al., 'Flight records say Russia sent Syria tons of cash'.
16 US Department of the Treasury, Office of Foreign Assets Control overview
    of sanctions on Iran: www.treasury.gov/resource-center/sanctions/Programs/
    Documents/iran.pdf.
17 John Williamson, 'The dollar and US power' in *The Power of Currencies and Currencies
    of Power*, ed. Alan Wheatley, International Institute for Strategic Studies, 2013, p. 83.
18 Giri Rajendran, 'Financial blockades: reserve currencies as instruments of coercion'
    in *The Power of Currencies and Currencies of Power*, p. 88.
19 *Reuters*, Babak Dehghanpisheh, 3 September 2018.
20 *Hurriyet Daily News*, 9 September 2018.
21 United States Department of the Treasury, 'Treasury and Commerce announce
    significant amendments to the Cuba sanctions regulations ahead of President
    Obama's historic trip to Cuba', 15 March 2016.
22 World Bank figures for 2014: data.worldbank.org/indicator/NY.GDP.MKTP.CD.
23 William T. Wilson, 'Washington, China and the rise of the Renminbi: are the dollar's
    days as the world's reserve currency numbered?', *Special Report* 171, 2015.
24 US Treasury data: ticdata.treasury.gov/Publish/mfh.txt.
25 Barry Eichengreen, *Exorbitant Privilege*, p. 135.
26 William T. Wilson, 'Washingon, China and the rise of the Renminbi'; Di
    Dongsheng, 'The Renminbi's rise and Chinese politics', in *The Power of Currencies
    and Currencies of Power*, p. 120.

Chapter 10

1   Andrey Ostroukh and Elena Fabrichnaya, 'Russian Central Bank, private banks lose $31 million in cyber attacks', *Reuters*, 6 December 2016.

2   Michael Corkery, 'Hackers $81 million sneak attack on world banking', *New York Times*, 30 April 2016.

3   Reuters, 'Federal Reserve was hacked more than 50 times in the past five years', *The Guardian*, 1 June 2016.

4   Peter Lloyd, 'Reserve Bank of Australia computer network breach blamed on Indonesia', *ABC News Online*, 2 December 2015; Anon., 'Central banks in Indonesia and South Korea hit by Anonymous cyber attacks, no losses reported', *Asian Correspondent*, 21 June 2016.

5   Waking Shark II Generic Scenario; Waking Shark II, Desktop Cyber Exercise, Report to Participants, 12 November 2013; Retired Member, 'Waking Shark II: a curate's egg?', *Finextra*, finextrablog.com, 9 April 2014.

6   Patrick Jenkins, 'Does cash have a future?', *Financial Times*, 12 May 2018.

BIBLIOGRAPHY

Books

Abbenhuis, Maartje M., *The Art of Staying Neutral: The Netherlands in the First World War, 1914–1918*, Amsterdam University Press, 2006.

Ahamed, Liaquat, *Lords of Finance: The Bankers Who Broke the World*, Penguin Press, 2009.

Beevor, Antony, *The Battle for Spain: The Spanish Civil War*, Penguin Books, 2006.

Bokarev et al., *Monetary Circulation of Russia*, Bank of Russia, 2010.

Bordo, M.D. and Capie, F. (eds), *Monetary Regimes in Transition*. Cambridge University Press, 1993.

Bowra, C.M., *Periclean Athens*, Weidenfeld & Nicholson, 1971.

Braudel, Fernand, *The Mediterranean and the Mediterranean World in the Age of Philip II*, 5th ed., Fontana Press, 1987.

Chalmers, Robert, *A History of Currency in the British Colonies, HMSO*, 1893.

Chernow, Ron, *Alexander Hamilton,* Penguin, 2005.

Chown, John, *A History of Money from AD 800*, Routledge, 1994.

Churchill, Winston S., *Marlborough: His Life and Times*, G.G. Harrap, 1947.

Coats, Warren, *One Currency for Bosnia*, Jameson Books Inc., 2007.

Conway, Ed, *The Summit: Bretton Woods, 1944: J.M. Keynes and the Reshaping of the Global Economy*, Pegasus Books, 2016.

Copnall, James, *A Poisonous Thorn in our Hearts: Sudan and South Sudan's Bitter and Incomplete Divorce*, Hurst, 2014.

Davies, Glyn, *History of Money*, University of Wales Press, 2010.

De Tocqueville, Alexis, *Democracy in America*, Everyman's Library, 1994.

Dean, Marjorie and Pringle, Robert, *The Central Banks*, Hamish Hamilton, 1994.

Del Mar, Alexander, *Barbara Villiers: A History of Monetary Crimes*, University Press of the Pacific, 2004.

Dillaye, Stephen D., *Assignats and Mandats: A True History*, Ulan Press, 1877.

Drake, Paul W., *The Money Doctor in the Andes: The Kemmerer Missions 1923–1933*, Duke University Press, 1989.

Eberhard, Wolfram, *A History of China*, H. Schuman, 1977.

Eichengreen, Barry, *Exorbitant Privilege: The Rise and Fall of the Dollar*, Oxford University Press, 2011.

Elton, G.R., *Reform and Reformation: England 1509–1588*, Harvard University Press, 1977.

Ferguson, Niall, *The Ascent of Money: A Financial History of the World*, Penguin, 2008.

Fergusson, Adam, *When Money Dies: The Nightmare of the Weimar Hyper-inflation*, Old Street Publishing, 2010.

Franklin, Benjamin, *A Modest Enquiry Into the Nature and Necessity of a Paper-Currency*, University of Virginia Library, 1729.

Gernet, Jacques, *A History of Chinese Civilization*, Cambridge University Press, 1996.

Glenny, Misha, *The Fall of Yugoslavia: The Third Balkan War*, Penguin Books, 1974.

Goethe, Johann Wolfgang von and Farie, Robert (trans.), *Campaign in France*, Chapman and Hall, 1849.

Grant, Isabel Frances, *The Social and Economic Development of Scotland Before 1603*, Oliver & Boyd, 1930.

Gray, Simon Thorburn, and Jacob Nell, *A New Currency for Iraq*, Central Banking, 2005.

Hardach, Gerd, *The First World War, 1914–1918*, Vol. 2. University of California Press, 1981.

Helleiner, Eric, *The Making of National Money: Territorial Currencies in Historical Perspective*, Cornell University Press, 2003.

Henze, Paul, *Eritrea's War: Confrontation, International Response, Outcome, Prospects*, Shama Books, 2001.

Horesh, Niv, *Chinese Money in Global Context: Historic Junctures Between 600 BCE and 2012*, Stanford University Press, 2013.

Isaacson, Walter, *Benjamin Franklin: An American Life*, Simon and Schuster, 2003.

Johnson, Brian, *The Politics of Money*, John Murray, 1970.

Johnson, Charles, *De Moneta of Nicholas Oresme*, Ludwig von Mises Institute, 1956.

Johnson, H. Clark, *Gold, France, and the Great Depression, 1919–1932*, Yale University Press, 1997.

Hanke, Steve H., Jonung, Lars and Schuler, Kurt, *Russian Currency and Finance: A Currency Board Approach to Reform*. Routledge, 1993.

Keynes, J.M., *Indian Currency and Finance*, Cambridge University Press for the Royal Economic Society, 1911.

Keynes, J.M., *The Economic Consequences of the Peace*, Penguin, 1995.

Kindleberger, Charles P., *A Financial History of Western Europe*, George Allen and Unwin, 1984.

King, Mervyn, *The End of Alchemy: Money, Banking, and the Future of the Global Economy*, WW Norton & Company, 2016.

Kirshner, Jonathan, *Currency and Coercion: The Political Economy of International Monetary Power*, Princeton University Press, 1995.

Kowalsky, Daniel, *Stalin and the Spanish Civil War*, Columbia University Press, 2004.

Kramnick, Isaac (ed.), *The Thomas Paine Reader*, Penguin, 1987.

Kwarteng, Kwasi, *War and Gold: A Five-Hundred-Year History of Empires, Adventures, and Debt*, Public Affairs, 2014.

Lauderbaugh, George, *The History of Ecuador*, ABC-CLIO, 2012.

LeBor, Adam, *Tower of Basel: The Shadowy History of the Secret Bank That Runs the World*, Public Affairs, 2013.

Lefebvre, Georges, *The French Revolution*, Routledge & Kegan, 1962.

LeRiche, Matthew and Arnold, Matthew, *South Sudan: From Revolution to Independence*, Oxford University Press, 2013.

Longmuir, Marilyn, *The Money Trail: Burmese Currencies in Crisis, 1937–1947*, Southeast Asia Publications, 2002.

Lucan, *Pharsalia*, trans. Robert Graves, Penguin Classics, 1956.

Martin, Felix, *Money: The Unauthorised Biography*, W.F. Howes Ltd, 2013.

Mason, R.H.P. and Caiger, J.G., *A History of Japan*, 2nd ed., Charles E. Tuttle, 1997.

Matthee, R., Floor, W. and Clawson, P., *The Monetary History of Iran*, I.B. Tauris, 2013.

Maurer, Noel, *The Power and the Money: The Mexican Financial System, 1876–1932*, Stanford University Press, 2002.

McCullough, David, *John Adams*, Simon and Schuster, 2002.

McLynn, Frank, *Villa and Zapata: A Biography of the Mexican Revolution*, Random House, 2001.

Melliss, C.L. and Cornelius, M., *New Currencies in the Former Soviet Union*, Bank of England, 1994.

Metzler, Mark, *Lever of Empire: The International Gold Standard and the Crisis of Liberalism in Prewar Japan*, University of California Press, 2006.

Pamuk, Şevket, *A Monetary History of the Ottoman Empire*, Cambridge University Press, 2000.

Parks, Tim, *Medici Money: Banking, Metaphysics, and Art in Fifteenth-Century Florence*, WW Norton & Company, 2005.

Petrov, Vladimir, *Money and Conquest: Allied Occupation Currencies in World War II*, Johns Hopkins Press, 1967.

Pintev, Svetoslav, *Currency Board Arrangements. Rationale for Their Introduction, Advantages and Disadvantages: The Case of Bulgaria*, German National Library, 2003.

Plutarch, *Fall of the Roman Empire*, Penguin, 1972.

Pugh, Peter, *The Highest Perfection: A History of De La Rue*, Aubrey Books, 2011.

Quinn, Frederick, *The French Overseas Empire*, Praeger, 2000.

Richards, John F., *The Mughal Empire*, Cambridge University Press, 2008.

Roberts, Richard, *Saving the City: The Great Financial Crisis of 1914*, Oxford University Press, 2013.

Sargent, Thomas J. and Velde, François R., *The Big Problem of Small Change*, Princeton University Press, 2002.

Schacht, Hjalmar, *The End of Reparations: The Economic Consequences of the War*, J. Cape, 1931.

Segur, Philipe Comte de, *A History of Napoleon's Expedition to Russia*, Project Gutenberg, 2006.

Selgin, George, *Good Money: Birmingham Button Makers, the Royal Mint and the Beginnings of a Modern Coinage 1775–1821*, University of Michigan Press, 2008.

Sinclair, David, *The Pound: A Biography*, Vintage, 2000.

Smith, Vera, *The Rationale of Central Banking and the Free Banking Alternative*, PS King, 1936.

Southard, Frank, *Some Currency and Exchange Experiences*, Department of Economics, Princeton University, 1946.

Spang, Rebecca L., *Stuff and Money in the Time of the French Revolution*, Harvard University Press, 2015.

Spufford, Peter, *Money and its Use in Medieval Europe*, Cambridge University Press, 1988.

Steil, Benn, *The Battle of Bretton Woods: John Maynard Keynes, Harry Dexter White, and the Making of a New World Order*, Princeton University Press, 2013.

Strangio, Donatella, *The Reasons for Underdevelopment: The Case of Decolonisation in Somaliland*, Springer Science & Business Media, 2011.

Tacitus, *The Annals of Imperial Rome*, Penguin Classics, 1996.

Tarnoff, Ben, *A Counterfeiter's Paradise: The Wicked Lives and Surprising Adventures of Three Early American Moneymakers*, Penguin, 2012.

Toniolo, Gianni and Clement, Piet, *Central Bank Cooperation at the Bank for International Settlements, 1930–1973*, Cambridge University Press, 2005.

Turnell, Sean, *Fiery Dragons: Banks, Moneylenders and Microfinance in Burma*, Nordic Institute of Asian Studies, 2009.

Vilar, Pierre, *A History of Gold and Money*, 3rd ed., Verso, 1984.

Voltaire, *History of Charles XII*, Everyman's Library, 1936.

Von Glahn, Richard, *Fountain of Fortune: Money and Monetary Policy in China, 1000–1700*, University of California Press, 1996.

Von Reden, Sitta, *Money in Classical Antiquity*, Cambridge University Press, 2010.

Wedgewood, C.V., *The Thirty Years War*, Methuen, 1981.

Wernham, R.B., *The New Cambridge Modern History: Volume 3, Counter-Reformation and Price Revolution, 1559–1610*, Cambridge University Press, 1968.

Wheatley, Alan (ed.), *The Power of Currencies and Currencies of Power*, Routledge, 2013.

Williams, Jonathan (ed.), *Money: A History*, British Museum Press, 1997.

Articles and Reports

'Afghanistan Switching to New Currency', Voice of America Online, 22 October 2002.

Abdelal, Rawi, 'Contested currency: Russia's rouble in domestic and international politics', *Journal of Communist Studies and Transition Politics*, Vol. 19, Issue 2 (2003), pp. 55–76.

Anon., 'Afghan currency replacement delayed', *Radio Free Europe Online*, 5 December 2002.

Anon., 'British and foreign extracts', *The Moreton Bay Courier*, 30 June 1849.

Anon., 'Central banks in Indonesia and South Korea hit by Anonymous cyber-attacks, no losses reported', *Asian Correspondent*, 21 June 2016.

Anon., 'NOTE FORGERIES: prosecution appeal fails leaders' sentences stand PRINCE AND NADOSY FOUR YEARS EACH (Reuter.)', *The Advocate* (Tasmania), 26 August 1926.

Anon., 'SA advises ZIM to join rand monetary area', *Radio VOP Online*, 10 July 2016.

Anon., 'The politics of trade', *The Economist*, 28 February 2002.

Bank for International Settlements, 15th Annual Report, 1945.

Banque de France, 'The Franc Zone', Fact sheet 127, 2010.

Bernanke, Ben and James, Harold, 'The gold standard, deflation and financial crisis in the Great Depression: an international comparison', *National Bureau of Economic Research, 1990.*'

Bordo M., Redish A., Shearer R.., 'Canada's monetary system in historical perspective: two faces of the exchange rate regime', Working Paper, University of British Columbia, 1999.

Bordo, M.D. and Jonung, L., 'The future of EMU: what does the history of monetary unions tell us?', *National Bureau of Economic Research*, 1999.

Bordo, Michael D., Simard, Dominique and White, Eugene N. 'France and the Bretton Woods international monetary system 1960 to 1968.' *International Monetary Systems in Historical Perspective*. Palgrave Macmillan, 1995. pp. 153–80.

Brathwaite, Trevor O.B., 'Monetary unions in the Caribbean context: the challenges faced by the Eastern Caribbean Union since the financial crisis', Eastern Caribbean Central Bank, March 2016.

Butlin, S.J., 'Foundations of the Australian monetary system 1788–1851', University of Sydney, 2002.

Capie, Forrest, 'Conditions in which very rapid inflation has appeared', *Carnegie-Rochester Conference Series on Public Policy*, 24, Issue 1, 1986, pp. 115–68.

Capie, Forrest, 'The development and evolution of the International Financial Architecture', *Elsevier Encyclopedia*, 2010.

Chiminva, Johannes, 'Sustainability of Rand Union', *The Financial Gazette*, 25 September 2009.

Cienski, Jan and Milne, Richard, 'Monetary union: Eurozone membership pros and cons', *The Financial Times*, 9 May 2013.

Cleveland, Tom, 'Do you know the history of the Afghani currency?', *News Central Asia*, 30 November 2012.

Corkery, Michael, 'Hackers $81 million sneak attack on world banking', *New York Times*, 30 April 2016.

Cropley, Ed, 'As Zimbabwe's money runs out, so does Mugabe's power', *Business Report*, 28 November 2016.

Dabrowski, Marek, Jermakowicz, W., Pankow, J., Kloc, K. and R. Antczak, 'The reasons for the collapse of the ruble zone', *Trade and Payments in Central and Eastern Europe's Transforming Economies: Handbook of Comparative Economic Policies* 6, 1997, pp. 145–69.

Deyell, John S., 'Akbar's currency system and monetary integration', *The Imperial Monetary System of Mughal India*, ed. Richards, J., 1987.

Dingli, Sophia. 'The politics of (re) unification.' *The Cyprus Review* 24, No. 2, 2012, pp. 29–6.

Duryea, Scott N., 'William Pitt, the Bank of England, and the 1797 suspension of specie payments: Central Bank war finance during the Napoleonic Wars', *Libertarian Papers,* Vol. 2, 2010.

Editorial Team, 'South Sudan rolls out her new currency', *The London Evening Post*, 19 July 2011.

Ellis, Eric, 'Afghanistan gets back to business', *Euromoney*, 4 September 2006.

'The European Union has announced new sanctions against Syria', European Institute for Export Compliance, exportcompliance.eu, 2 December 2011.

Fagiolo, Nicoletto, 'The CFA franc: Africa's financial anachronism', *NSNBC International Online*, 17 October 2015.

Foreman-Peck, James, 'Lessons from Italian Monetary Unification', No. E2005/4, Cardiff Economics Working Papers, 2005.

Fujimura, Manabu, 'Post conflict reconstruction of the Afghan economy', Asian Development Bank, 2004.

Fuller, H., 'From cowries to coins: money and colonialism in the Gold Coast and British West Africa in the early 20th century', *Money in Africa*, ed. C. Eagleton et al., British Museum Research Publications, 2009, pp. 54–61.

Gallarotti, Giulio M., 'The scramble for gold: monetary regime transformation in the 1870s', *Monetary Regimes in Transition*, 1993, pp. 15–67.

Girmay, Haileselassie, 'Ethiopia–Eritrea border conflict: the role nakfa played', Ethiopian Embassy.

Gligorov, Vladimir, 'Stabilization of a war economy: the case of Yugoslavia (Serbia and Montenegro)', East European Series 18, Institute for Advanced Studies, 1995.

Grandes, Martin, 'Macroeconomic convergence in Southern Africa: the rand zone experience', Working Paper No. 231, OECD Development Centre, December 2003.

Griffin, Michael, 'Money matters in Afghanistan', *Los Angeles Times*, 6 January 2002.

Hanke, Steve H. , '1997. A field report from Sarajevo and Pale', *Central Banking* 12, No. 3, 1996, pp. 36-40.

Hanke, Steve H. and Krus, Nicholas, 'World hyperinflations', Cato Working Paper, Cato Institute, 2012.

Hansson, Ardo H., 'Transforming an economy while building a nation: the case of Estonia', World Institute for Development Economics Research, 1993.

Herbert, Ross, 'The end of the Eritrean exception?', The South African Institute of International Affairs, 2002.

Hollander, David B., 'The demand for money in the Late Roman Republic', *The Monetary Systems of the Greeks and Romans*, ed. W.V. Harris, 2008.

Honohan, Patrick, 'Currency board or central bank? Lessons from the Irish Pound's link with sterling, 1928–79', CEPR Discussion Paper No. 1040, 1994 [accessed: ssrn.com/abstract=286599].

Huff, Gregg, and Majima, Shinobu, 'Financing Japan's World War II occupation of South East Asia', *The Journal of Economic History* 73, No. 4, 2013, pp. 937–77.

James, Harold, 'Monetary and fiscal unification in nineteenth-century Germany: what can kohl learn from Bismarck?', International Economics Section, Department of Economics, Princeton University, 1997.

Jefferis, Keith, 'Monetary and exchange rate management: policies and processes for stability and growth', International Growth Centre [accessed: www.theigc.org/event/monetary-and-exchange-rate-management-policies-and-processes-for-stability-and-growth/].

Kalyvas, Stathis N. and Sambanis, Nicholas, 'Bosnia's Civil War', *Understanding Civil War*, Yale University, 2005, p.191.

Karmin, Craig, 'Biography of the dollar', *New York: Crown Business*, 2008, p.116.

Kaufman, Marc, 'Afghans advised to unify currency', *The Washington Post*, 30 January 2002.

Kavari, Suta, 'Rand peg still beneficial', *BankWindhoek*, 14 January 2016.

Kemmerer, Edwin Walter, *Inflation and Revolution: Mexico's Experience of 1912–1917*, No. 04, HG229, K6, 1940.

Kifle, Temesgen, 'Can border demarcation help Eritrea to reverse the general slowdown in economic growth?', University of Bremen, 2004.

Klay, Andor, 'Hungarian counterfeit francs: a case of post-World War I political sabotage', *Slavic Review* 33, No. 1, 1974, pp. 107–13.

Krammer, Arnold, 'Russian counterfeit dollars: a case of early Soviet espionage', *Slavic Review* 30, No. 4, 1971, pp. 762–73.

Lata, Leenco, 'The Causes, mediation and settlement of the Ethio-Eritrean conflict' in *The Search for Peace: The Conflict between Ethiopia and Eritrea*, Proceedings of Scholarly Conference on the Ethiopia–Eritrea Conflict, Oslo, 2006, pp. 6–7.

Linzer, Dafna, Grabell, Michael and Larson, Jeff, 'Flight records say Russia sent Syria tons of cash' *ProPublica*, 26 November 2012.

Lloyd, Peter, 'Reserve Bank of Australia computer network breach blamed on Indonesia', *ABC News Online*, 2 December 2015.

M'bet, Allechi and Niamkey, Amlan Madeleine 'European economic integration and the Franc Zone: the future of the CFA franc after 1996: part I: historical background and a new evaluation of monetary co-operation in the CFA Ccountries', *Africa Portal*, 1993.

Ma, Debin, 'Money and monetary system in China in the 19th and 20th centuries: an overview', Economic History Working Papers, London School of Economics and Political Science, 2012.

Ma, Debin, 'The rise of a financial revolution in Republican China in 1900–1937: an institutional narrative', Economic History Working Papers, London School of Economics and Political Science, 2016.

Marawanyika, Godfrey and Latham, Brian, 'Dollar shortage forces Zimbabwe to delay military pay', *Bloomberg*, 19 June 2016.

Mardini, P. and Schuler, K., 'Free banking in Belgium 1835-1850,' for the conference Free Banking Systems: Diversity in Financial and Economic Growth, Lund University School of Economics and Management, 4–5 September 2014.

Marshall, Jonathan, 'Dirty wars: French and American piaster profiteering in Indochina, 1945–75', *Asia-Pacific Journal*, 12, No. 32, 2014.

Martín-Aceña, Pablo, Ruiz, Elena Martínez and Pons, María A., 'War and economics: Spanish Civil War finances revisited', *European Review of Economic History*, Vol. 16, No. 2, 2012, pp.144–65 [accessed: mpra.ub.uni-muenchen.de/22833/].

Mauri, Arnaldo, 'Eritrea's early stages in monetary and banking development', UNIMI Economics Working Paper No. 28, 2003 [accessed: ssrn.com/abstract=667266].

McGreal, Chris, 'Zimbabwe starts paying soldiers and other government workers in US dollars', *The Guardian*, 19 February 2009.

Meardon, Stephen, 'On Kindleberger and hegemony: from Berlin to MIT and back', Bowdoin College, 2013.

Mendoza, Carlos, 'Monetary authority: similar beginning but different trajectories: Bolivia, Ecuador and Guatemala in comparative perspective', 2004.

Metzger, Martina, 'The common monetary area in Southern Africa: a typical south-south coordination project?', *New Issues in Regional Monetary Coordination*, Palgrave Macmillan, 2006, pp. 147–64.

Morris, Ewan, 'Devilish devices or farmyard friends? The Free State coinage debate', *History Ireland* 12, No. 1, 2004, pp.24-8.

Morys, Matthias, 'Was the Bundesbank's credibility undermined during the process of German reunification?', LSE Working Paper, 2003.

Musonza, Brighton, 'Zimbabwe currency crisis: the rand and long history of trade with South Africa', *Zimbabwe Independent*, 12 May 2016.

Neil, R., 'Central banking and government policy: Canada 1871', University of Prince Edward Island [accessed: people.upei.ca/rneill/web_papers/1871_notes.html].

Newman, Eric P., 'The successful British counterfeiting of American paper money during the American Revolution', *British Numismatic Journal*, Vol. 29, 1958, pp. 174–87.

Nunes, Bastien, Valerio, de Souza, Costa, 'Banking in the Portuguese Colonial Empire 1864–1975', University of Lisbon Working Papers, 2010.

Oborne, Peter, 'Zimbabwe will sink into horror and depravity unless Mugabe quits now', *The Spectator*, 10 September 2016.

Occhino, Filippo, Oosterlink, Kim and White, Eugene, 'How Occupied France financed its own exploitation in World War II', NBER Working Paper 12137.

Okuk, James, 'Facts about Sudan and South Sudan bilateral relations', *South Sudan News Agency*, 27 May 2016.

Ostroukh, Andrey and Fabrichnaya, Elena, 'Russian central bank, private banks lose $31 mln in cyber attacks', *Reuters*, 16 December 2016.

Ow, Chwee-Huay, 'The currency board monetary system: the case of Singapore and Hong Kong', PhD dissertation, John Hopkins University, 1986.

Pauly, Louis W., 'The League of Nations and the foreshadowing of the International Monetary Fund', *Essays in International Finance*, No. 201, Princeton University, December 1996, pp. 1–47.

Powell, James, *A History of the Canadian dollar*, Bank of Canada, 2005 [accessed: www.bankofcanada.ca/2005/12/a-history-of-the-canadian-dollar-by-james-powell/].

Powell, John, *A History of the Gold Standard*, Bank of Canada, 2005 [accessed: www.bankofcanada.ca/wp-content/uploads/2010/07/dollar_book.pdf].

Pratschke, J., 'Establishing of Irish pound: backward glance', Economic and Social Research Institute, *Economic and Social Review*, Vol. 1, Issue 1, 1969, pp. 51–75 [accessed: hdl.handle.net/2262/68789].

Prydz, Kiringai, Demombynes et al., 'World Bank South Sudan Economic Brief', World Bank Group, April 2012.

Raza, Saima, 'Italian colonisation & Libyan resistance the Al-Sanusi of Cyrenaica (1911–1922)', *OGIRISI: A New Journal of African Studies* Vol. 9, No. 1, 2012, pp. 1–43.

Recknagel, Charles, 'Pakistan: Afghan currency blown by political winds', *Radio Free Europe Online*, 29 October 2001.

Retired Member, 'Waking Shark II: a curate's egg?' *Finextra*, finextrablog.com, 9 April 2014.

Rhodes, Karl, 'The counterfeiting weapon: attacks against American currency began in 1776', *Econ Focus*, Issue 1Q, Federal Reserve Bank of Richmond, 2012, pp. 34–7.

Riddell, Tom, 'Inflationary Impact of the Vietnam War', *Vietnam Generation*, Vol. 1, No. 1, Article 4, 1989 [accessed: digitalcommons.lasalle.edu/vietnamgeneration/vol1/iss1/4].

Rockoff, Hugh, 'How long did it take the United States to become an optimal currency area?', *National Bureau of Economic Research*, 124, April 2000.

Rockoff, Hugh, 'Until it's over, over there: the US economy in World War I', Working Paper 10580, *National Bureau of Economic Research*, 2004.

Samuels, David, 'Counterfeiting: notes on a scandal', *The Independent,* 24 August 2009.

Sandrock, John E., 'Italy's colonial empire: a paper money trail', *The Currency Collector* [accessed: www.thecurrencycollector.com/pdfs/Italys_Colonial_Empire_-_A_Paper_Money_Trail.pdf]

Şaul, Mahir, 'Money in colonial transition: cowries and francs in West Africa', *American Anthropologist*, Vol. 106, No. 1, 2004, pp. 71–84.

Scheidel, Walter, 'The divergent evolution of coinage in Eastern and Western Eurasia', in *The Monetary Systems of the Greeks and Romans*, ed. W.V. Harris, Oxford University Press, 2010.

Schuler, Kurt, 'Introduction to currency boards', in 'Monetary Politics in Post-Conflict Countries: Restoring Credibility' (archived webpage), Working Paper, American University, 2004, pp. 8–10.

Schuler, Kurt, 'Episodes from Asian monetary history: a brief history of Hong Kong monetary standards', *Asian Monetary Monitor*, Vol. 12, No. 5, September–October 1989, pp. 11–29.

Selassie, Bereket Habte, 'Dreams that turned to nightmares: the Ethio–Eritrean War of 1998–2000 and its aftermath' in *The Search for Peace: The Conflict between Ethiopia and Eritrea*, (ed. Leenco Lata), Proceedings of the Scholarly Conference on the Ethiopia–Eritrea Conflict, Oslo, 6–7 July 2006.

Shaban, Abdur Rahman Alfa, 'Zimbabwe to pay most December salaries in January 2017', *AfricaNews*, 15 December 2016.

Sly, Liz, 'Afghans see money value turn to dust', *Chicago Tribune*, 29 October 2002.

Soerg, M., Estonian Currency Board and Economic Performance, University of Tartu, Estonia, SATEB, 1998.

Solomon, Robert, 'The French exchange stabilization fund', Federal Reserve Bulletin, Board of Governors of the Federal Reserve System (US), January 1950, pp.35–9.

Staff Reporter, 'Zimbabwe army demands special dispensation on salaries', *Bulawayo 24 News*, 1 July 2016.

Starr, Martha A., 'Monetary politics in post-conflict countries: restoring credibility', Working Paper, American University, 2004.

Sy, Amadou, 'The implications of South Sudan's decision to float its currency', *Brookings Institute*, 18 December 2015.

Symes, P.J., 'Banknotes and banking in Ethiopia and Abyssinia', pjsymes.com.au, November 2013 [accessed: www.pjsymes.com.au/articles/Abyssinia.htm].

Sytas, Andrius, 'Lithuania joins Euro as tensions with neighbouring Russia rise', *Reuters*, 31 December 2014.

Talts, Mait, 'Eurodebate in Estonia: pros and contras in Estonian press', Institute for European Studies, November 1998.

Tesfay, Seyoum Yohannes, 'Eritrea–Ethiopia Arbitration: a "cure" based on neither diagnosis nor prognosis', *Mizan Law Review*, Vol. 6, No. 2, 2012, pp. 164–99.

Tsoi, Benjamin, 'The Constitutions (founding laws) and comparable features of select currency boards in the former British Empire', *Studies in Applied Economics*, John Hopkins University, October 2014.

Uche, Chibuike U., 'Banks and the West African Currency Board', *Money in Africa*, 2009.

Van Zyl, Lambertus, 'South Africa's experience of regional currency areas and the use of foreign currencies', *BIS Papers*, No. 17, May 2013.

Venner, Dwight, 'Eastern Caribbean Central Bank 2010/2011: Annual Report', *Eastern Caribbean Central Bank*, 2001.

Walker, Shaun, 'Plane loads of cash: flight records reveal Russia flew 30 tonnes of bank notes to Syrian regime', *The Independent*, 26 November 2012.

White, Eugene N., 'Measuring the French Revolution's inflation: the tableaux de dépréciation', *Histoire & Mesure*, 1991, pp. 245–74.

Wigan, Henry, 'The effects of the 1925 Portuguese bank note crisis', London School of Economics Working Papers, 2004.

Williamson, John, 'The dollar and US power', in *The Power of Currencies and Currencies of Power*, ed. Wheatley, Alan, International Institute for Strategic Studies, 2013.

Wilson, William T., 'Washington, China, and therRise of the Renminbi: Are the dollar's days as the global reserve currency numbered?', *Special Report* 171, 2015.

Zupcević, Merima and Čaušević, Fikret, 'Case study: Bosnia and Herzegovina', McGill University and the World Bank, 2009.

Government Papers

Hamilton, Alexander and United States Department of the Treasury, 'Report on a National Bank, December 13, 1790', in Hamilton, Alexander and United States Department of the Treasury, *Official Reports on Publick Credit, a National Bank, Manufactures, and a Mint*, William McKean, 1821, pp. 67–118 [accessed: fraser.stlouisfed.org/title/3647/toc/525926?start_page=67].

HM Government (UK), *Bank Charter Act 1844*.

HM Government (UK), *Indian Councils Act 1861.*

Irish Senate, *Coinage Act 1926, Second Stage*, 27 January 1926.

Organisation of East Caribbean States, 'Economic Union Treaty: frequently asked questions', 2008 [accessed: ctrc.sice.oas.org/CARICOM/OECS/FAQs_OECS_Integration.pdf].

Perez Vasquez, Carlos (trans.), 'The political constitution of the Mexican United States', Clause 10, Article 123, 1917 (trans. 2005).

The National Archives website (UK): Discovery, 'West African Currency Board', CO94, 1880–1974 [accessed: discovery.nationalarchives.gov.uk/details/record?catid=3643&catln=3].

United Kingdom, Trade and Payments Agreement between His Majesty's Government and the Government of the Turkish Republic, 4 May 1945.

United Nations Missions in Sudan, 'The comprehensive peace agreement between the government of the Republic of the Sudan and the Sudan People's Liberation Movement/Sudan People's Liberation Army', *Naivasha*, 26 May 2004.

United Nations Treaty Depositary (League of Nations Treaties), 'International Convention for the Suppression of the Counterfeiting of Currency', *United Nations Treaty Collection*, Vol. 12, 20 April 1929.

United Nations, 'Letter from Benon Sevan to Mohammed al-Douri', Office of the Iraq Programme, 13 February 2001.

United Nations, Annex 4, Article VII, 'The general framework agreement for peace in Bosnia and Herzegovina', Organization for Security and Co-operation in Europe, 14 December 1995.

United States Department of the Treasury, 'Treasury and commerce announce significant amendments to the Cuba sanctions regulations ahead of President Obama's historic trip to Cuba', 15 March 2016.

United States State Department, 'Nixon and the end of the Bretton Woods system 1971–1973', *Milestones in the History of US Foreign Relations*, Office of the Historian.

United States, 'Hearing before the subcommittee on government operations abroad of the permanent subcommittee on investigations of the committee on government operations', United States Senate, Eighty-third Congress, first session, 20–21 October 1953.

Werner, Pierre, 'Report to the council and the commission on the realisation by stages of economic and monetary union in the community', *Bulletin of the European Communities*, Supplement 11/1970, 8 October 1970.

Financial Institute and Policy Group Papers

Institute for Economics and Peace, 'Economic consequences of war on the US Economy', 2011 [accessed: visionofhumanity.org/app/uploads/2017/04/The-Economic-Consequences-of-War-on-US-Economy_0.pdf].

International Monetary Fund, 'East Caribbean currency union, financial system stability assessment', 15 April 2004 [accessed: www.imf.org/external/pubs/ft/scr/2004/cr04293.pdf].

International Monetary Fund, 'Eritrea: selected issues and statistical appendix', June 2003 [accessed: www.imf.org/external/pubs/ft/scr/2003/cr03166.pdf].

International Monetary Fund, 'The Federal Democratic Republic of Ethiopia: selected issues and statistical appendix', 28 January 2005 [accessed: www.imf.org/en/

Publications/CR/Issues/2016/12/31/The-Federal-Democratic-Republic-of-Ethiopia-Selected-Issues-and-Statistical-Appendix-18012].

International Monetary Fund, 'World economic outlook', October 1992.

Kwon, Goohoon, 'Experiences with monetary integration and lessons for Korean unification', IMF Working Paper, International Monetary Fund, 1997.

Lainela, Seija and Sutela, Pekka, 'Introducing new currencies in the Baltic countries', Bank of Finland Institute for Economies in Transition, 1993.

Mosel, Irina and Henderson, Emily, 'Markets in crises: South Sudan case study', Humanitarian Policy Group, 2015.

Schuler, Kurt and Bernkopf, Mark, 'Who was at Bretton Woods?', Centre for Financial Stability, 2014.

White, Eugene, 'France and the Failure to modernize macroeconomic institutions', 12th International Economic History Congress, Madrid, 25 August 1998.

White, Eugene, 'Making the French pay: the costs and consequences of the Napoleonic reparations', NBER working paper series, Working Paper 7438.

Worrell, DeLisle, 'A currency union for the Caribbean', IMF Working Paper, February 2003, pp. 1–35 [accessed: ssrn.com/abstract=879110].

Websites and Webpages

Bank of Ghana: www.bog.gov.gh.

Bank of Italy: www.bancaditalia.it.

Bundesbank: www.bundesbank.de/en.

CameroonPostline: cameroonpostline.com.

Central Bank of Sri Lanka: cbsl.gov.lk.

Federal Reserve: www.federalreserve.gov.

Globalsecurity.org, 'Yemeni Civil War: 1990–1994': www.globalsecurity.org/military/world/war/yemen1.htm.

Gomez-Galvariatto, Aurora, 'The transformation of the Mexican banking system from the Porfiriato to 1925.' worldbhc.org: www.worldbhc.org/files/full%20program/A4_B4_TheTransformationoftheMexicanBankingSystemfromthePorfiriatoto1925.pdf.

Interpol: www.interpol.int.

McMahon, Tim, 'Confederate inflation rates (1861–1865)', inflationdata.com: inflationdata.com/articles/confederate-inflation.

National Bank of Belgium, 'A brief history of Belgian banknotes and coins': www.nbb.be/en/notes-and-coins/belgian-currency/brief-history-belgian-banknotes-and-coins.

Prendergast, Simon, 'Constitutionalist Cartones', *The Paper Money of Sonora*: www.papermoneyofsonora.com/history/constitutionalist-cartones.html.

Prendergast, Simon, 'The Legal Status of the Monclova Issue', *The Paper Money of Sondora*, www.papermoneyofsonora.com/history/monclova/legal-status.html.

Reserve Bank of Australia: www.rba.gov.au.

Reserve Bank of New Zealand: www.rbnz.govt.nz.

Trading Economics: www.tradingeconomics.com.

UK Public Spending: www.ukpublicspending.co.uk.

United States Department of the Treasury: www.treasury.gov.

United States Department of the Treasury, 'Iran sanctions', Office of Foreign Assets Control: www.treasury.gov/resource-center/sanctions/programs/pages/iran.aspx.

United States Department of the Treasury, 'Treasury reporting rates of exchange', Bureau of the Fiscal Service: fiscal.treasury.gov/reports-statements/treasury-reporting-rates-exchange.

University of Quebec at Montreal: uqam.ca.

World Gold Council: www.gold.org

World Integrated Trade Solution (WITS), World Bank: wits.worldbank.org.

Newspapers

The Advocate.
African Business.
Der Spiegel.
The Gateshead Observer.
The Guardian.

Television

'The Superdollar Plot', *Panorama*, BBC, 20 June 2004.

INDEX